American Intervention, 1917:

SENTIMENT, SELF-INTEREST, OR IDEALS?

American Intervention, 1917

Edited with an Introduction by

DANIEL M. SMITH, *University of Colorado*

SENTIMENT,

SELF-INTEREST,

OR IDEALS?

Houghton Mifflin Company · *Boston*

CONTENTS

II. *Commerce and Neutral Rights*

Contents

III. *The Challenge of the U-Boat*

IV. *America Enters the War*

V.   *The War in Retrospect*

INTRODUCTION

For over thirty years the causes of American involvement in World War I have excited controversy among scholars and laymen alike — a debate which in the 1920's and 1930's was all too frequently characterized by emotion rather than objectivity. Until 1917 most citizens believed that the wisest policy for the United States was one of abstention from the politics, alliances, and wars of the Old World. George Washington in his *Farewell Address* allegedly had given solemn warning to his countrymen to adhere to an isolationist course — actually he had advised as "little *political* connection" as possible with Europe and the avoidance of permanent alliances — and in the years thereafter, characterized by American expansion to the Pacific, peace and prosperity had seemingly resulted from following his advice. Ignored were the facts that advances in communications and transportation made the Atlantic and Pacific Ocean barriers less effective than in the past. In addition, many citizens were unaware of the beneficence to America of the relatively stable European balance of power and the century of general peace which prevailed after the fall of Napoleon.

When in the summer of 1914 Europe exploded into what was to become the most destructive war of the modern era, most Americans assumed that their country had no vital interests either in the origins or in the outcome of that struggle. It was simply one more of the dynastic and nationalistic conflicts which, from time immemorial, had plagued the Old World and from which the United States was happily removed by distance, interests, and policy. The formal proclamation of neutrality by President Woodrow Wilson adhered to the traditionally neutral practices of the nation, and his subsequent appeal for neutrality of private speech and thought was widely applauded by the American public as a statesmanlike gesture to insulate the United States from Europe's foolish and irrational conflict. Even though the events of the war soon made the latter injunction impossible for most Americans, including the President himself, to follow, the nearly universal desire for peace and faith in neutrality continued to buttress the administration in its relations with the European belligerents. The economic ties with the Entente Powers (initially, Great Britain, France, and Russia) that resulted from British control of the seas and hence of access to the American market, were accepted by most citizens as valuable to the nation's economy and as consistent with past American practices and the dictates of neutrality. Why should the New World not continue to profit from the needs and

follies of the Old? Again, when Germany launched the first of its submarine campaigns, the majority of the people approved Wilson's defense
of national rights, honor, and lives against that novel and ruthless
challenge. Yet as late as the presidential election campaign of 1916, after
repeated crises with Germany over the U-boat issue and the issuance of
an American threat to sever diplomatic relations, sentiment for continued neutrality prevailed generally throughout the country. Not until
early 1917 and the coming of unrestricted submarine warfare did a
majority of Americans reluctantly support entrance into the war.

America at war speedily transformed the struggle from a defense of
national rights and honor against the submarine challenge into a great
crusade for the universal triumph of democracy over autocracy and the
achievement of perpetual peace through the establishment of a global
collective security organization, the League of Nations. War passions and
idealism were aroused to a high intensity, with the result that the actual
causes and immediate aims of America's involvment were largely for-
gotten and noble goals impossible of complete achievement became the
rallying slogans of the hour. The inevitable disenchantment after the
war was over caused many citizens to question if the sacrifices of belligerency had been justified after all. Had it been wise or worthy to
enter the struggle? Why had America abandoned its cherished neutrality
to enter such a futile conflict?

The tide of disillusionment and isolationist sentiment increased in the
1920's and early 1930's. That intervention in 1917 had been a woeful
and costly mistake which must not be repeated when Europe again
experienced a major war increasingly became a popular truism. Scholars
began to study closely the events of 1914–1917 which had led America to
war in an effort to discover what had gone wrong and who had failed
in leadership. These studies were greatly affected by the prevailing
tendency toward an economic interpretation of history, together with a
heightened awareness of the importance of mass psychology and the
role of propaganda. "Revisionists" — those who would revise or alter
sharply the previously accepted explanations of why America had gone
to war — denied that the government had been genuinely neutral in
1914–1917 and had been forced into hostilities only by submarine attacks
upon its ocean commerce; far from the war having been made in Berlin,
these writers asserted that it had been largely forced upon Germany by
America. Pro-Ally sentiment on the part of important officials and
prominent citizens, close and unneutral economic entanglement with the
Allied Powers (as the Entente came to be called), the effects of British
propaganda, and the pro-Ally and anti-German foreign policies pursued
by the Wilson administration inevitably had led to conflict and hostilities
with the Central Powers of Germany and Austria-Hungary. Historians
such as H. C. Peterson and Charles C. Tansill varied in the emphasis
placed upon any one of these factors as *casus belli*, but they agreed that,
whatever the precise mechanism, belligerency had resulted from the

imperfections in America's policy of neutrality. Either the nation had been drawn into the conflict by its own unneutral sentiments and economic interests or its pro-Ally policies had led a hurt and enraged Germany to retaliate with U-boat warfare.

Defenders of Wilson's neutrality policies, who did not believe that intervention had been an avoidable mistake, sought to refute such criticisms and insisted that he had made every effort consistent with the nation's rights and honor to stay out of the war. Charles Seymour was the historian most representative of that point of view. The contraband trade with the Allies, he asserted, had been completely neutral and its one-sided character resulted simply from the fact of German naval weakness. Both belligerent camps had been requested to respect neutral rights and sharp protests had been directed at the violations by each side; Allied infractions had affected only property, however, while the U-boat endangered lives as well. Finally, Seymour maintained, the evidence indicated that despite the prevalence of pro-Ally sentiment, the United States would have remained at peace but for the intolerable challenge to its rights and honor presented by Germany's ruthless submarine warfare.

Since 1945, with the waning of old passions and debates and from the perspective of another global holocaust, scholars such as Arthur S. Link and Ernest R. May have broadened the study of American involvement to include not only policies and politics in the United States but in the principal belligerent countries as well. Economics, propaganda, and ancient ties and sentiment have all been reconsidered and the attitudes of Wilson and his advisers subjected to close scrutiny. Elements of practical and realistic thought about the significance of the European war for American security and long term political and economic interests have been detected in the attitudes of Wilson and his aides, which complement, and perhaps modify, the idealistic and moralistic convictions previously emphasized by students of the period.

Several basic questions must be raised and answered by the student seeking to understand the causes of American involvement in World War I. Was the United States genuinely neutral in its policies toward both belligerent sides? Or did propaganda and economic ties to the Allies seriously lessen, impair, and finally destroy that neutrality? Why did Germany launch unrestricted submarine warfare, and did it alone explain America's entry into the war? What was the effect of security considerations in the formulation of American policies and the decision to intervene in 1917? And did ideological concepts of the war as a struggle between democracy and autocracy, involving the future peace and stability of the world, play a significant role in the transition from neutrality to belligerency? The editor hopes that the following selection of documents and secondary readings will enable the student to understand better this complex and extraordinarily significant period in American and world history.

 I

THE IMPACT OF
THE GREAT WAR
ON AMERICA

PART ONE

Neutrality Proclaimed

Two rival blocs had formed in Europe at the turn of the century: the Central Powers of Germany, Austria-Hungary and Italy and the Triple Entente of France, Russia and Great Britain. The resultant arms race and competition for security and prestige had threatened to end in war on several occasions prior to 1914, but each time the crisis had been narrowly averted. On June 28, 1914, a Serbian nationalist's shots at Sarajevo felled the heir to the Austro-Hungarian throne, the Archduke Franz Ferdinand, and set in motion a series of events culminating in a general war between the rival camps. Determined to defend its multi-national empire against Serbian nationalism, Austria served an ultimatum on Serbia and then declared war. Within a few weeks, Great Britain, France, and Russia, later joined by Japan and Italy, were at war with the Central Powers and their eventual allies, Turkey and Bulgaria. The most destructive war in modern history was underway. When it finally ended, nearly four and one-half years later, after incredible losses of life and treasure, the political map of Europe had been shattered almost beyond recognition. The age of European primacy was nearly over.

President Woodrow Wilson's proclamation on August 4, 1914, announced that the United States would remain aloof from the war, and in accordance with the statutes it defined the duties incumbent upon a neutral nation. Wilson subsequently requested citizens to seek neutrality of thought and speech as well.

1 · The Proclamation of Neutrality by President Wilson

WHEREAS a state of war unhappily exists between Austria-Hungary and Servia and between Germany and Russia and between Germany and France;

And WHEREAS the United States is on terms of friendship and amity with the contending powers, and with the persons inhabiting their several dominions;

And WHEREAS there are citizens of the United States residing within the territories or dominions of each of the said belligerents and carrying on commerce, trade, or other business or pursuits therein;

And WHEREAS there are subjects of each of the said belligerents residing within the territory or jurisdiction of the United States, and carrying on commerce, trade, or other business or pursuits therein;

And WHEREAS the laws and treaties of the United States, without interfering with the free expression of opinion and sympathy, or with the commercial manufacture or sale of arms or munitions of war, nevertheless impose upon all persons who may be within their territory and jurisdiction the duty of an impartial neutrality during the existence of the contest;

And WHEREAS it is the duty of a neutral government not to permit or suffer the making of its waters subservient to the purposes of war;

Now, therefore, I, WOODROW WILSON, President of the United States of America, in order to preserve the neutrality of the United States and of its citizens and of persons within its territory and jurisdiction, and to enforce its laws and treaties, and in order that all persons, being warned of the general tenor of the laws and treaties of the United States in this behalf, and of the law of nations, may thus be prevented from any violation of the same, do hereby declare and proclaim that by certain provisions of the act approved on the 4th day of March, A.D. 1909, commonly known as the "Penal Code of the United States," the following acts are forbidden to be done, under severe penalties, within the territory and jurisdiction of the United States, to wit. . . .

And I do further declare and proclaim that the statutes and the treaties of the United States and the law of nations alike require that no person, within the territory and jurisdiction of the United States, shall take part, directly or indirectly, in the said wars, but shall remain at peace with all

1 *Papers Relating to the Foreign Relations of the United States, 1914, Supplement* (Washington: Government Printing Office, 1928), pp. 547–551. Hereafter this series will be cited as *Foreign Relations, 1914, Supplement.*

of the said belligerents, and shall maintain a strict and impartial neutrality.

And I do hereby enjoin all citizens of the United States, and all persons residing or being within the territory or jurisdiction of the United States, to observe the laws thereof, and to commit no act contrary to the provisions of the said statutes or treaties or in violation of the law of nations in that behalf.

And I do hereby warn all citizens of the United States, and all persons residing or being within its territory or jurisdiction that, while the free and full expression of sympathies in public and private is not restricted by the laws of the United States, military forces in aid of a belligerent cannot lawfully be originated or organized within its jurisdiction; and that, while all persons may lawfully and without restriction by reason of the aforesaid state of war manufacture and sell within the United States arms and munitions of war, and other articles ordinarily known as "contraband of war," yet they cannot carry such articles upon the high seas for the use or service of a belligerent, nor can they transport soldiers and officers of a belligerent, or attempt to break any blockade which may be lawfully established and maintained during the said wars without incurring the risk of hostile capture and the penalties denounced by the law of nations in that behalf.

And I do hereby give notice that all citizens of the United States and others who may claim the protection of this Government, who may misconduct themselves in the premises, will do so at their peril, and that they can in no wise obtain any protection from the Government of the United States against the consequences of their misconduct. . . .

2 · Appeal for Neutrality of Thought and Speech

An appeal by the President of the United States to the citizens of the Republic, requesting their assistance in maintaining a state of neutrality during the present European war; presented in the Senate, August 19, 1914, and ordered to be printed

MY FELLOW COUNTRYMEN: I suppose that every thoughtful man in America has asked himself, during these last troubled weeks, what influ-

---

2 *Foreign Relations, 1914, Supplement,* pp. 551–552.

ence the European war may exert upon the United States, and I take the liberty of addressing a few words to you in order to point out that it is entirely within our own choice what its effects upon us will be and to urge very earnestly upon you the sort of speech and conduct which will best safeguard the nation against distress and disaster.

The effect of the war upon the United States will depend upon what American citizens say and do. Every man who really loves America will act and speak in the true spirit of neutrality, which is the spirit of impartiality and fairness and friendliness to all concerned. The spirit of the nation in this critical matter will be determined largely by what individuals and society and those gathered in public meetings do and say, upon what newspapers and magazines contain, upon what ministers utter in their pulpits, and men proclaim as their opinions on the street.

The people of the United States are drawn from many nations, and chiefly from the nations now at war. It is natural and inevitable that there should be the utmost variety of sympathy and desire among them with regard to the issues and circumstances of the conflict. Some will wish one nation, others another, to succeed in the momentous struggle. It will be easy to excite passion and difficult to allay it. Those responsible for exciting it will assume a heavy responsibility, responsibility for no less a thing than that the people of the United States, whose love of their country and whose loyalty to its Government should unite them as Americans all, bound in honor and affection to think first of her and her interests, may be divided in camps of hostile opinion, hot against each other, involved in the war itself in impulse and opinion if not in action.

Such divisions among us would be fatal to our peace of mind and might seriously stand in the way of the proper performance of our duty as the one great nation at peace, the one people holding itself ready to play a part of impartial mediation and speak the counsels of peace and accommodation, not as a partisan, but as a friend.

I venture, therefore, my fellow countrymen, to speak a solemn word of warning to you against that deepest, most subtle, most essential breach of neutrality which may spring out of partisanship, out of passionately taking sides. The United States must be neutral in fact as well as in name during these days that are to try men's souls. We must be impartial in thought as well as in action, must put a curb upon our sentiments as well as upon every transaction that might be construed as a preference of one party to the struggle before another.

My thought is of America. I am speaking, I feel sure, the earnest wish and purpose of every thoughtful American that this great country of ours, which is, of course, the first in our thoughts and in our hearts, should show herself in this time of peculiar trial a nation fit beyond others to exhibit the fine poise of undisturbed judgment, the dignity of self-control, the efficiency of dispassionate action; a nation that neither sits in judgment upon others nor is disturbed in her own counsels and which keeps herself fit and free to do what is honest and disinterested and truly serviceable for the peace of the world.

Shall we not resolve to put upon ourselves the restraints which will bring to our people the happiness and the great and lasting influence for peace we covet for them?

WOODROW WILSON

PART TWO

Public Reaction to the War

The following excerpts from *The Literary Digest* summarize American newspaper editorial opinion on the responsibility for the outbreak of the European war and provide some insight into the state of public opinion in the early months of the conflict. Although most Americans had applauded the President's plea for neutrality, the pull of Old World loyalties and emotions aroused by the war made impartiality of thought and sentiment virtually impossible. Of a population of nearly 92 million people in 1914, almost a third were "hyphenated" Americans (either born abroad or with one or both parents as immigrants). German-Americans numbering over eight million, and large numbers of Irish-Americans and Scandinavian-Americans were inclined to sympathize with the German cause. Conversely, three million recent immigrants from Great Britain and millions of Italian-Americans and Russian-Americans were drawn toward the Allies, while the bulk of the "older" Americans were also at least mildly pro-Ally, the result of their English heritage and of America's traditional friendship with France.

3 · Blaming Germany for the War

Bitter protests are coming from German newspapers, German societies, and many German Americans of high standing among us against what they declare to be unfair treatment by the newspapers of this country. They complain of anti-German editorials, of "abysmal ignorance concerning German conditions," and of suppression or obscure display of news favorable to Germany. Our editors find no difficulty in acquitting themselves of blame for unfairness in handling the news, replying that practically no military information is allowed to leak through the German frontiers, and that practically all our press reports undergo a censorship in Brussels, Paris, or London before reaching us. But when blamed for anti-German sentiments, many editorial writers hasten to make a distinction between the German people, whom they highly honor, and the German Government, which they hold primarily responsible for a general European war. And this position is one which weeklies like *The Outlook*, *The Independent*, and *Harper's Weekly* hold, tho they are careful to present the German viewpoint. Most spokesmen for Germany, however, reject such efforts to distinguish between the rulers and the nation, and reiterate, in a series of letters and statements to the press, their view of the war as one forced on Germany or as a necessary conflict between Slav and Teuton, the latter, of course, standing for civilization. They agree with the Kaiser that the war is "the result of ill will existing for years against the strength and prosperity of the German Empire." . . .

The repeated statement in the American press that the Kaiser and a Prussian military autocracy forced a war which the German people do not want is ridiculed by many Germans here. Take, for instance, these paragraphs from the New York *Staats-Zeitung*, perhaps the leading German-American daily:

"It is frequently stated here that the attitude of the American people is directed not against the German people, but against the Kaiser. He is the one to be 'defeated.' The intention is to 'free' the German people from the Kaiser and his régime. What groundless folly! The Kaiser is good enough for the German people. Even the Socialists have shouldered their guns. . . .

"You can not separate the German Kaiser from the German people. It will be in the interests of both countries to avoid any permanent disarrangement of the friendly feeling between the German and American people."

Professor Ernst Richard, of Columbia University, President of the German-American Peace Society, heads a German-American committee of protest against the attitude of the American press. He argues that

---

3 *The Literary Digest*, 49:293–295 (August 22, 1914).

Germany is not an autocracy, that her army is "a citizens' army" for national defense, and says of the Kaiser: "I have been often assured by German working men that the people, by a free vote, would vote for the Kaiser and against having a republic." And he plainly informs our editors that "it will take a long time and strong proof of good will before Germany and Austria will forget for which side the American public stood in this, their fight for the defense of the Western world against Muscovitism and all that it implies."

These protests from our German fellow citizens are quite justified, in the opinion of the Milwaukee *Free Press*, which has "gone through our exchanges since the beginning of this war in an endeavor to find a just and reasonably correct representation of Germany's position," and has "not found one." The Chicago *News*, Boston *Traveler*, and Hartford *Times* fear that we are making up our minds hastily and without sufficient knowledge about Germany's position, and that public opinion here may be unwarrantably inflamed against the Kaiser. A Socialist daily, the New York *Call*, finds one cause of this "undeniable disposition to unload the responsibility for the war upon the Kaiser" in the feeling among business men that the German Fleet must be annihilated before the seas will again be open for commerce.

Turning now to the other side, we find Mr. Horace White writing to the Boston *Herald* that there is no prejudice or political feeling against Germany in this country, "but much that is favorable, and justly so." If, he says, "our opinions have undergone a change within a few days, it is due to the belief that if the German Emperor had simply sat still and done nothing, the present European war would not have taken place." With this statement, and the statement of the Paris *Temps* that the war is "a war of piracy," thrust upon the allies by Germany, many of our newspaper editors agree. And strong editorials expressing that viewpoint appear in papers like the Lowell *Courier-Citizen*, Brooklyn *Citizen*, and Philadelphia *North American*. The obsession that precipitated and supports the war is not confined to Germany's rulers, says the New York *Journal of Commerce*, but "has evidently extended to the mass of the subjects of the Empire and filled them with enthusiastic loyalty."

> "It is the policy of blood and iron, of the mailed fist, of preparation for war as a means of preserving peace and dictating its terms, the militarism that has begotten a swollen pride and a brutal cast of loyal patriotism under a dominating power, which has bred this obsession that all the world is in arms against Germany, and that she must fight and conquer or die as a great Power of the earth."

Nevertheless a distinction is insisted upon by those who, like the Syracuse *Post-Standard*, see American sympathy generally felt "against the German Emperor — not against the German people," and they include, among newspapers, names like the Worcester *Gazette*, Rochester *Herald*, Springfield *Republican*, New York *Globe*, *World*, *Tribune*, *Times*, *Eve-*

ning Post, St. Louis *Republic,* Philadelphia *Press,* Baltimore *News,* and Salt Lake *Herald-Republican.* The New York *Times* endeavors at some length to prove that there is no newspaper prejudice against Germany. Our papers, indeed, have put upon the Emperor a large part of the responsibility for the war. . . . "Not since the rise of the first Napoleon," says the Colorado Springs *Gazette,* "has there been an instance of a ruler so obsessed by the craze for military glory and imperial aggrandizement." And the New York *World* declares that "wantonly and deliberately the Kaiser has plunged his sword into the heart of civilization," and there can be only one answer to his challenge —

> "German autocracy has made itself the enemy of mankind. Its destruction will be the emancipation of the German people themselves as well as the salvation of European republicanism."

4 · *American Sympathies in the War*

Much talk is heard about American sympathy in the European War, but thus far it has had no basis except hearsay or very limited personal observation. Do a majority of the American press or the American people favor the Germans or the Allies? To approach an answer to this question we have obtained statements from between 350 and 400 editors, telling their own attitudes and the feelings of their communities toward the warring nations. We need hardly say that we give the result of this inquiry entirely without partizanship, and purely for our readers' information. The replies cover the country from the Atlantic to the Pacific and from Mexico to the Canadian border. They can not very well be woven into a connected narrative, but the reader who scans the summary presented here will find the country divided into large areas where the feeling is preponderately for one side or the other, or is so mixed as to be neutral. Yet the sympathy on either side is that of the distant observer. No belligerency is evident anywhere. Reports of pro-German sentiment follow pretty closely the geographical distribution of our German-American population, but at the same time a number of editors report a more favorable feeling toward Germany now than at the start of the war, so both sides can exact some comfort from the findings. We hear frequently from sections of the Middle West, in which the Germans preponderate, that "this is a German community — we are for the Germans." Or it is related of other districts that the "extreme partizanship" of the

German-Americans has awakened a good deal of active sympathy for the Allies. But no matter in what territory we come upon downright supporters of the Allies, we are nearly always assured by our informants that "not Germany or the Germans" do they and their readers condemn, but "Prussian militarism." The reproaches to the Kaiser for having plunged the German people into war are severe by pro-Ally partizans in some quarters. In others it is noticed not unfavorably that the local Germans are "very loyal to the Fatherland and the Kaiser." Finally, in some middle-sized towns of mixed population we even find a general tone of absolute neutrality. The citizens are said to have only one idea about the war, and that is to see it over and done with at the earliest possible day. In the larger cities, such as New York, Chicago, and others, the sentiment of the community is aptly described as "very mixed," because of the great and various foreign population. Looking at the matter in wider scope, that is, in the Government's geographical divisions of the country, we are struck with an old fact discovered anew. The marked leaning of New England toward the Allies may be the effect of the lineage of the majority of the inhabitants, just as the pro-German tendency of the Central States or of regions in the far Northwest proceeds from the heavy population of Germans and German-Americans in this region. In the Southern and Southwestern States, whose people are principally of English ancestry, sympathy inclines to the Allies, while the Western States to the Coast seem of the same bent, tho less markedly. Part explanation of this condition is found in the statement of one authority that in certain sections "the Teutonic element is far in the minority." Nor must it be overlooked that in neighborhoods which were "on the fence," so to speak, at the beginning of the war, American resentment against so-called "censored" British dispatches works for German sentiment, just as the Belgian invasion has influenced some "neutral" minds against Germany. The following summary shows in cold figures the complete returns to our inquiry. To these must be added the warmth of personality as exprest in the statements of the editors.

Attitude of the Press. Of the 367 replies, 105 editors report that they favor the Allies, 20 favor the Germans, and 242 are neutral.

Of the pro-Ally editors 34 are in the Eastern States, 13 in the Central, 47 in the Southern, and 11 in the Western.

Only one pro-German editor hails from the Eastern States, while 10 are from the Central, 5 from the Southern, and 4 from the Western group.

The neutral editors number 43 in the Eastern states, 112 in the Central, 51 in the Southern, and 36 in the Western.

Attitude of the People. The feeling of the cities and towns represented is reported as favoring the Allies in 189 cases, for the Germans in 38, and neutral or divided in 140.

The pro-Ally cities and towns heard from total 52 in the Eastern division, 40 in the Central, 71 in the Southern, and 26 in the Western.

The pro-German communities are 2 in the Eastern group, 29 in the Central, 4 in the Southern, and 3 in the Western.

Cities and towns reckoned as neutral or divided number 24 in the Eastern States, 66 in the Central, 28 in the Southern, and 22 in the Western. . . .

PART THREE

The Role of Propaganda

A large minority of German-Americans, Irish-Americans and others were attracted to the cause of the Central Powers, some vociferously so. The great majority of Americans, however, because of cultural, ethnic, and economic ties to Great Britain and the traditional Franco-American friendship dating back to the American Revolution, were mildly to strongly pro-Entente in sympathies and convictions. Both belligerent sides engaged in propaganda in the United States. German and British activities were extensive and well-organized, but in the long run Great Britain scored the greater victory in the battle of words. Exploiting language affinities and its control of the more direct channels of communication between Europe and America, the British were also aided immeasurably by the fact that the war was fought largely on Belgian and French soil — Germany obviously was the invader and seemed to many to be an aggressive militaristic power responsible with its ally Austria for initiating the conflict.

Much of the British propaganda effort depicted the rulers of Germany as ruthlessly autocratic and imperialistic and the German army as brutal and inhumane in its treatment of civilians in the war areas and zones of occupation. An official committee headed by James, Viscount Bryce, a respected former ambassador to Washington who had written much — and sympathetically — about the United States, investigated charges of German atrocities and issued its report in May, 1915. It consisted of testimony, some of which was of the second or third-hand variety, which alleged against German troops deliberate destruction of civilian property and buildings of historical and cultural value, sexual crimes, use of civilians as shields for military action, and other outrages. While scholars have questioned the reliability of many of the stories recounted in the Report, it does seem that the German army was severe in its treatment of civilian populations in the invaded areas and utilized terror for purposes of intimidation. Moreover, Lord Bryce's high reputation and popularity in America lent credence to the British charges. The Report was issued during the *Lusitania* crisis in May 1915 and had a profound effect on American opinion.

13

5 · The Bryce Report: German Treatment of Belgian Civilians

In the minds of Prussian officers War seems to have become a sort of sacred mission, one of the highest functions of the omnipotent State, which is itself as much an Army as a State. Ordinary morality and the ordinary sentiment of pity vanish in its presence, superseded by a new standard which justifies to the soldier every means that can conduce to success, however shocking to a natural sense of justice and humanity, however revolting to his own feelings. The Spirit of War is deified. Obedience to the State and its War Lord leaves no room for any other duty or feeling. Cruelty becomes legitimate when it promises victory. Proclaimed by the heads of the army, this doctrine would seem to have permeated the officers and affected even the private soldiers, leading them to justify the killing of non-combatants as an act of war, and so accustoming them to slaughter that even women and children become at last the victims. It cannot be supposed to be a national doctrine, for it neither springs from nor reflects the mind and feelings of the German people as they have heretofore been known to other nations. It is a specifically military doctrine, the outcome of a theory held by a ruling caste who have brooded and thought, written and talked and dreamed about War until they have fallen under its obsession and been hypnotised by its spirit.

The doctrine is plainly set forth in the German Official Monograph on the usages of War on land, issued under the direction of the German staff. This book is pervaded throughout by the view that whatever military needs suggest becomes thereby lawful, and upon this principle, as the diaries show, the German officers acted.

If this explanation be the true one, the mystery is solved, and that which seemed scarcely credible becomes more intelligible though not less pernicious. This is not the only case that history records in which a false theory, disguising itself as loyalty to a State or to a Church, has perverted the conception of Duty, and becomes a source of danger to the world. . . .

(a) *Killing of Non-Combatants.* The killing of civilians in Belgium has been already described sufficiently. Outrages on the civilian popula-

---

5 Great Britain, *Report of the Committee on Alleged German Outrages* (London: His Majesty's Stationery Office, 1915), pp. 44–61.

14

tion of the invaded districts, the burning of villages, the shooting of innocent inhabitants and the taking of hostages, pillage and destruction continued as the German armies passed into France. . . .

A proclamation (a specimen of which was produced to the Committee) issued at Reims, and placarded over the town, affords a clear illustration of the methods adopted by the German Higher Command. The population of Reims is warned that on the slightest disturbance part or the whole of the city will be burnt to the ground and all the hostages taken from the city (a long list of whom is given in the proclamation) immediately shot. . . .

Naturally soldiers in a foreign country, with which they were unacquainted, cannot be expected always to give accurately the names of villages through which they passed on their marches, but this does not prevent their evidence from being definite as to what they actually saw in the farms and houses where the German troops had recently been. Many shocking outrages are recorded. Three examples here may suffice, others are given in the Appendix. A sergeant who had been through the retreat from Mons, and then taken part in the advance from the Marne, and who had been engaged in driving out some German troops from a village, states that his troop halted outside a bakery just inside the village. It was a private house where baking was done, "not like our bakeries here." Two or three women were standing at the door. The women motioned them to come into the house, as did also three civilian Frenchmen who were there. They took them into a garden at the back of the house. At the end of the garden was the bakery. They saw two old men — between 60 and 70 years of age — and one old woman lying close to each other in the garden. All three had the scalps cut right through and the brains were hanging out. They were still bleeding. Apparently they had only just been killed. The three French civilians belonged to this same house. One of them spoke a few words of English. He gave them to understand that these three had been killed by the Germans because they had refused to bake bread for them.

Another witness states that two German soldiers took hold of a young civilian named D. and bound his hands behind his back, and struck him in the face with their fists. They then tied his hands in front and fastened the cord to the tail of the horse. The horse dragged him for about 50 yards and then the Germans loosened his hands and left him. The whole of his face was cut and torn and his arms and legs were bruised. On the following day one of his sisters, whose husband was a soldier, came to their house with her four children. His brother, who was also married and who lived in a village near Valenciennes, went to fetch the bread for his sister. On the way back to their house he met a patrol of Uhlans, who took him to the market place at Valenciennes and then shot him. About 12 other civilians were also shot in the market place. The Uhlans then burned 19 houses in the village, and afterwards burned the corpses of the civilians, including that of his brother. His father and his uncle afterwards went to see the dead body of his brother, but the German soldiers refused to allow them to pass.

A lance-corporal in the Rifles, who was on patrol duty with five privates during the retirement of the Germans after the Marne, states that they entered a house in a small village and took ten Uhlans prisoners and then searched the house and found two women and two children. One was dead, but the body not yet cold. The left arm had been cut off just below the elbow. The floor was covered with blood. The woman's clothing was disarranged. The other woman was alive but unconscious. Her right leg had been cut off above the knee. There were two little children, a boy about 4 or 5 and a girl of about 6 or 7. The boy's left hand was cut off at the wrist and the girl's right hand at the same place. They were both quite dead. The same witness states that he saw several women and children lying dead in various other places, but says he could not say whether this might not have been accidentally caused in legitimate fighting.

The evidence before us proves that, in the parts of France referred to, murder of unoffending civilians and other acts of cruelty, including aggravated cases of rape, carried out under threat of death, and sometimes actually followed by murder of the victim, were committed by some of the German troops.

(*b*) *The Treatment of Women and Children.* The evidence shows that the German authorities, when carrying out a policy of systematic arson and plunder in selected districts, usually drew some distinction between the adult male population on the one hand and the women and children on the other. It was a frequent practice to set apart the adult males of the condemned district with a view to the execution of a suitable number — preferably of the younger and more vigorous — and to reserve the women and children. . . .

We find many well-established cases of the slaughter (often accompanied by mutilation) of whole families, including not infrequently that of quite small children. In two cases it seems to be clear that preparations were made to burn a family alive. These crimes were committed over a period of many weeks and simultaneously in many places, and the authorities must have known or ought to have known that cruelties of this character were being perpetrated, nor can anyone doubt that they could have been stopped by swift and decisive action on the part of the heads of the German army.

The use of women and even children as a screen for the protection of the German troops is referred to in a later part of this Report. From the number of troops concerned, it must have been commanded or acquiesced in by officers, and in some cases the presence and connivance of officers is proved.

The cases of violation, sometimes under threat of death, are numerous and clearly proved. We referred here to comparatively few out of the many that have been placed in the Appendix, because the circumstances are in most instances much the same. They were often accompanied with cruelty, and the slaughter of women after violation is more than once credibly attested.

It is quite possible that in some cases where the body of a Belgian or a French woman is reported as lying in the roadside pierced with bayonet wounds or hanging naked from a tree, or else as lying gashed and mutilated in a cottage kitchen or bedroom, the woman in question gave some provocation. She may by act or word have irritated her assailant, and in certain instances evidence has been supplied both as to the provocation offered and as to the retribution inflicted: —

"Just before we got to Melen," says a witness, who had fallen into the hands of the Germans on August 5th, "I saw a woman with a child in her arms standing on the side of the road on our left-hand side watching the soldiers go by. Her name was G . . . . , aged about sixty-three, and a neighbour of mine. The officer asked the woman for some water in good French. She went inside her son's cottage to get some and brought it immediately he had stopped. The officer went into the cottage garden and drank the water. The woman then said, when she saw the prisoners, 'Instead of giving you water you deserve to be shot.' The officer shouted to us, 'March.' We went on, and immediately I saw the officer draw his revolver and shoot the woman and child. One shot killed both." . . .

In considering the question of provocation it is pertinent to take into account the numerous cases in which old women and very small children have been shot, bayoneted, and even mutilated. Whatever excuse may be offered by the Germans for the killing of grown-up women, there can be no possible defence for the murder of children, and if it can be shown that infants and small children were not infrequently bayoneted and shot it is a fair inference that many of the offences against women require no explanation more recondite than the unbridled violence of brutal or drunken criminals.

It is clearly shown that many offences were committed against infants and quite young children. On one occasion children were even roped together and used as a military screen against the enemy, on another three soldiers went into action carrying small children to protect themselves from flank fire. A shocking case of the murder of a baby by a drunken soldier at Malines is thus recorded by one eye-witness and confirmed by another: —

"One day when the Germans were not actualling [*sic*] bombarding the town I left my house to go to my mother's house in High Street. My husband was with me. I saw eight German soldiers, and they were drunk. They were singing and making a lot of noise and dancing about. As the German soldiers came along the street I saw a small child, whether boy or girl I could not see, come out of a house. The child was about two years of age. The child came into the middle of the street so as to be in the way of the soldiers. The soldiers were walking in twos. The first line of two passed the child; one of the second line, the man on the left, stepped aside and drove his bayonet with both hands into the child's stomach, lifting the child into the air on his bayonet and carrying it away on his bayonet, he and his comrades still singing. The child screamed when the soldier struck it with his bayonet, but not afterwards."

These, no doubt, were for the most part the acts of drunken soldiers, but an incident has been recorded which discloses the fact that even sober and highly-placed officers were not always disposed to place a high value on child life. Thus the General, wishing to be conducted to the Town Hall at Lebbeke, remarked in French to his guide, who was accompanied by a small boy: "If you do not show me the right way I will shoot you and your boy." There was no need to carry the threat into execution, but that the threat should have been made is significant.

We cannot tell whether these acts of cruelty to children were part of the scheme for inducing submission by inspiring terror. . . .

Conclusions. From the foregoing pages it will be seen that the Committee have come to a definite conclusion upon each of the heads under which the evidence has been classified.

It is proved —

(i) That there were in many parts of Belgium deliberate and systematically organised massacres of the civil population, accompanied by many isolated murders and other outrages.

(ii) That in the conduct of the war generally innocent civilians, both men and women, were murdered in large numbers, women violated, and children murdered.

(iii) That looting, house burning, and the wanton destruction of property were ordered and countenanced by the officers of the German Army, that elaborate provision had been made for systematic incendiarism at the very outbreak of the war, and that the burnings and destruction were frequent where no military necessity could be alleged, being indeed part of a system of general terrorization.

(iv) That the rules and usages of war were frequently broken, particularly by the using of civilians, including women and children, as a shield for advancing forces exposed to fire, to a less degree by killing the wounded and prisoners, and in the frequent abuse of the Red Cross and the White Flag.

Sensible as they are of the gravity of these conclusions, the Committee conceive that they would be doing less than their duty if they failed to record them as fully established by the evidence. Murder, lust, and pillage prevailed over many parts of Belgium on a scale unparalleled in any war between civilised nations during the last three centuries.

Our function is ended when we have stated what the evidence establishes, but we may be permitted to express our belief that these disclosures will not have been made in vain if they touch and rouse the conscience of mankind, and we venture to hope that as soon as the present war is over, the nations of the world in council will consider what means can be provided and sanctions devised to prevent the recurrence of such horrors as our generation is now witnessing.

6 · *American Reaction to the Bryce Report*

Because the American people have had an object-lesson in the torpedoing of the *Lusitania,* and because, as the New York *Herald* remarks, "they know James Bryce," the Bryce Commission's report on alleged German atrocities in Belgium and northern France has attracted far more attention in the American press, and has won, apparently, a far wider credence than did the somewhat similar reports previously issued by France and Belgium. "The Bryce report has sharply directed the attention of civilized humanity to Germany's manner of conducting her warfare," says the New Haven *Journal-Courier,* and the Boston *Herald,* until now rather skeptical of the many stories of atrocities with which the press have been deluged since the war began, is convinced that "all dispute as to the character of the German conquest of Belgium may now be laid aside." "A civilized and neutral world, recalling what it knew of Germany and Germans, found it impossible to believe that the things reported in Belgium represented German deliberate and reasoned policy," remarks the New York *Tribune,* "but all such incredulity, so far as the United States is concerned, sank with the *Lusitania.*" Before bringing in a final verdict, however, the New York *Evening Mail* calls for a further investigation by an international commission. "The honor of humanity itself and the credit of the faith of Christendom," exclaims *The Evening Mail,* "demand that either these terrible charges shall be disproved, or that the men guilty of the committing, ordering, or permitting the outrages shall be held up, on the fullest authority, to the scourging scorn of the whole world." "The testimony of the Bryce Commission is such that general

6 *The Literary Digest,* 50:1257–1259 (May 29, 1915).

denials from the German side are no longer sufficient," says the New York *Globe*, which hopes that "Germany will never have applied against her civilians the rules that her soldiers applied in Belgium."

The British Commission, which carried on its investigation independently of the French and Belgian commissions, based its conclusions on the depositions of more than 1,200 eyewitnesses of the incidents described, and upon the corroboratory evidence found in diaries kept by German soldiers. The personnel of the Commission is as follows: Viscount Bryce, author of "The American Commonwealth," and from 1907 to 1912 British Ambassador at Washington; Sir Frederick Pollock, Sir Edward Clarke, Sir Alfred Hopkinson, and Sir Kenelm E. Digby, all eminent in the domain of English law; Herbert A. L. Fisher, historian and economist; and Harold Cox, editor of *The Edinburgh Review*. These highly trained men, "bound," as the New York *Sun* remarks, "by their education, pursuits, experience, and habits of mind to seek and know facts," confess that they began their work "with doubts whether a positive result would be obtained." But after five months of investigation they are convinced that in the early weeks of the war "murder, lust, and pillage prevailed over many parts of Belgium on a scale unparalleled in any war between civilized nations during the last three centuries," and they find the following conclusions "definitely established by the evidence". . . .

"That is how Germany makes war," comments *The Republican*. The authorities responsible for the program of "frightfulness" in Belgium, remarks the Washington *Herald*, are "the same authorities who sank the *Lusitania* and murdered 115 Americans because England interfered with her commerce, and because they doubted America's neutrality." "No denunciation could add to the force of this plain tale," says the Philadelphia *Public Ledger,* and the Waterbury *Republican* remarks: "The work done in some parts of Belgium proves that civilized people are not fit to make war upon one another." As a result of this "tale of systematic butchery, of remorseless and calculated terrorism," and of the "*Lusitania* horror," remarks the New York *Evening Post,* Germany "stands now branded with a mark of infamy such as in our time has not been stamped upon the face of any people." "The last hope that German atrocities in Belgium might have been exaggerated is dissipated by Viscount Bryce's report," says the Louisville *Courier-Journal,* and the Philadelphia *Public Ledger* thinks that the word of the Commission "will be accepted by Americans as final."

At the same time many papers, like the Boston *Globe*, remind us that the report is "not a verdict," but "a partizan statement, full of partizan, tho strong, evidence." Herman Ridder, in the *New Yorker Staats-Zeitung,* dismisses the report as "a rehash of stories long since twice told and long ago disproved."

Still other papers point out that the Bryce report, if true, is damning to German militarism, but not to the German people. Thus the St. Louis

Republic remarks: "There is abundant evidence that the German private and non-commissioned officer regarded this policy of 'frightfulness' exactly as American privates, corporals, and sergeants would have regarded it, and that only the cast-iron discipline of the German military machine forced them to become the unwilling instruments of it." The incongruity between these alleged atrocities and what we know of the German character is further emphasized by another St. Louis paper, *The Star*, which says:

> "It is difficult to reconcile these brutal methods of making war with the kindly heart we so well know lies in the breast of the individual German. The German who shoots down civilians, burns villages, executes hostages, drops bombs upon sleeping towns far from the scene of war, and blows up ships loaded with non-combatant men, women, and children is a different man from the German of peace, industry, and home love.
>
> "What makes the difference? An education, from the cradle to the grave, through three generations of Prussian militarism — a complete surrender of the individual body, mind, and conscience to the State, ruled solely by the military thought."

"Germans everywhere," says the Indianapolis *News*, "should realize the danger to their national character from a continued subordination to the military caste, which is alone responsible for whatever wrong was done in Belgium." The Bryce report, says the Newark *News*, "brings Prussian militarism before the bar as that militarism never has been brought before"; and in the Nashville *News-Leader* we read:

> "The Kaiser himself, the Crown Prince, the high admiral, the general staff, and the army commanders — these are the real criminals. Humanity will never be satisfied, and justice will never be done, until these men, stript of their honors and their dignity, stand in the common dock of international crime and receive the sentence they deserve for the murder of non-combatants, the ravishing of women, and the mutilation of children."

PART FOUR

American Officials View the War
William Jennings Bryan:
Advocate of Peace

William Jennings Bryan, Democratic nominee for the presidency in 1896, 1900, and 1908, was named Secretary of State by President Wilson in 1913. The appointment was a political one and aroused much criticism; the portly Nebraskan was too closely identified with agrarian radicalism in the view of many conservative Americans. Bryan's obvious lack of experience in foreign affairs and his provincial habits and manner (such as lecturing on the Chautauqua circuit and insisting on the substitution of grape juice for alcoholic beverages at diplomatic functions) made him the target of much ridicule at home and abroad. Unquestionably he was one of the most unsophisticated secretaries of state in recent American history.

Inclined toward pacifism and convinced that the United States had a great moral mission of encouraging the spread of peace and democracy in the world, Bryan told an audience in 1913 that: "I made up my mind before I accepted the offer of Secretaryship of State that I would not take the office if I thought there was to be a war during my tenure. . . . I believe there will be no war while I am Secretary of State, and I believe there will be no war so long as I live." (*New York Times*, May 13, 1913). The following excerpt indicates his approach to the war. (Sir Cecil Spring-Rice was the British Ambassador to the United States).

7 · Bryan Discusses the War with the British Ambassador

"Bryan spoke to me about peace as he always does. He sighs for the Nobel Prize, and besides that he is a really convinced peaceman. He has just given me a sword beaten into a ploughshare six inches long to serve as a paper-weight. It is adorned with quotations from Isaiah and himself. No one doubts his sincerity, but that is rather embarrassing for us at the present moment, because he is always at us with peace propositions. This time, he said he could not understand why we could not say what we were fighting for. The nation which continued war had as much responsibility as the country which began it. The United States was the one great Power which was outside the struggle, and it was their duty to do what they could to put an end to it. — I felt rather cross and said that the United States were signatories to the Hague Convention, which had been grossly violated again and again without one word from the principal neutral nation. They were now out of court. They had done nothing to prevent the crime, and now they must not prevent the punishment. — He said that all the Powers concerned had been disappointed in their ambitions. Germany had not taken Paris. France had not retaken Alsace, England had not cleared the seas of the German navy. The last month had made no appreciable difference in the relative positions of the armies, and there was now no prospect of an issue satisfactory to any Power. Why should they not make peace now, if they had to make peace a year hence after another year's fruitless struggle. It would be far wiser if each said what it was fighting for and asked the United States to help them in arriving at a peaceful conclusion. — I asked him if he thought that under present circumstances Germany would give up Belgium and compensate her for her suffering. If not, how could the United States Government go on record as condoning a peace which would put the seal on the most disgraceful act of tyranny and oppression committed in modern times? I didn't believe there was a man in the country not a German or a Jew who could advocate such a cause. — He got rather angry and said that if that was what we wanted, why did we not say so. He added, 'Who can tell who was really responsible for what had happened in Belgium or whether the treaty wasn't only a pretext?' I reminded him that he was a great admirer of Gladstone, who was like him, a great lover of peace, and that Gladstone had always maintained that

---

7 Sir Cecil Spring-Rice to Sir Arthur Nicolson, November 13, 1914, in Stephen Gwynn, ed., *The Life and Letters of Sir Cecil Spring-Rice* (Boston: Houghton Mifflin Co., 1929 — 2 vols.), II, 240–241. Reprinted by permission.

if we had gone to war for Belgium in 1870, we should have gone to war for freedom and for public right and to save human happiness from being invaded by a tyrannous and lawless power, and that in such a war as that while the breath continued in his body he was ready to engage. This rather surprised him as he had read in the newspapers that Gladstone had always maintained that the Belgian Treaty was not binding."

PART FIVE

Robert Lansing: A Realist in the State Department

R obert Lansing, who succeeded Bryan as Secretary of State after his resignation in June, 1915, combined a realistic appraisal of the war with ideological considerations. Short of stature, formal and reserved in manner, Lansing was a New York lawyer with much experience in international arbitrations. He had traveled extensively abroad and was a close student of world affairs. Married to the daughter of John Watson Foster, Secretary of State in the administration of President Benjamin Harrison, Lansing had been associated with the State Department in several capacities since 1892. He served as Counselor of the State Department (the equivalent of the later Undersecretary) for a year prior to Bryan's resignation. Lansing held the post of Secretary of State until February, 1920, and exerted considerable influence on Wilsonian foreign policies in the neutrality and war periods. The following memorandum was written as a policy guide soon after he had replaced Bryan and during the *Lusitania* crisis.

8 · *Consideration and Outline of Policies*

July 11, 1915

I have come to the conclusion that the German Government is utterly hostile to all nations with democratic institutions because those who compose it see in democracy a menace to absolutism and the defeat of the German ambition for world domination. Everywhere German agents are plotting and intriguing to accomplish the supreme purpose of their Government.

Only recently has the conviction come that democracy throughout the world is threatened. Suspicions of the vaguest sort only a few months [ago] have been more and more confirmed. From many sources evidence has been coming until it would be folly to close one's eyes to it.

German agents have undoubtedly been at work in Mexico arousing anti-American feeling and holding out false hopes of support. The proof is not conclusive but is sufficient to compel belief. Germans also appear to be operating in Haiti and San Domingo and are probably doing so in other Latin American republics.

I think that this is being done so that this nation will have troubles in America and be unable to take part in the European War if a repetition of such outrages as the LUSITANIA sinking should require us to act. It may even go further and have in mind the possibility of a future war with this Republic in case the Allies should be defeated.

In these circumstances the policies we adopt are vital to the future of the United States and, I firmly believe to the welfare of mankind, for I see in the perpetuation of democracy the one hope of universal peace and progress for the world. Today German absolutism is the great menace to democracy.

I think that we should, therefore, adopt the following for the present and pursue these policies until conditions materially change:

1. The settlement for the time being at least of present submarine controversy because the American people are still much divided on the merits of the war. As it progresses, I believe, that the real objects of the German Government will be disclosed and there will be united opposition. Meanwhile we should get ready to meet the worst.

2. A rigorous and continuing prosecution of all plots in this country and a vigilant watch on Germans and their activities here.

---

8 Private Memoranda Books, The Papers of Robert Lansing (Manuscripts Division, Library of Congress).

3. Secret investigations of German activities in Latin America, particularly Mexico, and the adoption of means to frustrate them.

4. The cultivation of a Pan American doctrine with the object of alienating the American republics from European influence, especially the German influence. . . .

8. The actual participation of this country in the war in case it becomes evident that Germany will be the victor. A triumph for German imperialism *must not be.* We ought to look forward to this possibility and make ready to meet it.

There is a future possibility which does not change the foregoing policies but which emphasizes the last one. It is that the war may end in a draw or with the German Empire dominant over their enemies.

The argument could then be made by the German Government that, in spite of the fact that the world was arrayed against it, it succeeded in preventing the defeat of the Empire, and that having thus proved its superior efficiency it should be continued and supported as the agency best fitted to restore the German nation to a state of prosperity.

I believe that this argument would be potent with the German people, who are in the habit of unquestioning obedience to their rulers in thought as well as action. Of course the terrible cost of the war, when the time to consider that arrives, will weaken the argument for the people will ask what is the recompense for the great sacrifices they have made, the great sufferings which they have endured, and the Government will have nothing to show. The nation may then rise and demand a change to a political system in which their voice will be supreme. But, if the argument should prevail and the present military oligarchy should be perpetuated, then what?

My judgment is that the German Government, cherishing the same ambition of world empire which now possesses it, would with its usual vigor and thoroughness prepare to renew its attack on democracy. I think, however, that it would not pursue the course taken in this war which had failed because it would realize that the democratic nations would be more watchful and less trustful and better prepared to resist. It would probably endeavor to sow dissentions [*sic*] among the nations with liberal institutions and seek an alliance with other governments based to a more or less degree on the principle of absolutism.

The two powers, which would probably be approached by Germany, would be Russia and Japan, which are almost as hostile to democracy as Germany and which have similar ambitions of territorial expansion.

These three great empires would constitute an almost irresistable [*sic*] coalition against the nations with republican and liberal monarchical institutions. It would be the old struggle of absolutism against democracy, an even greater struggle than the one now in progress. The outcome would be doubtful, with, as it seems to me, the chances in favor of the autocratic allies.

The success of these three empires would mean a division for the time being at least of the world among them. I imagine that Germany would be master of Western Europe, of Africa and probably of the Americas; that Russia would dominate Scandinavia, and Western and Southern Asia; and Japan would control the Far East, the Pacific and possibly the West Coast of North America.

Their success would mean the overthrow of democracy in the world, the suppression of individual liberty, the setting up of evil ambitions, the subordination of the principles of right and justice to physical might directed by arbitrary will, and the turning back of the hands of human progress two centuries.

These, I believe, would be the consequences of the triumph of this triple alliance of autocratic empires, a triumph which even the most optimistic cannot deny to be a reasonable expectation.

The remedy seems to me to be plain. It is that Germany must not be permitted to win this war and to break even, though to prevent it this country is forced to take an active part. This ultimate necessity must be constantly in our minds in all our controversies with the belligerents. American public opinion must be prepared for the time, which may come, when we will have to cast aside our neutrality and become one of the champions of democracy.

We must in fact risk everything rather than leave the way open for a new combination of powers, stronger and more dangerous to liberty than the Central Allies are today.

PART SIX

Colonel House and the National Interests

Colonel Edward M. House — his title was an honorary one — was a wealthy and able Texan interested in politics and reform. He became the intimate friend and trusted private counselor of President Wilson and was sent to Europe in several futile efforts at promoting mediation and peace. A small and physically unimpressive man, the Colonel greatly enjoyed his role as the "grey eminence" in politics and diplomacy. With a justified sense of the importance of that role, he earned the gratitude of future historians by keeping extensive diaries. These reveal that in general he believed that a limited Allied victory would best serve the interests of the world by checking overweening German ambitions but still leaving that nation strong enough to serve as a counterpoise to Russian expansionist tendencies. He repeatedly recorded such views in his diary: "it was not good for the United States to have peace brought about until Germany was sufficiently beaten to cause her to consent to a fundamental change in her military policy. . . ." (December 3, 1914, House Diary, The Papers of Colonel Edward M. House [Yale University Library]); and "it was clear that it would not do to permit the Allies to go down in defeat, for if they did, we would follow in natural sequence." (October 13, 1915, House Diary).

9 · Colonel House to the President

PRIDE'S CROSSING, MASSACHUSETTS
August 22, 1914

DEAR GOVERNOR:

Thinking that I might see you soon has caused me to hope that I might tell you in person of how splendidly I think you are meeting the difficult situations that come to you day by day.

Your Address on Neutrality is one of the finest things you have ever done, and it has met with universal approbation. Every day editorials of the Republican press speak of you as if you were of their party instead of being the idol of ours. . . .

Of course the war continues to be a most disturbing and uncertain element. I am sorry that Japan injected herself into the general *mêlée*, for it will place an additional strain upon us not to become involved.

The saddest feature of the situation to me is that there is no good outcome to look forward to. If the Allies win, it means largely the domination of Russia on the Continent of Europe; and if Germany wins, it means the unspeakable tyranny of militarism for generations to come.

Fundamentally the Germans are playing a rôle that is against their natural instincts and inclinations, and it shows how perverted men may become by habit and environment.

Germany's success will ultimately mean trouble for us. We will have to abandon the path which you are blazing as a standard for future generations, with permanent peace as its goal and a new international ethical code as its guiding star, and build up a military machine of vast proportions. . . .

---

9 Charles Seymour, ed., *The Intimate Papers of Colonel House* (Boston & N.Y.: Houghton Mifflin Co., 1926–28, 4 vols.), I, 284–285. Reprinted by permission.

Woodrow Wilson: A Determined Neutralist

President Woodrow Wilson has been described as a theologian in politics. Steeped in the tenets of Presbyterianism, he brought a deep sense of morality to public issues. Trained first as a lawyer, he soon began a long and brilliant career as a teacher, writer, and administrator prior to entering the more boisterous world of politics. Wilson agreed with Bryan that the United States should use its power and influence in behalf of world peace, morality, and progress, an approach which has been described as one of "missionary diplomacy."

Although sympathetic to the Entente cause and initially inclined to view the Central Powers as primarily responsible for the war, Wilson soon came to a more balanced appraisal of the origins of the great conflict. Still, he remained mildly pro-Ally in sentiment and was quick to appreciate the arguments of his counselors that American interests would not be served by a German triumph. Yet he was long convinced that a termination of the war without a decisive victory for either side would be best both for America and for the cause of future world peace and stability. Until early 1917 he clearly believed that a policy of neutrality for the United States was morally and materially right. The selection from *Mr. Miller of "The Times"* is from an off-the-record interview granted to a reporter from the *New York Times*. The remaining selections are excerpts from Wilson's addresses given in early 1916 in support of his preparedness program for strengthening the army and navy against unnamed, but obvious, perils.

10 · Wilson and the War

August 30, 1914: . . . The President spoke with deep feeling of the war. He said it made him heartsick to think of how near we had come to averting this great disaster, and he thought if it had been delayed a little longer, it could never have happened, because the nations would have gotten together in the way I had outlined.

I told in detail of my suggestion to Sir Edward Grey and other members of the Cabinet, that the surest guaranty of peace was for the principals to get together frequently and discuss matters with frankness and freedom, as Great Britain and the United States were doing. He agreed that this was the most effective method and he again expressed deep regret that the war had come too soon to permit the inauguration of such procedure. He wondered whether things might have been different if I had gone sooner. I thought it would have made no difference, for the reason that the Kaiser was at Corfu and it was impossible for me to approach him sooner than I did. . . .

I was interested to hear him express as his opinion what I had written him some time ago in one of my letters, to the effect that if Germany won it would change the course of our civilization and make the United States a military nation. He also spoke of his deep regret, as indeed I did to him in that same letter, that it would check his policy for a better international ethical code.

He felt deeply the destruction of Louvain, and I found him as unsympathetic with the German attitude as is the balance of America. He goes even further than I in his condemnation of Germany's part in this war, and almost allows his feeling to include the German people as a whole rather than the leaders alone. He said German philosophy was essentially selfish and lacking in spirituality. When I spoke of the Kaiser building up the German machine as a means of maintaining peace, he said, "What a foolish thing it was to create a powder magazine and risk someone's dropping a spark into it!"

He thought the war would throw the world back three or four centuries. I did not agree with him. He was particularly scornful of Germany's disregard of treaty obligations, and was indignant at the German Chancellor's designation of the Belgian Treaty as being "only a scrap of paper." . . .

❊   ❊   ❊   ❊   ❊

November 4, 1914 [conference between Wilson and House]: We passed to the question of a reserve army. He baulked somewhat at first

---

10 House Diary entries, in Seymour, *Intimate Papers,* I, 292–293, 298–299. House returned from a trip to Europe as the war began.

32

and said he thought the labor people would object because they felt that a large army was against their interests. He did not believe there was any necessity for immediate action; he was afraid it would shock the country. He made the statement that no matter how the great war ended, there would be complete exhaustion; and, even if Germany won, she would not be in a condition seriously to menace our country for many years to come. I combated this idea, stating that Germany would have a large military force ready to act in furthering the designs which the military party evidently have in mind. He said she would not have the men. I replied that she could not win unless she had at least two or three million men under arms at the end. He evidently thought the available men would be completely wiped out.

I insisted it was time to do a great constructive work for the army and one which would make the country too powerful for any nation to think of attacking us. He told me there was reason to suspect that the Germans had laid throughout the country concrete foundations for great guns, similar to those they laid in Belgium and France. He almost feared to express this knowledge aloud, for, if the rumor got abroad, it would inflame our people to such an extent that he would be afraid of the consequences. . . .

In speaking of the building-up of our army, I thought if the Allies were successful there would be no need for haste; but if the Germans were successful and we then began our preparations, it would be almost equivalent to a declaration of war, for they would know we were directing our preparations against them. I therefore urged that we start without delay, so that we might be ready and avoid being placed in such a position. . . .

II · *Memorandum of Interview with the President, Dec. 14, 1914*

The President hopes for a deadlock in Europe. During the half hour I was with him he talked mainly on this subject. He praised *The Times* for its fair spirit in printing the chief documents of the war, and for its editorial analysis of them. He said he could not foresee what would come

11 As Quoted in F. Fraser Bond, *Mr. Miller of "The Times"* © 1931 by The New York Times Company. Reprinted by permission.

of it all, but he thought the greatest advantages for all concerned in the war, including the neutral nations, would accrue from a deadlock that "will show to them the futility of employing force in the attempt to resolve their differences." The rest of what he said I will give as nearly as I can recollect in his own words.

The Powers are making the most tremendous display of force in history. If the result of it all is merely to wear each other down without coming to a decision, the point will at length be reached when they will be glad to say, we have tried both bluff and force, and since neither could avail, there remains the alternative of trying to reason out our differences according to the principles of right and justice. So I think that the chances of a just and equitable peace, and of the only possible peace that will be lasting, will be happiest if no nation gets the decision by arms; and the danger of an unjust peace, one that will be sure to invite further calamities, will be if some one nation or group of nations succeeds in enforcing its will upon the others.

It will be found before long that Germany is not alone responsible for the war, and that some other nations will have to bear a portion of the blame in our eyes. The others will be blamed and it might be well if there were no exemplary triumph and punishment. I believe thoroughly that the settlement should be for the advantage of the European nations regarded as people and not for any nation imposing its governmental will upon alien peoples. Bismarck was longheaded when he urged Germany not to take Alsace and Lorraine.

It seems to me that the Government of Germany must be profoundly changed, and that Austria-Hungary will go to pieces altogether — ought to go to pieces for the welfare of Europe.

As for Russia, I cannot help sympathizing with its aims to secure natural outlets for its trade with the world, and a proper settlement should permit this.

"If the decision is not to be reached wholly by the forces of reason and justice after the trial at arms is found futile, if the decision by arms should be in favor of the nations that are parties of the Triple Entente; I cannot regard this as the ideal solution, at the same time I cannot see now that it would hurt greatly the interests of the United States if either France or Russia or Great Britain should finally dictate the settlement. England has already extended her empire as far as she wants to — in fact she has got more than she wants — and she now wishes to be let alone in order that she may bend all her energies to the task of consolidating the parts of her empire. Russia's ambitions are legitimate, and when she gets the outlets she needs her development will go on and the world will be benefited." . . .

12 · Excerpts From President Wilson's Preparedness Speeches (at Pittsburgh and Cleveland, January 29, 1916)

. . . What is it that we want to defend? You do not need to have me answer that question for you; it is your own thought. We want to defend the life of this Nation against any sort of interference. We want to maintain the equal right of this Nation as against the action of all other nations, and we wish to maintain the peace and unity of the Western Hemisphere. Those are great things to defend, and in their defense sometimes our thought must take a great sweep, even beyond our own borders. Do you never stop to reflect just what it is that America stands for? If she stands for one thing more than another, it is for the sovereignty of self-governing peoples, and her example, her assistance, her encouragement, has thrilled two continents in this Western World with all the fine impulses which have built up human liberty on both sides of the water. She stands, therefore, as an example of independence, as an example of free institutions, and as an example of disinterested international action in the maintenance of justice. These are very great things to defend, and wherever they are attacked America has at least the duty of example, has at least the duty of such action as it is possible for her with self-respect to take, in order that these things may not be neglected or thrust on one side. . . .

  ❈ ❈ ❈ ❈ ❈

I suppose that from the first America has had one peculiar and particular mission in the world. Other nations have grown rich, my fellow citizens, other nations have been as powerful as we in material resources in comparison with the other nations of the world, other nations have built up empires and exercised dominion; we are not peculiar in any of these things, but we are peculiar in this, that from the first we have dedicated our forces to the service of justice and righteousness and peace. We have said: "Our chief interest is not in the rights of property, but in the rights of men; our chief interest is in the spirits of men that they might be free, that they might enjoy their lives unmolested so long as they observed the just rules of the game, that they might deal with their fellowmen with their heads erect, the subjects and servants of no man;

12 *President Wilson's State Papers and Addresses* (New York: The Review of Reviews Co., 1918), pp. 163, 168–169.

the servants only of the principles upon which their lives rested." And America has done more than care for her own people and think of her own fortunes in these great matters. She has said ever since the time of President Monroe that she was the champion of the freedom and the separate sovereignty of peoples throughout the Western Hemisphere. She is trustee for these ideals and she is pledged, deeply and permanently pledged, to keep these momentous promises.

She not only, therefore, must play her part in keeping this conflagration from spreading to the people of the United States; she must also keep this conflagration from spreading on this side of the sea. These are matters in which our very life and our whole pride are embedded and rooted, and we can never draw back from them. And I, my fellow citizens, because of the extraordinary office with which you have intrusted me, must, whether I will or not, be your responsible spokesman in these great matters. It is my duty, therefore, when impressions are deeply borne in upon me with regard to the national welfare to speak to you with the utmost frankness about them, and that is the errand upon which I have come away from Washington.

 II

COMMERCE AND
NEUTRAL RIGHTS

PART ONE

The Contraband Trade

International law and practice permitted neutrals to trade freely with other neutrals and to continue commerce with the belligerents in peaceful goods except when a valid blockade had been established. (A legal blockade was defined as one in which sufficient vessels were maintained off the blockaded area to prevent egress and ingress; a "paper blockade" was one in which inadequate naval forces were present.) Neutral citizens could also sell to a belligerent arms and other war materials, although at the risk of interception and confiscation by the opposing belligerent side. World War I was unique, however, in that the United States was the one great industrial neutral country, trading extensively in war goods with one side only. British control of the seas meant that the Entente alone had access to the American market.

Within a short time the American economy rallied from a prewar recession and began to experience a booming prosperity as the result of Allied war purchases. Exports to the Allies increased over 184% by 1917 and American trade with the European neutrals also mounted over peacetime levels. Vast amounts of meat, lard, wheat, copper, cotton and other commodities were exported to Europe. An almost entirely new munitions industry was created to meet Allied needs, with exports of explosives and arms totalling over a billion dollars in value by 1917. German public opinion was embittered by the one-sided commerce and German–American relations were correspondingly affected. Although Germany earlier had protested the arms trade, on April 4, 1915, the Austrian government lodged the separate and lengthier objection which follows. Baron Stephen Burian, Austria's Foreign Secretary, recorded in his memoirs the reaction of the Austro-Hungarian government to the American defense of the trade.

38

1 · Contraband Trade Circular

October 15, 1914

The Department of State has received numerous inquiries from American merchants and other persons as to whether they could sell to governments or nations at war contraband articles without violating the neutrality of the United States, and the Department has also received complaints that sales of contraband were being made on the apparent supposition that they were unneutral acts which this Government should prevent.

In view of the number of communications of this sort which have been received it is evident that there is a widespread misapprehension among the people of this country as to the obligations of the United States as a neutral nation in relation to trade in contraband and as to the powers of the Executive branch of the Government over persons who engage in it. For this reason it seems advisable to make an explanatory statement on the subject for the information of the public.

In the first place it should be understood that, generally speaking, a citizen of the United States can sell to a belligerent government or its agent any article of commerce which he pleases. He is not prohibited from doing this by any rule of international law, by any treaty provisions, or by any statute of the United States. It makes no difference whether the articles sold are exclusively for war purposes, such as firearms, explosives, etc., or are foodstuffs, clothing, horses, etc., for the use of the army or navy of the belligerent.

Furthermore, a neutral government is not compelled by international law, by treaty, or by statute to prevent these sales to a belligerent. Such sales, therefore, by American citizens do not in the least affect the neutrality of the United States.

It is true that such articles as those mentioned are considered contraband and are, outside the territorial jurisdiction of a neutral nation, subject to seizure by an enemy of the purchasing government, but it is the enemy's duty to prevent the articles reaching their destination, not the duty of the nation whose citizens have sold them. If the enemy of the purchasing nation happens for the time to be unable to do this that is for him one of the misfortunes of war; the inability, however, imposes on the neutral government no obligation to prevent the sale.

Neither the President nor any executive department of the Government possesses the legal authority to interfere in any way with trade

1 *Foreign Relations, 1914, Supplement*, pp. 573–574.

between the people of this country and the territory of a belligerent. There is no act of Congress conferring such authority or prohibiting traffic of this sort with European nations, although in the case of neighboring American Republics Congress has given the President power to proclaim an embargo on arms and ammunition when in his judgment it would tend to prevent civil strife.

For the Government of the United States itself to sell to a belligerent nation would be an unneutral act, but for a private individual to sell to a belligerent any product of the United States is neither unlawful nor unneutral, nor within the power of the Executive to prevent or control.

The foregoing remarks, however, do not apply to the outfitting or furnishing of vessels in American ports or of military expeditions on American soil in aid of a belligerent. These acts are prohibited by the neutrality laws of the United States.

2 · *The Austro-Hungarian Minister of Foreign Affairs to the American Ambassador*

VIENNA, *June 29, 1915.*

The far-reaching effects which result from the fact that for a long time the traffic in munitions of war to the greatest extent has been carried on between the United States of America on the one hand and Great Britain and its allies on the other, while Austria-Hungary as well as Germany have been absolutely excluded from the American market, have from the very beginning attracted the most serious attention of the Imperial and Royal Government. . . .

Although the Imperial and Royal Government is absolutely convinced that the attitude of the Federal Government in this connection emanates from no other intention than to maintain the strictest neutrality and to conform to the letter of the provisions of international treaties, nevertheless the question arises whether the conditions as they have developed during the course of the war, certainly independently of the will of the Federal Government, are not such as in effect thwart the intentions of the Washington Cabinet or even actually oppose them. In the affirmative

---

2 *Papers Relating to the Foreign Relations of the United States, 1915, Supplement* (Washington: G.P.O., 1928), pp. 790–793.

case — and affirmation, in the opinion of the Imperial and Royal Government, can not be doubted — then immediately follows the further question whether it would not seem possible, even imperative, that appropriate measures be adopted toward bringing into full effect the desire of the Federal Government to maintain an attitude of strict parity with respect to both belligerent parties. The Imperial and Royal Government does not hesitate to answer also this question unqualifiedly in the affirmative. . . .

According to all authorities on international law who concern themselves more particularly with the question now under consideration, a neutral government may not permit traffic in contraband of war to be carried on without hindrance when this traffic assumes such a form or such dimensions that the neutrality of the nation becomes involved thereby.

If any one of the various criteria which have been laid down in science in this respect be used as a basis in determining the permissibility of commerce in contraband, one reaches the conclusion from each of these criteria that the exportation of war requisites from the United States, as is being carried on in the present war, is not to be brought into accord with the demands of neutrality.

The question now before us is surely not whether American industries which are engaged in the manufacture of war material should be protected from loss in the export trade that was theirs in times of peace. Rather has that industry soared to unimagined heights. In order to turn out the huge quantities of arms, ammunition, and other war material of every description ordered in the past months by Great Britain and her allies from the United States, not only the full capacity of the existing plants, but also their transformation and enlargement and the creation of new large plants, as well as a flocking of workmen of all trades into that branch of industry, in brief, far-reaching changes of economic life encompassing the whole country, became necessary. From no quarter, then, can there come any question of the right of the American Government to prohibit, through the issuance of an embargo, that enormous exportation of war implements that is openly carried on and, besides, is commonly known to be availed of by only one of the parties to the war. If the Federal Government would exercise that power it possesses, it could not lay itself open to blame if, in order to keep within the requirements of the law of the land, it adopted the course of enacting a law. For while the principle obtains that a neutral state may not alter the rules in force within its province concerning its attitude toward belligerents while war is being waged, yet this principle, as clearly appears from the preamble to the thirteenth Hague convention, suffers an exception in the case "où l'expérience acquise en démontrerait la nécessité pour la sauvegarde de ses droits" [where experience has shown the necessity thereof for the protection of its rights].

Moreover, this case is already established for the American Government through the fact that Austria-Hungary, as well as Germany, is cut off from all commercial intercourse with the United States of America without the existence of a legal prerequisite therefor — a legally constituted blockade.

In reply to the possible objection that, notwithstanding the willingness of American industry to furnish merchandise to Austria-Hungary and Germany as well as to Great Britain and her allies, it is not possible for the United States of America to trade with Austria-Hungary and Germany as the result of the war situation, it may be pointed out that the Federal Government is undoubtedly in a position to improve the situation described. It would be amply sufficient to confront the opponents of Austria-Hungary and Germany with the possibility of the prohibition of the exportation of foodstuffs and raw materials in case legitimate commerce in these articles between the Union and the two Central Powers should not be allowed. If the Washington Cabinet should find itself prepared for an action in this sense, it would not only be following the tradition always held in such high regard in the United States of contending for the freedom of legitimate maritime commerce, but would also earn the high merit of nullifying the wanton efforts of the enemies of Austria-Hungary and Germany to use hunger as an ally.

The Imperial and Royal Government may therefore, in the spirit of the excellent relations which have never ceased to exist between the Austro-Hungarian Monarchy and the United States of America, appeal to the Federal Government in sincere friendship, in view of the expositions here set forth, to subject its previously adopted standpoint in this so important question to a mature reconsideration. A revision of the attitude observed by the Government of the Union in the sense of the views advocated by the Imperial and Royal Government would, according to the convictions of the latter, be not only within the bounds of the rights and obligations of a neutral government, but also in close keeping with those principles dictated by true humanity and love of peace which the United States has ever written on its banner. . . .

3 · The Secretary of State to President Wilson

WASHINGTON, *July 8, 1915.*

DEAR MR. PRESIDENT: I think that we could dismiss the Austrian statement regarding the sale of arms and ammunition with an acknowledgement, as you suggest in your note of yesterday, but it seems to me that it offers an excellent opportunity to make a full and clear statement of our attitude. While the communication would be addressed to Vienna, we could by making the correspondence public present the matter in a favorable and, I believe, convincing way to the American people.

Home consumption would be the real purpose; an answer to Austria the nominal purpose.

Convinced of the strength of our position and the desirability of placing the case frankly before the people in order to remove the opposition to sales of war materials, which many persons have on moral grounds and not because of pro-Germany sympathy, it seems to me advisable to prepare an answer to the Austrian communication, which I will submit to you as soon as it is drafted.

Faithfully yours,

ROBERT LANSING

4 · The Secretary of State to the Ambassador in Austria-Hungary

WASHINGTON, *August 12, 1915.*

The Government of the United States has given careful consideration to the statement of the Imperial and Royal Government in regard to the exportation of arms and ammunition from the United States to the countries at war with Austria-Hungary and Germany. The Government of

---

3 *Papers Relating to the Foreign Relations of the United States; The Lansing Papers, 1914–1920* (Washington: G.P.O., 1940, 2 vols.), I, 122–123.
4 *Foreign Relations, 1915, Supplement,* pp. 794–798.

43

the United States notes with satisfaction the recognition by the Imperial and Royal Government of the undoubted fact that its attitude with regard to the exportation of arms and ammunition from the United States is prompted by its intention to "maintain the strictest neutrality and to conform to the letter of the provisions of international treaties," but is surprised to find the Imperial and Royal Government implying that the observance of the strict principles of the law under the conditions which have developed in the present war is insufficient, and asserting that this Government should go beyond the long-recognized rules governing such traffic by neutrals and adopt measures to "maintain an attitude of strict parity with respect to both belligerent parties."

To this assertion of an obligation to change or modify the rules of international usage on account of special conditions the Government of the United States can not accede. The recognition of an obligation of this sort, unknown to the international practice of the past, would impose upon every neutral nation a duty to sit in judgment on the progress of a war and to restrict its commercial intercourse with a belligerent whose naval successes prevented the neutral from trade with the enemy. The contention of the Imperial and Royal Government appears to be that the advantages gained to a belligerent by its superiority on the sea should be equalized by the neutral powers by the establishment of a system of non-intercourse with the victor. The Imperial and Royal Government confines its comments to arms and ammunition, but if the principle for which it contends is sound, it should apply with equal force to all articles of contraband. A belligerent controlling the high seas might possess an ample supply of arms and ammunition, but be in want of food and clothing. On the novel principle that equalization is a neutral duty, neutral nations would be obligated to place an embargo on such articles because one of the belligerents could not obtain them through commercial intercourse.

But if this principle, so strongly urged by the Imperial and Royal Government, should be admitted to obtain by reason of the superiority of a belligerent at sea, ought it not to operate equally as to a belligerent superior on land? Applying this theory of equalization, a belligerent who lacks the necessary munitions to contend successfully on land ought to be permitted to purchase them from neutrals, while a belligerent with an abundance of war stores or with the power to produce them should be debarred from such traffic.

Manifestly the idea of strict neutrality now advanced by the Imperial and Royal Government would involve a neutral nation in a mass of perplexities which would obscure the whole field of international obligation, produce economic confusion, and deprive all commerce and industry of legitimate fields of enterprise, already heavily burdened by the unavoidable restrictions of war.

In this connection it is pertinent to direct the attention of the Imperial and Royal Government to the fact that Austria-Hungary and Germany, particularly the latter, have during the years preceding the present European war produced a great surplus of arms and ammunition, which they sold throughout the world and especially to belligerents. Never during that period did either of them suggest or apply the principle now advocated by the Imperial and Royal Government. . . .

In view of the foregoing statements, this Government is reluctant to believe that the Imperial and Royal Government will ascribe to the United States a lack of impartial neutrality in continuing its legitimate trade in all kinds of supplies used to render the armed forces of a belligerent efficient, even though the circumstances of the present war prevent Austria-Hungary from obtaining such supplies from the markets of the United States, which have been and remain, so far as the action and policy of this Government are concerned, open to all belligerents alike.

But, in addition to the question of principle, there is a practical and substantial reason why the Government of the United States has from the foundation of the Republic to the present time advocated and practiced unrestricted trade in arms and military supplies. It has never been the policy of this country to maintain in time of peace a large military establishment or stores of arms and ammunition sufficient to repel invasion by a well-equipped and powerful enemy. It has desired to remain at peace with all nations and to avoid any appearance of menacing such peace by the threat of its armies and navies. In consequence of this standing policy the United States would, in the event of attacks by a foreign power, be at the outset of the war seriously, if not fatally, embarrassed by the lack of arms and ammunition and by the means to produce them in sufficient quantities to supply the requirements of national defense. The United States has always depended upon the right and power to purchase arms and ammunition from neutral nations in case of foreign attack. This right, which it claims for itself, it can not deny to others.

A nation whose principle and policy it is to rely upon international obligations and international justice to preserve its political and territorial integrity, might become the prey of an aggressive nation whose policy and practice it is to increase its military strength during times of peace with the design of conquest, unless the nation attacked can, after war had been declared, go into the markets of the world and purchase the means to defend itself against the aggressor.

The general adoption by the nations of the world of the theory that neutral powers ought to prohibit the sale of arms and ammunition to belligerents would compel every nation to have in readiness at all times sufficient munitions of war to meet any emergency which might arise and to erect and maintain establishments for the manufacture of arms and ammunition sufficient to supply the needs of its military and naval forces throughout the progress of a war. Manifestly the application of this theory would result in every nation becoming an armed camp, ready to resist aggression and tempted to employ force in asserting its rights rather than appeal to reason and justice for the settlement of international disputes.

Perceiving, as it does, that the adoption of the principle that it is the duty of a neutral to prohibit the sale of arms and ammunition to a belligerent during the progress of a war would inevitably give the advantage to the belligerent which had encouraged the manufacture of munititions in time of peace and which had laid in vast stores of arms and ammunition in anticipation of war, the Government of the United States is convinced that the adoption of the theory would force militarism on the world and work against that universal peace which is the desire and purpose of all nations which exalt justice and righteousness in their relations with one another.

The Government of the United States in the foregoing discussion of the practical reason why it has advocated and practiced trade in munitions of war, wishes to be understood as speaking with no thought of expressing or implying any judgment with regard to the circumstances of the present war, but as merely putting very frankly the argument in this matter which has been conclusive in determining the policy of the United States. . . .

The Government of the United States deems it unnecessary to extend further at the present time a consideration of the statement of the Austro-Hungarian Government. The principles of international law, the practice of nations, the national safety of the United States and other nations without great military aid and naval establishments, the prevention of increased armies and navies, the adoption of peaceful methods for the adjustment of international differences, and, finally, neutrality itself are opposed to the prohibition by a neutral nation of the exportation of arms, ammunition, or other munitions of war to belligerent powers during the progress of the war.

5 · *Austria's Reaction to Lansing's Defense*

America's skilfully drafted reply . . . sidetracked the question by debating against my alleged assertion of an obligation "to change or modify the rules of international usage on account of special conditions," and

---

5 Baron Stephen Burian, *Austria in Dissolution* (New York: George H. Doran Co., 1925), pp. 118–121. Reprinted by permission.

also "that the advantages gained to a belligerent by its superiority on the sea should be equalised by the neutral Powers by the establishment of a system of non-intercourse with the victor." . . .

The object of my answering Note on the 24th September was to show that American neutrality, even if formally brought into line with what was admissible according to international law, pressed heavily upon the Central Powers, since the spirit of true impartiality was obscured by the practical workings of the system.

I had been far from striving to secure that neutral America should to a certain extent equalise the chances of the two sides by prohibiting the export of arms. Our view was rather that the excessive export of war material would not have been permissible even if it had been destined for the countries of both sides. I merely protested against the economic life of the United States being devoted to the production and export of war material on a huge scale, through the creation of new factories and the extension and conversion of existing ones.

Thereby, though perhaps not deliberately, effective assistance was actually rendered to one of the combatants. The comparisons adduced with other wars failed, because in the cases mentioned the combatants were able to supply themselves with war material from many different countries. In the world war the United States was the only Power who really counted for deliveries on such a scale. This is what gave the export of war material from the United States its special significance and its distinctive character.

If the Federal government had taken up the standpoint that it was impossible for the United States to trade with the Central Powers on account of the military position, it was in their power to make it possible. It was not the maritime successes of England and her allies that caused legitimate trade between America and the Central Powers entirely to cease, but the measures taken by the Entente Powers which were contrary to international law, and which the United States government too regarded as illegitimate.

The exchange of Notes on the neutrality question did not in any way alter the situation. American war material played a very great part in European theatres of war until finally the American armies came over and decided the war against us. It may therefore to-day seem otiose to spend time in describing the shades of a neutrality which was destined to pass into open hostility. But the very fact that it did so proves how right we were in feeling the basis of hostility underlying American neutrality. This attitude of mind, which never gave the benefit of extenuating circumstances to the Central Powers, especially Germany, and always indulged in the severest criticism, necessitated the most cautious handling of our relations with the United States, in order to avoid such dangerous situations as might arise from various incidents, and finally occurred in connection with the U-boats.

PART TWO

Loans to the Belligerents

British seapower kept open the channels of trade between the United States and the Entente Powers. But the diminishing
dollar credits of the Allies soon presented financial difficulties which
threatened to curtail their expanding war trade with America. A neutral
state could either permit or prohibit the extension of credits and loans
by its citizens to belligerent governments, as long as the ruling applied
impartially to all the warring powers. In accordance with President
Wilson's expressed desire that the United States remain neutral in spirit
as well as deed, the government in 1914 discouraged public and banking
loans to the belligerents. As a consequence, the financial prosperity
which Allied purchases had created was jeopardized. The so-called
Bryan Loan Ban, which was not a legal prohibition but a statement of
the administration's attitude, was rescinded after the Secretary of the
Treasury, William G. McAdoo, and the Secretary of State discussed the
problem with President Wilson in September, 1915. The way was then
open for belligerents to arrange large public and banking loans in the
United States, which reached a total of over $2 billion by early 1917
and helped transform the country from a debtor to a creditor nation.
American markets, however, remained largely inaccessible to the Central
Powers, so that loans tended to benefit the Entente almost exclusively.

6 · The Secretary of State to President Wilson

WASHINGTON, *August 10, 1914.*

My DEAR MR. PRESIDENT: I beg to communicate to you an important matter which has come before the Department. Morgan Company of New York have asked whether there would be any objection to their making a loan to the French Government and also the Rothschilds — I suppose that is intended for the French Government. I have conferred with Mr. Lansing[1] and he knows of no legal objection to financing this loan, but I have suggested to him the advisability of presenting to you an aspect of the case which is not legal but I believe to be consistent with our attitude in international matters. It is whether it would be advisable for this Government to take the position that it will not approve of any loan to a belligerent nation. The reasons that I would give in support of this proposition are:

First: Money is the worst of all contrabands because it commands everything else. The question of making loans contraband by international agreement has been discussed, but no action has been taken. I know of nothing that would do more to prevent war than an international agreement that neutral nations would not loan to belligerents. While such an agreement would be of great advantage, could we not by our example hasten the reaching of such an agreement? We are the one great nation which is not involved and our refusal to loan to any belligerent would naturally tend to hasten a conclusion of the war. We are responsible for the use of our influence through example and as we cannot tell what we can do until we try, the only way of testing our influence is to set the example and observe its effect. This is the fundamental reason in support of the suggestion submitted.

Second: There is a special and local reason, it seems to me, why this course would be advisable. Mr. Lansing observed in the discussion of the subject that a loan would be taken by those in sympathy with the country in whose behalf the loan was negotiated. If we approved of a loan to France we would not, of course, object to a loan to Great Britain, Germany, Russia, Austria, or to any other country, and if loans were made to these countries our citizens would be divided into two groups, each group loaning money to the country which it favors and this money could not be furnished without expressions of sympathy. These expres-

---

[1] Lansing was then Counselor in the State Department.

sions of sympathy are disturbing enough when they do not rest upon pecuniary interests — they would be still more disturbing if each group was pecuniarily interested in the success of the nation to whom its members had loaned money.

Third: The powerful financial interests which would be connected with these loans would be tempted to use their influence through the newspapers to support the interests of the Government to which they had loaned because the value of the security would be directly affected by the result of the war. We would thus find our newspapers violently arrayed on one side or the other, each paper supporting a financial group and pecuniary interest. All of this influence would make it all the more difficult for us to maintain neutrality, as our action on various questions that would arise would affect one side or the other and powerful financial interests would be thrown into the balance. . . .

With assurances [etc.]   W. J. BRYAN

7 · *The Secretary of State to J. P. Morgan and Company*

DEPARTMENT OF STATE,
Washington, August 15, 1914.

Inquiry having been made as to the attitude of this government in case American bankers are asked to make loans to foreign governments during the war in Europe, the following announcement is made:

There is no reason why loans should not be made to the governments of neutral nations, but in the judgment of this Government, loans by American bankers to any foreign nation which is at war are inconsistent with the true spirit of neutrality.

W. J. BRYAN

---

7 *Foreign Relations, 1914, Supplement,* p. 580.

8 · The Vice President of the National City Bank to the Acting Secretary of State

New York, *October 23, 1914.*

Mr. Counsellor: Supplementing our conversation of this morning, I desire to call your particular attention to the following conditions now existing in this country and abroad.

The outbreak of the European War came at a time when this country owed a large amount to Europe, particularly to England in the form of short time drafts, maturing between the outbreak of the war and the end of the year. The amount, while large, was not abnormal, considering the volume of our trade relations and was directly due to the anticipated shipment of cotton during the autumn.

War conditions, as you are aware, have made cotton bills unavailable for the settlement of this balance against us and it can only be wiped out by the shipment of the goods, in lieu of the cotton, that are now needed and desired by the various European countries. This is true, regardless of any temporary bridging over of the situation, and it has been the policy of the National City Bank, as far as possible and proper, to stimulate the unprecedented and unusual buying that is now going on in this country by foreign governments and their nationals. Since the beginning of the war this bank alone has received cabled instructions for the payment of in excess of $50,000,000 for American goods and the volume of this business is increasing. Owing to war conditions, this buying is necessarily for cash and it is of such magnitude that the cash credits of the European governments are being fast depleted. Lately we have been urged by manufacturers who are customers of the bank and, in some cases, by representatives of the foreign governments, to provide temporary credits for these purchases. For that purpose we have recently arranged to advance the Norwegian Government some three million dollars, practically all of which is to be expended for cereals in this country. Very recently the Russian Government has placed directly, and through agents, large orders with American manufacturers — such large orders that their cash credit has been absorbed and they have asked us to allow an overdraft, secured by gold deposited in their state bank, of some five million dollars.

---

8 *Foreign Relations, Lansing Papers,* I, 136–137. After discussion of the proposed short-term credits with President Wilson, on October 23, 1914, Lansing let the bankers know that the administration had no objections.

Some of our clients have been asked to take short time Treasury warrants of the French Government in payment for goods and have, in turn, asked us if we could discount them or purchase warrants direct from the French Government for the purpose of replenishing their cash balances. We have also been asked by European interests practically the same question as to English Consols and Treasury securities. Some of our German correspondents have approached us with the suggestion that, without naming a particular security, we sell securities to increase their cash account with us, and we have little doubt this is indirectly for the purposes of the German Government.

We strongly feel the necessity of aiding the situation by temporary credits of this sort, otherwise the buying power of these foreign purchasers will dry up and the business will go to Australia, Canada, Argentine and elsewhere. It may in the end come back to us, but the critical time for American finance in our International relations is during the next three or four months and, if we allow these purchases to go elsewhere, we will have neglected our foreign trade at the time of our greatest need and greatest opportunity.

It is the desire of the National City Bank to be absolutely in accord with the policies of our own Government, both in its legal position and in the spirit of its operations and, while very anxious to stimulate our foreign trade, we do not wish to, in any respect, act otherwise than in complete accord with the policy of our government.

For the purpose of enabling them to make cash payments for American goods, the Bank is disposed to grant short time banking credits to European governments, both belligerent and neutral, and where necessary or desirable replenish their cash balances on this side by the purchase of short time Treasury warrants. Such purchases would necessarily be limited to the legal capacity of the bank and, as these warrants are bearer warrants without interest, they could not and would not be made the subject of a public issue. These securities could be sold abroad or be readily available as collateral in our foreign loans and would be paid at maturity in dollars or equivalent in foreign exchange.

This business which I have attempted to describe to you, we deem necessary to the general good and we desire to proceed along the lines indicated unless it is objectionable from the Government's standpoint, in which case we assume that you will advise us.

Very respectfully yours,

SAMUEL McROBERTS

9 · The Secretary of State to President Wilson

WASHINGTON, September 6, 1915.

MY DEAR MR. PRESIDENT: Doubtless Secretary McAdoo has discussed with you the necessity of floating government loans for the belligerent nations, which are purchasing such great quantities of goods in this country, in order to avoid a serious financial situation which will not only affect them but this country as well.

Briefly, the situation, as I understand it, is this: Since December 1st, 1914, to June 30, 1915, our exports have exceeded our imports by nearly a billion dollars, and it is estimated that the excess will be from July 1st to December 31, 1915, a billion and three quarters. Thus for the year 1915 the excess will be approximately two and [a] half billions of dollars.

It is estimated that the European banks have about three and [a] half billions of dollars in gold in their vaults. To withdraw any considerable amount would disastrously affect the credit of the European nations, and the consequence would be a general state of bankruptcy.

If the European countries cannot find means to pay for the excess of goods sold to them over those purchased from them, they will have to stop buying and our present export trade will shrink proportionately. The result would be restriction of outputs, industrial depression, idle capital and idle labor, numerous failures, financial demoralization, and general unrest and suffering among the laboring classes.

Probably a billion and three quarters of the excess of European purchases can be taken care of by the sale of American securities held in Europe and by the transfer of trade balances of oriental countries, but that will leave three quarters of a billion to be met in some other way. Furthermore, even if that is arranged, we will have to face a more serious situation in January, 1916, as the American securities held abroad will have been exhausted.

I believe that Secretary McAdoo is convinced and I agree with him that there is only one means of avoiding this situation which would so seriously affect economic conditions in the country, and that is the flotation of large bond issues by the belligerent governments. Our financial institutions have the money to loan and wish to do so. On account of

---

9 *Foreign Relations, Lansing Papers,* I, 144–147. The abandonment of the loan policy was signalled by a statement published in the *New York Times* on September 14, 1915, that "assurances had been received that if it were arranged as a straight credit arrangement, no objection would be offered by the State Department on the score of a possible violation of neutrality."

the great balance of trade in our favor the proceeds of these loans would be expended here. The result would be a maintenance of the credit of the borrowing nations based on their gold reserve, a continuance of our commerce at its present volume and industrial activity with the consequent employment of capital and labor and national prosperity.

The difficulty is — and this is what Secretary McAdoo came to see me about — that the Government early in the war announced that it considered "war loans" to be contrary to "the true spirit of neutrality." A declaration to this effect was given to the press about August 15, 1914, by Secretary Bryan. The language is as follows: "In the judgment of this Government loans by American bankers to any foreign nation at war is inconsistent with the true spirit of neutrality."

In October, 1914, after a conference with you, I gave my "impressions" to certain New York bankers in reference to "credit loans," but the general statement remained unaffected. In drafting the letter of January 20, 1915, to Senator Stone I sought to leave out a broad statement and to explain merely the reasons for distinguishing between "general loans" and "credit loans." However, Mr. Bryan thought it well to repeat the August declaration and it appears in the first sentence of division 13 of the letter, a copy of which I enclose.

On March 31, 1915, another press statement was given out from the Department which read as follows:

"The State Department has from time to time received information directly or indirectly to the effect that belligerent nations had arranged with Banks in the United States for credits in various sums. While loans to belligerents have been disapproved, this Government has not felt that it was justified in interposing objection to the credit arrangements which have been brought to its attention. It has neither approved these nor disapproved — it has simply taken no action in the premises and expressed no opinion."

Manifestly the Government has committed itself to the policy of discouraging general loans to belligerent governments. The practical reasons for the policy at the time we adopted it were sound, but basing it on the ground that loans are "inconsistent with the true spirit of neutrality" is now a source of embarrassment. This latter ground is as strong today as it was a year ago, while the practical reasons for discouraging loans have largely disappeared. We have more money than we can use. Popular sympathy has become crystallized in favor of one or another of the belligerents to such an extent that the purchase of bonds would in no way increase the bitterness of partisanship or cause a possibly serious situation.

Now, on the other hand, we are face to face with what appears to be a critical economic situation, which can only be relieved apparently by the investment of American capital in foreign loans to be used in liquidating the enormous balance of trade in favor of the United States.

Can we afford to let a declaration as to our conception of "the true spirit of neutrality" made in the first days of the war stand in the way of our national interests which seem to be seriously threatened?

If we cannot afford to do this, how are we to explain away the declaration and maintain a semblance of consistency?

My opinion is that we ought to allow the loans to be made for our own good, and I have been seeking some means of harmonizing our policy, so unconditionally announced, with the flotation of general loans. As yet I have found no solution to the problem.

Secretary McAdoo considers that the situation is becoming acute and that something should be done at once to avoid the disastrous results which will follow a continuance of the present policy.

Faithfully yours,

ROBERT LANSING

PART THREE

In Defense of America's Neutrality Policies

American trade with the Entente nations was increased by the extension to them of financial credits, a development which further exacerbated pro-German sentiment. Professor Hugo Münsterberg of Harvard University summed up the criticisms which many pacifists and pro-Germans had raised against this and other neutrality policies of the Wilson administration. The Bryan-Stone Letter was intended as a public rebuttal to these allegations. (William J. Stone of Missouri was chairman of the Senate Foreign Relations Committee.)

10 · President Wilson to the Acting Secretary of State

WASHINGTON, *December 1, 1914.*

MY DEAR MR. LANSING: I would be very much obliged if you would read the enclosed letter from Professor Münsterberg and send me a memorandum, if you would be so kind, of the answers and comments that might be made upon his statements. Here at last is a very definite summing up of the matters upon which German anti-administration feeling in this country is being built up, and perhaps it would be wise to take very serious notice of it. The case they make out is *prima facie* very plausible indeed.

Cordially and sincerely yours,

WOODROW WILSON

[ENCLOSURE]

CAMBRIDGE, MASS., *November 19, 1914.*

DEAR MR. PRESIDENT: A few days ago I wrote to you from New York in reply to your very kind letter of November 10th that I begged to postpone my reply until I reached my desk in Cambridge. Now after my return I indeed ask your permission to enter into some detail with regard to the neutrality question. But let me assure you beforehand that I interpret your inquiry as referring exclusively to the views which are expressed to me by American citizens who sympathize with the German cause or who are disturbed by the vehement hostility to Germany on the part of the American press.

My remarks refer in no way to the views of official Germany. . . .

Let me emphasize three points to which my correspondents refer most frequently. First, all cables sent by and received by wire pass uncensored, while all wireless news is censored. This reacts against Germany, because England sends all her news by cable, whereas Germany alone uses the wireless. The matter is of grave importance. Second, the policy of the administration with regard to the holding up, detaining and searching of Germans and Austrians from neutral and American vessels is a reversal of the American policy established in 1812. It has excited no end of bitterness. Third, the United States permitted the violation by England of the Hague Convention and international law in connection

10 *Foreign Relations, Lansing Papers,* I, 161–165.

with conditional and unconditional contraband.[1] The United States, for instance, has not protested against the transference of copper from the conditional to the absolute list, although on former occasions the United States has taken a spirited stand against onesided interpretations of international agreements. . . . The United States, moreover, insisted that conditional contraband can be sent in neutral or in American bottoms even to belligerent nations, provided it was not consigned to the government, the military or naval authorities or to any contractors known to represent the belligerent government. By permitting this new interpretation the United States practically supports the starving out policy of the Allies. The nation by reversing its own policy thus seriously handicaps Germany and Austria in their fight for existence. . . .

Many of the complaints refer more to the unfriendly spirit than to the actual violation of the law. Here above all belongs the unlimited sale of ammunition to the belligerents. The administration originally advised Mr. Morgan that the making of loans to the nations at war would not be looked upon with favor by the President, and Mr. Morgan cancelled the plans. This attitude has been given up; the State Department has emphasized that money and arms may be sold to the belligerents, while evidently the friends of peace had firmly hoped that the President would denounce the sale of ammunition or any other sale which would be likely to prolong the war. Indeed our friends of peace must regret this encouraging attitude with reference to the sale of agencies of destruction, but the friends of Germany cannot forget that this sympathetic attitude of the State Department under the conditions which objectively exist is not only helpful to the prolongation of the war, but helpful exclusively to the Allies against Central Europe. The favorite interpretation of the Germans is even that the government makes itself a party to the violation of neutrality by giving clearance papers to vessels loaded with war material for England and France. They say, moreover, that the President as Commander-in-Chief of the Army and Navy could and did restrain the shipment of war material into Mexico. Hence he has the same power to restrain the shipment of such material to Europe. . . .

---

[1] Conditional contraband, as opposed to absolute contraband goods such as arms, consisted of materials which could be used either for military or peaceful purposes and could be seized by an enemy if the former could be demonstrated. Absolute contraband was subject to seizure whenever intercepted.

II · The Secretary of State to the Chairman of the Senate Committee on Foreign Relations

WASHINGTON, *January 20, 1915.*

DEAR MR. STONE: I have received your letter of the 8th instant, referring to frequent complaints or charges made in one form or another through the press that this Government has shown partiality to Great Britain, France, and Russia against Germany and Austria during the present war, and stating that you have received numerous letters to the same effect from sympathizers with the latter powers. You summarize the various grounds of these complaints and ask that you be furnished with whatever information the Department may have touching these points of complaint, in order that you may be informed as to what the true situation is in regard to these matters.

In order that you may have such information as the Department has on the subjects referred to in your letter, I will take them up *seriatim.*

(1) *Freedom of communication by submarine cables versus censored communication by wireless.* The reason that wireless messages and cable messages require different treatment by a neutral government is as follows:

Communications by wireless can not be interrupted by a belligerent. With a submarine cable it is otherwise. The possibility of cutting the cable exists, and if a belligerent possesses naval superiority the cable is cut, as was the German cable near the Azores by one of Germany's enemies and as was the British cable near Fanning Island by a German naval force. Since a cable is subject to hostile attack, the responsibility falls upon the belligerent and not upon the neutral to prevent cable communication.

A more important reason, however, at least from the point of view of a neutral government, is that messages sent out from a wireless station in neutral territory may be received by belligerent warships on the high seas. If these messages, whether plain or in cipher, direct the movements of warships or convey to them information as to the location of an enemy's

---

public or private vessels, the neutral territory becomes a base of naval operations, to permit which would be essentially unneutral.

As a wireless message can be received by all stations and vessels within a given radius, every message in cipher, whatever its intended destination, must be censored; otherwise military information may be sent to warships off the coast of a neutral. It is manifest that a submarine cable is incapable of becoming a means of direct communication with a warship on the high seas. Hence its use can not, as a rule, make neutral territory a base for the direction of naval operations. . . .

(4) *Submission without protest to British violations of the rules regarding absolute and conditional contraband as laid down in the Hague conventions, the Declaration of London, and international law.* There is no Hague convention which deals with absolute or conditional contraband, and, as the Declaration of London is not in force, the rules of international law only apply. As to the articles to be regarded as contraband, there is no general agreement between nations. It is the practice for a country, either in time of peace or after the outbreak of war, to declare the articles which it will consider as absolute or conditional contraband. It is true that a neutral government is seriously affected by this declaration, as the rights of its subjects or citizens may be impaired. But the rights and interests of belligerents and neutrals are opposed in respect to contraband articles and trade and there is no tribunal to which questions of difference may be readily submitted.

The record of the United States in the past is not free from criticism. When neutral, this Government has stood for a restricted list of absolute and conditional contraband. As a belligerent, we have contended for a liberal list, according to our conception of the necessities of the case.

The United States has made earnest representations to Great Britain in regard to the seizure and detention by the British authorities of all American ships or cargoes *bona fide* destined to neutral ports, on the ground that such seizures and detentions were contrary to the existing rules of international law. It will be recalled, however, that American courts have established various rules bearing on these matters. The rule of "continuous voyage" has been not only asserted by American tribunals but extended by them. They have exercised the right to determine from the circumstances whether the ostensible was the real destination. They have held that the shipment of articles of contraband to a neutral port "to order," from which, as a matter of fact, cargoes had been transshipped to the enemy, is corroborative evidence that the cargo is really destined to the enemy instead of to the neutral port of delivery. It is thus seen that some of the doctrines which appear to bear harshly upon neutrals at the present time are analogous to or outgrowths from policies adopted by the United States when it was a belligerent. The Government therefore can not consistently protest against the application of rules which it has followed in the past, unless they have not been practiced as heretofore. . . .

(6) *Submission without protest to interference with American trade to neutral countries in conditional and absolute contraband.* The fact that the commerce of the United States is interrupted by Great Britain is consequent upon the superiority of her Navy on the high seas. History shows that whenever a country has possessed that superiority our trade has been interrupted and that few articles essential to the prosecution of the war have been allowed to reach its enemy from this country. The Department's recent note to the British Government, which has been made public, in regard to detentions and seizures of American vessels and cargoes, is a complete answer to this complaint.

Certain other complaints appear aimed at the loss of profit in trade, which must include, at least in part, trade in contraband with Germany; while other complaints demand the prohibition of trade in contraband, which appear to refer to trade with the Allies.

(7) *Submission without protest to interruption of trade in conditional contraband consigned to private persons in Germany and Austria, thereby supporting the policy of Great Britain to cut off all supplies from Germany and Austria.* As no American vessel, so far as known, has attempted to carry conditional contraband to Germany or Austria-Hungary, no ground of complaint has arisen out of the seizure or condemnation by Great Britain of an American vessel with a belligerent destination. Until a case arises and the Government has taken action upon it, criticism is premature and unwarranted. The United States in its note of December 28 to the British Government strongly contended for the principle of freedom of trade in articles of conditional contraband not destined to the belligerent's forces. . . .

(9) *The United States has not interfered with the sale to Great Britain and her allies of arms, ammunition, horses, uniforms, and other munitions of war, although such sales prolong the conflict.* There is no power in the Executive to prevent the sale of ammunition to the belligerents.

The duty of a neutral to restrict trade in munitions of war has never been imposed by international law or by municipal statute. It has never been the policy of this Government to prevent the shipment of arms or ammunition into belligerent territory, except in the case of neighboring American Republics, and then only when civil strife prevailed. Even to this extent the belligerents in the present conflict, when they were neutrals, have never, so far as the records disclose, limited the sale of munitions of war. It is only necessary to point to the enormous quantities of arms and ammunition furnished by manufacturers in Germany to the belligerents in the Russo-Japanese war and in the recent Balkan wars to establish the general recognition of the propriety of the trade by a neutral nation.

It may be added that on the 15th of December last, the German Ambassador, by direction of his Government, presented a copy of a memorandum of the Imperial German Government which, among other things, set forth the attitude of that Government toward traffic in contraband of war by citizens of neutral countries. The Imperial Government stated that "under the general principles of international law, no exception can be taken to neutral States letting war material go to Germany's enemies from or through neutral territory," and that the adversaries of Germany in the present war are, in the opinion of the Imperial Government, authorized to "draw on the United States contraband of war and especially arms worth billions of marks." These principles, as the Ambassador stated, have been accepted by the United States Government in the statement issued by the Department of State on October 15 last, entitled "Neutrality and trade in contraband." Acting in conformity with the propositions there set forth, the United States has itself taken no part in contraband traffic, and has, so far as possible, lent its influence toward equal treatment for all belligerents in the matter of purchasing arms and ammunition of private persons in the United States. . . .

(11) *British warships are permitted to lie off American ports and intercept neutral vessels.* The complaint is unjustified from the fact that representations were made to the British Government that the presence of war vessels in the vicinity of New York Harbor was offensive to this Government, and a similar complaint was made to the Japanese Government as to one of its cruisers in the vicinity of the port of Honolulu. In both cases the warships were withdrawn.

It will be recalled that in 1863 the Department took the position that captures made by its vessels after hovering about neutral ports would not be regarded as valid. In the Franco-Prussian war, President Grant issued a proclamation warning belligerent warships against hovering in the vicinity of American ports for purposes of observation or hostile acts. The same policy has been maintained in the present war, and in all of the recent proclamations of neutrality the President states that such practice by belligerent warships is "unfriendly and offensive." . . .

(13) *Change of policy in regard to loans to belligerents.* War loans in this country were disapproved because inconsistent with the spirit of neutrality. There is a clearly defined difference between a war loan and the purchase of arms and ammunition. *The policy of disapproving of war loans affects all governments alike, so that the disapproval is not an unneutral act.* The case is entirely different in the matter of arms and ammunition, because prohibition of export not only might not, but in this case would not, operate equally upon the nations at war. Then, too, the

reason given for the disapproval of war loans is supported by other considerations which are absent in the case presented by the sale of arms and ammunitions. The taking of money out of the United States during such a war as this might seriously embarrass the Government in case it needed to borrow money, and it might also seriously impair this Nation's ability to assist the neutral nations which, though not participants in the war, are compelled to bear a heavy burden on account of the war, and, again, a war loan, if offered for popular subscription in the United States, would be taken up chiefly by those who are in sympathy with the belligerent seeking the loan. The result would be that great numbers of the American people might become more earnest partisans, having material interest in the success of the belligerent whose bonds they hold. These purchases would not be confined to a few, but would spread generally throughout the country, so that the people would be divided into groups of partisans, which would result in intense bitterness and might cause an undesirable, if not a serious, situation. On the other hand, contracts for and sales of contraband are mere matters of trade. The manufacturer, unless peculiarly sentimental, would sell to one belligerent as readily as he would to another. No general spirit of partisanship is aroused — no sympathies excited. The whole transaction is merely a matter of business.

This Government has not been advised that any general loans have been made by foreign governments in this country since the President expressed his wish that loans of this character should not be made. . . .

(20) *General unfriendly attitude of Government toward Germany and Austria.* If any American citizens, partisans of Germany and Austria-Hungary, feel that this administration is acting in a way injurious to the cause of those countries, this feeling results from the fact that on the high seas the German and Austro-Hungarian naval power is thus far inferior to the British. It is the business of a belligerent operating on the high seas, not the duty of a neutral, to prevent contraband from reaching an enemy. Those in this country who sympathize with Germany and Austria-Hungary appear to assume that some obligation rests upon this Government in the performance of its neutral duty to prevent all trade in contraband, and thus to equalize the difference due to the relative naval strength of the belligerents. No such obligation exists; it would be an unneutral act, an act of partiality on the part of this Government, to adopt such a policy if the Executive had the power to do so. If Germany and Austria-Hungary can not import contraband from this country, it is not, because of that fact, the duty of the United States to close its markets to the Allies. The markets of this country are open upon equal terms to all the world, to every nation, belligerent or neutral.

The foregoing categorical replies to specific complaints are sufficient answer to the charge of unfriendliness to Germany and Austria-Hungary.

I am [etc.]   W. J. BRYAN

PART FOUR

Protests Against Allied Maritime Warfare

While trade with the Entente flourished, American commerce with the Central Powers was disrupted by the British navy and by restrictions on traffic with the European neutrals. Although international law and practice made contraband goods consigned to the belligerents subject to confiscation, no legal grounds justified the interruption of trade between neutral powers. British confiscation of conditional contraband (materials which could be used either for military or peaceful purposes), and the restrictions imposed by the Allied blockade on American trade with European neutrals, occasioned lengthy — but futile — diplomatic protests by the State Department. The British government maintained that many goods shipped from the United States to European neutrals were actually intended for re-export to the enemy. Such goods, they argued, were involved in a "continuous voyage" from neutral source to enemy consumer and were thus subject to seizure. The contention of the American government, however, was that such shipments ("broken voyage") were not subject to confiscation unless the interceptor could clearly prove an enemy destination. Since the Allied Powers controlled the seas and were determined to throttle the enemy, the seizures continued. (Walter Hines Page was the American Ambassador to Great Britain; and Sir Edward Grey was the British Foreign Secretary.)

12 · The Secretary of State to the Ambassador in Great Britain

DEPARTMENT OF STATE,
Washington, December 26, 1914.

The present condition of American foreign trade resulting from the frequent seizures and detentions of American cargoes destined to neutral European ports has become so serious as to require a candid statement of the views of this Government in order that the British Government may be fully informed as to the attitude of the United States toward the policy which has been pursued by the British authorities during the present war.

You will, therefore, communicate the following to His Majesty's Principal Secretary of State for Foreign Affairs, but in doing so you will assure him that it is done in the most friendly spirit and in the belief that frankness will better serve the continuance of cordial relations between the two countries than silence, which may be misconstrued into acquiescence in a course of conduct which this Government can not but consider to be an infringement upon the rights of American citizens.

The Government of the United States has viewed with growing concern the large numbers of vessels laden with American goods destined to neutral ports in Europe, which have been seized on the high seas, taken into British ports and detained sometimes for weeks by the British authorities. During the early days of the war this Government assumed that the policy adopted by the British Government was due to the unexpected outbreak of hostilities and the necessity of immediate action to prevent contraband from reaching the enemy. For this reason it was not disposed to judge this policy harshly or protest it vigorously, although it was manifestly very injurious to American trade with the neutral countries of Europe. This Government, relying confidently upon the high regard which Great Britain has so often exhibited in the past for the rights of other nations, confidently awaited amendment of a course of action which denied to neutral commerce the freedom to which it was entitled by the law of nations.

This expectation seemed to be rendered the more assured by the statement of the Foreign Office early in November that the British Government were satisfied with guarantees offered by the Norwegian, Swedish, and Danish Governments as to non-exportation of contraband goods when consigned to named persons in the territories of those Governments, and

---

12 *Foreign Relations, 1914, Supplement*, pp. 372–375.

that orders had been given to the British fleet and customs authorities to restrict interference with neutral vessels carrying such cargoes so consigned to verification of ship's papers and cargoes.

It is, therefore, a matter of deep regret that, though nearly five months have passed since the war began, the British Government have not materially changed their policy and do not treat less rigorously ships and cargoes passing between neutral ports in the peaceful pursuit of lawful commerce, which belligerents should protect rather than interrupt. The greater freedom from detention and seizure which was confidently expected to result from consigning shipments to definite consignees, rather than "to order," is still awaited.

It is needless to point out to His Majesty's Government, usually the champion of the freedom of the seas and the rights of trade, that peace, not war, is the normal relation between nations and that the commerce between countries which are not belligerents should not be interfered with by those at war unless such interference is manifestly an imperative necessity to protect their national safety, and then only to the extent that it is a necessity. It is with no lack of appreciation of the momentous nature of the present struggle in which Great Britain is engaged and with no selfish desire to gain undue commercial advantage that this Government is reluctantly forced to the conclusion that the present policy of His Majesty's Government toward neutral ships and cargoes exceeds the manifest necessity of a belligerent and constitutes restrictions upon the rights of American citizens on the high seas which are not justified by the rules of international law or required under the principle of self-preservation.

The Government of the United States does not intend at this time to discuss the propriety of including certain articles in the lists of absolute and conditional contraband, which have been proclaimed by His Majesty. Open to objection as some of these seem to this Government, the chief ground of present complaint is the treatment of cargoes of both classes of articles when bound to neutral ports.

Articles listed as absolute contraband, shipped from the United States and consigned to neutral countries, have been seized and detained on the ground that the countries to which they were destined have not prohibited the exportation of such articles. Unwarranted as such detentions are, in the opinion of this Government, American exporters are further perplexed by the apparent indecision of the British authorities in applying their own rules to neutral cargoes. For example, a shipment of copper from this country to a specified consignee in Sweden was detained because, as was stated by Great Britain, Sweden had placed no embargo on copper. On the other hand, Italy not only prohibited the export of copper, but, as this Government is informed, put in force a decree that shipments to Italian consignees or "to order," which arrive in ports of

Italy, can not be exported or transshipped. The only exception Italy makes is of copper which passes through that country in transit to another country. In spite of these decrees, however, the British Foreign Office has thus far declined to affirm that copper shipments consigned to Italy will not be molested on the high seas. Seizures are so numerous and delays so prolonged that exporters are afraid to send their copper to Italy, steamship lines decline to accept it, and insurers refuse to issue policies upon it. In a word, a legitimate trade is being greatly impaired through uncertainty as to the treatment which it may expect at the hands of the British authorities.

We feel that we are abundantly justified in asking for information as to the manner in which the British Government propose to carry out the policy which they have adopted, in order that we may determine the steps necessary to protect our citizens, engaged in foreign trade, in their rights and from the serious losses to which they are liable through ignorance of the hazards to which their cargoes are exposed.

In the case of conditional contraband the policy of Great Britain appears to this Government to be equally unjustified by the established rules of international conduct. As evidence of this, attention is directed to the fact that a number of the American cargoes which have been seized consist of foodstuffs and other articles of common use in all countries which are admittedly relative contraband. In spite of the presumption of innocent use because destined to neutral territory, the British authorities made these seizures and detentions without, so far as we are informed, being in possession of facts which warranted a reasonable belief that the shipments had in reality a belligerent destination, as that term is used in international law. Mere suspicion is not evidence and doubts should be resolved in favor of neutral commerce, not against it. The effect upon trade in these articles between neutral nations resulting from interrupted voyages and detained cargoes is not entirely cured by reimbursement of the owners for the damages which they have suffered, after investigation has failed to establish an enemy destination. The injury is to American commerce with neutral countries as a whole through the hazard of the enterprise and the repeated diversion of goods from established markets.

It also appears that cargoes of this character have been seized by the British authorities because of a belief that, though not originally so intended by the shippers, they will ultimately reach the territory of the enemies of Great Britain. Yet this belief is frequently reduced to a mere fear in view of the embargoes which have been decreed by the neutral countries to which they are destined on the articles composing the cargoes.

That a consignment "to order" of articles listed as conditional contraband and shipped to a neutral port raises a legal presumption of enemy destination appears to be directly contrary to the doctrine previously held by Great Britain and thus stated by Lord Salisbury during the South African War:

> Foodstuffs, though having a hostile destination, can be considered as contraband of war only if they are for the enemy forces; it is not sufficient that they are capable of being so used, it must be shown that this was in fact their destination at the time of their seizure.

With this statement as to conditional contraband the views of this Government are in entire accord, and upon this historic doctrine, consistently maintained by Great Britain when a belligerent as well as a neutral, American shippers were entitled to rely.

The Government of the United States readily admits the full right of a belligerent to visit and search on the high seas the vessels of American citizens or other neutral vessels carrying American goods and to detain them *when there is sufficient evidence to justify a belief that contraband articles are in their cargoes;* but His Majesty's Government, judging by their own experience in the past, must realize that this Government can not without protest permit American ships or American cargoes to be taken into British ports and there detained for the purpose of searching generally for evidence of contraband, or upon presumptions created by special municipal enactments which are clearly at variance with international law and practice.

This Government believes and earnestly hopes His Majesty's Government will come to the same belief, that a course of conduct more in conformity with the rules of international usage, which Great Britain has strongly sanctioned for many years, will in the end better serve the interests of belligerents as well as those of neutrals.

Not only is the situation a critical one to the commercial interests of the United States, but many of the great industries of this country are suffering because their products are denied long-established markets in European countries, which, though neutral, are contiguous to the nations at war. Producers and exporters, steamship and insurance companies are pressing, and not without reason, for relief from the menace to transatlantic trade which is gradually but surely destroying their business and threatening them with financial disaster.

The Government of the United States, still relying upon the deep sense of justice of the British nation, which has been so often manifested in the intercourse between the two countries during so many years of uninterrupted friendship, expresses confidently the hope that His Majesty's Government will realize the obstacles and difficulties which their present policy has placed in the way of commerce between the United States and the neutral countries of Europe, and will instruct their officials to refrain from all unnecessary interference with the freedom of trade between nations which are sufferers, though not participants, in the present conflict; and will in their treatment of neutral ships and cargoes conform more closely to those rules governing the maritime relations between belligerents and neutrals, which have received the sanction of the civilized world, and which Great Britain has, in other wars, so strongly and successfully advocated.

In conclusion, it should be impressed upon His Majesty's Government that the present condition of American trade with the neutral European countries is such that, if it does not improve, it may arouse a feeling contrary to that which has so long existed between the American and British peoples. Already it is becoming more and more the subject of public criticism and complaint. There is an increasing belief, doubtless not entirely unjustified, that the present British policy toward American trade is responsible for the depression in certain industries which depend upon European markets. The attention of the British Government is called to this possible result of their present policy to show how widespread the effect is upon the industrial life of the United States and to emphasize the importance of removing the cause of complaint.

BRYAN

13 · *The Ambassador in Great Britain to the Secretary of State*

LONDON, *January 7, 1915.*

Following is the text of Sir Edward Grey's note:

FOREIGN OFFICE, *January 7, 1915.*

. . . Let me say at once that we entirely recognize the most friendly spirit referred to by your excellency, and that we desire to reply in the same spirit and in the belief that, as your excellency states, frankness will best serve the continuance of cordial relations between the two countries.

His Majesty's Government cordially concur in the principle enunciated by the Government of the United States that a belligerent, in dealing with trade between neutrals, should not interfere unless such interference is necessary to protect the belligerent's national safety, and then only to the extent to which this is necessary. We shall endeavour to keep our

---

13 *Foreign Relations, 1915, Supplement,* pp. 299–302.

action within the limits of this principle on the understanding that it admits our right to interfere when such interference is not with *bona fide* trade between the United States and another neutral country, but with trade in contraband destined for the enemy's country, and we are ready, whenever our action may unintentionally exceed this principle, to make redress.

We think that much misconception exists as to the extent to which we have, in practice, interfered with trade. Your excellency's note seems to hold His Majesty's Government responsible for the present condition of trade with neutral countries, and it is stated that, through the action of His Majesty's Government, the products of the great industries of the United States have been denied long-established markets in European countries which, though neutral, are contiguous to the seat of war. Such a result is far from being the intention of His Majesty's Government, and they would exceedingly regret that it should be due to their action. I have been unable to obtain complete or conclusive figures showing what the state of trade with these neutral countries has been recently, and I can therefore only ask that some further consideration should be given to the question whether United States trade with these neutral countries has been so seriously affected. The only figures as to the total volume of trade that I have seen are those for the exports from New York for the month of November 1914, and they are as follows, compared with the month of November 1913:

Exports from New York for November 1913
[and] November 1914, respectively

Denmark	$558,000	$7,101,000
Sweden	377,000	2,858,000
Norway	477,000	2,318,000
Italy	2,971,000	4,781,000
Holland	4,389,000	3,960,000

. . . Your excellency's note refers in particular to the detention of copper. The figures taken from official returns for the export of copper from the United States for Italy for the months during which the war has been in progress up to the end of the first three weeks of December are as follows:

1913	£ 15,202,000
1914	£ 36,285,000

Norway, Sweden, Denmark, and Switzerland are not shown separately for the whole period in the United States returns, but are included in the heading "Other Europe"; that is, Europe other than the United Kingdom, Russia, France, Belgium, Austria, Germany, Holland, and Italy. The corresponding figures under this heading are as follows:

1913	£ 7,271,000
1914	£ 35,347,000

With such figures the presumption is very strong that the bulk of copper consigned to these countries has recently been intended, not for their own use, but for that of a belligerent who can not import it direct. It is therefore an imperative necessity for the safety of this country while it is at war that His Majesty's Government should do all in their power to stop such part of this import of copper as is not genuinely destined for neutral countries. . . .

I can not believe that, with such figures before them and in such cases as those just mentioned, the Government of the United States would question the propriety of the action of His Majesty's Government in taking suspected cargoes to a prize court, and we are convinced that it can not be in accord with the wish either of the Government or of the people of the United States to strain the international code in favor of private interests so as to prevent Great Britain from taking such legitimate means for this purpose as are in her power.

With regard to the seizure of foodstuffs to which your excellency refers, His Majesty's Government are prepared to admit that foodstuffs should not be detained and put into a prize court without presumption that they are intended for the armed forces of the enemy or the enemy government. We believe that this rule has been adhered to in practice hitherto, but if the United States Government have instances to the contrary, we are prepared to examine them, and it is our present intention to adhere to the rule, though we can not give an unlimited and unconditional undertaking in view of the departure by those against whom we are fighting from hitherto accepted rules of civilization and humanity and the uncertainty as to the extent to which such rules may be violated by them in future.

From the 4th of August last to the 3d of January the number of steamships proceeding from the United States for Holland, Denmark, Norway, Sweden, and Italy has been 773. Of these there are 45 which have had consignments or cargoes placed in the prize court while of the ships themselves only 8 have been placed in the prize court and 1 of these has since been released. It is, however, essential under modern conditions that where there is real ground for suspecting the presence of contraband, the vessels should be brought into port for examination: in no other way can the right of search be exercised, and but for this practice it would have to be completely abandoned. Information was received by us that special instructions had been given to ship rubber from the United States under another designation to escape notice, and such cases have occurred in several instances. Only by search in a port can such cases, when suspected, be discovered and proved. The necessity for examination in a port may also be illustrated by a hypothetical instance, connected with cotton, which has not yet occurred. Cotton is not specifically mentioned in your excellency's note, but I have seen public statements made in the United States that the attitude of His Majesty's Government with regard to cotton has been ambiguous, and thereby responsible for depression in the cotton trade. There has never been any foundation for this allegation. His Majesty's Government have never put cotton on the list of contraband; they have throughout the war kept it on the free list; and, on every occasion when questioned on the point, they have stated their intention of adhering to this practice. But information has reached us that, precisely because we have declared our intention of not interfering with cotton, ships carrying cotton will be specially selected to carry concealed contraband; and we have been warned that copper will be concealed in bales of cotton. Whatever suspicions we have entertained, we have not so far made these a ground for detaining any ship carrying cotton, but should we have information giving us real reason to believe in the case of a particular ship that the bales of cotton concealed copper or other contraband, the only way to prove our case would be to examine and weigh the bales; a process that could be carried out only by bringing the vessel into a port. In such a case, or if examination justified the action of His Majesty's Government, the case shall be brought before a prize court and dealt with in the ordinary way. . . .

We are confronted with the growing danger that neutral countries contiguous to the enemy will become on a scale hitherto unprecedented a base of supplies for the armed forces of our enemies and for materials for manufacturing armament. The trade figures of imports show how strong this tendency is, but we have no complaint to make of the attitude of the governments of those countries, which so far as we are aware have not departed from proper rules of neutrality. We endeavour in the interest of our own national safety to prevent this danger by intercepting goods really destined for the enemy without interfering with those which are *bona fide* neutral. . . .

Pending a more detailed reply, I would conclude by saying that His Majesty's Government do not desire to contest the general principles of law on which they understand the note of the United States to be based, and desire to restrict their action solely to interference with contraband destined for the enemy. His Majesty's Government are prepared, whenever a cargo coming from the United States is detained, to explain the case on which such detention has taken place, and would gladly enter into any arrangement by which mistakes can be avoided and reparation secured promptly when any injury to the neutral owners of a ship or cargo has been improperly caused, for they are most desirous in the interest both of the United States and of other neutral countries that British action should not interfere with the normal importation and use by the neutral countries of goods from the United States.

I have [etc.]   E. Grey

14 · Order in Council of March 11, 1915

WHEREAS the German Government has issued certain orders which, in violation of the usages of war, purport to declare the waters surrounding the United Kingdom a military area, in which all British and allied merchant vessels will be destroyed irrespective of the safety of the lives of passengers and crew, and in which neutral shipping will be exposed to similar danger in view of the uncertainties of naval warfare; and . . .

WHEREAS such attempts on the part of the enemy give to His Majesty an unquestionable right of retaliation; and

WHEREAS His Majesty has therefore decided to adopt further measures in order to prevent commodities of any kind from reaching or leaving Germany, though such measures will be enforced without risk to neutral ships or to neutral or non-combatant life and in strict observance of the dictates of humanity; and

WHEREAS the Allies of His Majesty are associated with him in the steps now to be announced for restricting further the commerce of Germany;

His Majesty is therefore pleased, by and with the advice of his Privy Council, to order and it is hereby ordered as follows:

1. No merchant vessel which sailed from her port of departure after the 1st March 1915 shall be allowed to proceed on her voyage to any German port.

Unless the vessel receives a pass enabling her to proceed to some neutral or allied port to be named in the pass, goods on board any such vessel must be discharged in a British port and placed in the custody of the marshal of the Prize Court. Goods so discharged, not being contraband of war, shall, if not requisitioned for the use of His Majesty, be restored by order of the Court, upon such terms as the Court may in the circumstances deem to be just, to the person entitled thereto.

2. No merchant vessel which sailed from any German port after the 1st March 1915 shall be allowed to proceed on her voyage with any goods on board laden at such port.

All goods laden at such port must be discharged in a British or allied port. Goods so discharged in a British port shall be placed in the custody of the marshal of the Prize Court, and, if not requisitioned for the use of His Majesty, shall be detained or sold under the direction of the Prize Court. The proceeds of goods so sold shall be paid into Court and dealt with in such manner as the Court may in the circumstances deem to be just.

---

14 *Foreign Relations, 1915, Supplement,* pp. 144–145.

Provided, that no proceeds of the sale of such goods shall be paid out of Court until the conclusion of peace, except on the application of the proper officer of the Crown, unless it be shown that the goods had become neutral property before the issue of this Order.

Provided also, that nothing herein shall prevent the release of neutral property laden at such enemy port on the application of the proper officer of the Crown.

3. Every merchant vessel which sailed from her port of departure after the 1st March 1915 on her way to a port other than a German port, carrying goods with an enemy destination, or which are enemy property, may be required to discharge such goods in a British or allied port. Any goods so discharged in a British port shall be placed in the custody of the marshal of the Prize Court, and, unless they are contraband of war, shall, if not requisitioned for the use of His Majesty, be restored by order of the Court, upon such terms as the Court may in the circumstances deem to be just to the person entitled thereto.

Provided, that this Article shall not apply in any case falling within Articles 2 or 4 of this Order.

4. Every merchant vessel which sailed from a port other than a German port after the 1st March 1915 having on board goods which are of enemy origin or are enemy property may be required to discharge such goods in a British or allied port. Goods so discharged in a British port shall be placed in the custody of the marshal of the Prize Court, and, if not requisitioned for the use of His Majesty, shall be detained or sold under the direction of the Prize Court. The proceeds of goods so sold shall be paid into Court and dealt with in such manner as the Court may in the circumstances deem to be just.

Provided, that no proceeds of sale of such goods shall be paid out of Court until the conclusion of peace except on the application of the proper officer of the Crown, unless it be shown that the goods had become neutral property before the issue of this order.

Provided also, that nothing herein shall prevent the release of neutral property of enemy origin on the application of the proper officer of the Crown.

5. Any person claiming to be interested in, or to have any claim in respect of, any goods (not being contraband of war) placed in the custody of the marshal of the Prize Court under this order, or in the proceeds of such goods, may forthwith issue a writ in the Prize Court against the proper officer of the Crown and apply for an order that the goods should be restored to him, or that their proceeds should be paid to him, or for such other order as the circumstances of the case may require.

The practice and procedure of the Prize Court shall, so far as applicable, be followed *mutatis mutandis* in any proceedings consequential upon this Order.

6. A merchant vessel which has cleared for a neutral port from a British or allied port, or which has been allowed to pass having an ostensible destination to a neutral port, and proceeds to an enemy port, shall, if captured on any subsequent voyage, be liable to condemnation.

7. Nothing in this Order shall be deemed to affect the liability of any vessel or goods to capture or condemnation independently of this Order.

8. Nothing in this Order shall prevent the relaxation of the provisions of this Order in respect of the merchant vessels of any country which declares that no commerce intended for or originating in Germany or belonging to German subjects shall enjoy the protection of its flag.

15 · *The Secretary of State to the Ambassador in Great Britain*

WASHINGTON, *March 30, 1915*

You are instructed to deliver the following to His Majesty's Government . . . :

The Government of the United States has given careful consideration to the subjects treated in the British notes of March 13 and March 15, and to the British order in council of the latter date.

These communications contain matters of grave importance to neutral nations. They appear to menace their rights of trade and intercourse not only with belligerents but also with one another. They call for frank comment in order that misunderstandings may be avoided. The Government of the United States deems it its duty, therefore, speaking in the sincerest spirit of friendship, to make its own view and position with regard to them unmistakably clear.

The order in council of the 15th of March would constitute, were its provisions to be actually carried into effect as they stand, a practical assertion of unlimited belligerent rights over neutral commerce within the whole European area, and an almost unqualified denial of the sovereign rights of the nations now at peace.

This Government takes it for granted that there can be no question what those rights are. A nation's sovereignty over its own ships and citizens under its own flag on the high seas in time of peace is, of course, unlimited; and that sovereignty suffers no diminution in time of war, except in so far as the practice and consent of civilized nations has

---

limited it by the recognition of certain now clearly determined rights, which it is conceded may be exercised by nations which are at war.

A belligerent nation has been conceded the right of visit and search, and the right of capture and condemnation, if upon examination a neutral vessel is found to be engaged in unneutral service or to be carrying contraband of war intended for the enemy's government or armed forces. It has been conceded the right to establish and maintain a blockade of an enemy's ports and coasts and to capture and condemn any vessel taken in trying to break the blockade. It is even conceded the right to detain and take to its own ports for judicial examination all vessels which it suspects for substantial reasons to be engaged in unneutral or contraband service and to condemn them if the suspicion is sustained. But such rights, long clearly defined both in doctrine and practice, have hitherto been held to be the only permissible exceptions to the principle of universal equality of sovereignty on the high seas as between belligerents and nations not engaged in war.

It is confidently assumed that His Majesty's Government will not deny that it is a rule sanctioned by general practice that, even though a blockade should exist and the doctrine of contraband as to unblockaded territory be rigidly enforced, innocent shipments may be freely transported to and from the United States through neutral countries to belligerent territory without being subject to the penalties of contraband traffic or breach of blockade, much less to detention, requisition, or confiscation.

Moreover the rules of the Declaration of Paris of 1856 — among them that free ships make free goods — will hardly at this day be disputed by the signatories of that solemn agreement.

His Majesty's Government, like the Government of the United State[s], have often and explicitly held that these rights represent the best usage of warfare in the dealings of belligerents with neutrals at sea. . . . And no claim on the part of Great Britain of any justification for interfering with these clear rights of the United States and its citizens as neutrals could be admitted. To admit it would be to assume an attitude of unneutrality toward the present enemies of Great Britain which would be obviously inconsistent with the solemn obligations of this Government in the present circumstances; and for Great Britain to make such a claim would be for her to abandon and set at naught the principles for which she has consistently and earnestly contended in other times and circumstances.

The note of His Majesty's Principal Secretary of State for Foreign Affairs which accompanies the order in council, and which bears the same date, notifies the Government of the United States of the establishment of a blockade which is, if defined by the terms of the order in council, to include all the coasts and ports of Germany and every port of possible access to enemy territory. But the novel and quite unprecedented feature of that blockade, if we are to assume it to be properly so defined, is that it embraces many neutral ports and coasts, bars access to them, and subjects all neutral ships seeking to approach them to the same suspicion that would attach to them were they bound for the ports of the enemies of Great Britain, and to unusual risks and penalties.

It is manifest that such limitations, risks, and liabilities placed upon the ships of a neutral power on the high seas, beyond the right of visit and search and the right to prevent the shipment of contraband already referred to, are a distinct invasion of the sovereign rights of the nation whose ships, trade, or commerce are interfered with.

The Government of the United States is, of course, not oblivious to the great changes which have occurred in the conditions and means of naval warfare since the rules hitherto governing legal blockade were formulated. It might be ready to admit that the old form of "close" blockade with its cordon of ships in the immediate offing of the blockaded ports is no longer practicable in face of an enemy possessing the means and opportunity to make an effective defense by the use of submarines, mines, and aircraft; but it can hardly be maintained that, whatever form of effective blockade may be made use of, it is impossible to conform at least to the spirit and principles of the established rules of war. If the necessities of the case should seem to render it imperative that the cordon of blockading vessels be extended across the approaches to any neighboring neutral port or country, it would seem clear that it would still be easily practicable to comply with the well-recognized and reasonable prohibition of international law against the blockading of neutral ports by according free admission and exit to all lawful traffic with neutral ports through the blockading cordon. This traffic would of course include all outward-bound traffic from the neutral country and all inward-bound traffic to the neutral country except contraband in transit to the enemy. Such procedure need not conflict in any respect with the rights of the belligerent maintaining the blockade since the right would remain with the blockading vessels to visit and search all ships either entering or leaving the neutral territory which they were in fact, but not of right, investing.

The Government of the United States notes that in the order in council His Majesty's Government give as their reason for entering upon a course of action, which they are aware is without precedent in modern warfare, the necessity they conceive themselves to have been placed under to retaliate upon their enemies for measures of a similar nature which the latter have announced it their intention to adopt and which they have to some extent adopted; but the Government of the United States, recalling the principles upon which His Majesty's Government have hitherto been scrupulous to act, interprets this as merely a reason for certain extraordinary activities on the part of His Majesty's naval forces and not as an excuse for or prelude to any unlawful action. If the course pursued by the present enemies of Great Britain should prove to be in fact tainted by illegality and disregard of the principles of war sanctioned by enlightened nations, it can not be supposed, and this Government does not for a moment suppose, that His Majesty's Government would wish the same taint to attach to their own actions or would cite such illegal acts as in any sense or degree a justification for similar practices on their part in so far as they affect neutral rights. . . .

This Government notes with gratification that "wide discretion is afforded to the prize court in dealing with the trade of neutrals in such manner as may in the circumstances be deemed just, and that full provision is made to facilitate claims by persons interested in any goods placed in the custody of the marshal of the prize court under the order"; that "the effect of the order in council is to confer certain powers upon the executive officers of His Majesty's Government"; and that "the extent to which these powers will be actually exercised and the degree of severity with which the measures of blockade authorized will be put into operation are matters which will depend on the administrative orders issued by the Government and the decisions of the authorities especially charged with the duty of dealing with individual ships and cargoes according to the merits of each case." This Government further notes with equal satisfaction the declaration of the British Government that "the instructions to be issued by His Majesty's Government to the fleet and to the customs officials and executive committees concerned will impress upon them the duty of acting with the utmost dispatch consistent with the object in view, and of showing in every case such consideration for neutrals as may be compatible with that object, which is, succinctly stated, to establish a blockade to prevent vessels from carrying goods for or coming from Germany."

In view of these assurances formally given to this Government, it is confidently expected that the extensive powers conferred by the order in council on the executive officers of the Crown will be restricted by "orders issued by the Government" directing the exercise of their discretionary powers in such a manner as to modify in practical application those provisions of the order in council which, if strictly enforced, would violate neutral rights and interrupt legitimate trade. Relying on the faithful performance of these voluntary assurances by His Majesty's Government the United States takes it for granted that the approach of American merchantmen to neutral ports situated upon the long line of coast affected by the order in council will not be interfered with when it is known that they do not carry goods which are contraband of war or goods destined to or proceeding from ports within the belligerent territory affected. . . .

The possibilities of serious interruption of American trade under the order in council are so many, and the methods proposed are so unusual and seem liable to constitute so great an impediment and embarrassment to neutral commerce that the Government of the United States, if the order in council is strictly enforced, apprehends many interferences with its legitimate trade which will impose upon His Majesty's Government heavy responsibilities for acts of the British authorities clearly subversive of the rights of neutral nations on the high seas. It is, therefore, expected that His Majesty's Government, having considered these possibilities, will take the steps necessary to avoid them, and, in the event that they should unhappily occur, will be prepared to make full reparation for every act, which under the rules of international law constitutes a violation of neutral rights.

As stated in its communication of October 22, 1914, "This Government will insist that the rights and duties of the United States and its citizens in the present war be defined by the existing rules of international law and the treaties of the United States, irrespective of the provisions of the Declaration of London, and that this Government reserves to itself the right to enter a protest or demand in each case in which those rights and duties so defined are violated, or their free exercise interfered with, by the authorities of the British Government."

In conclusion you will reiterate to His Majesty's Government that this statement of the views of the Government of the United States is made in the most friendly spirit, and in accordance with the uniform candor which has characterized the relations of the two Governments in the past, and which has been in large measure the foundation of the peace and amity existing between the two nations without interruption for a century.

BRYAN

PART FIVE

The View from
Washington and London

Despite the failure of Washington to secure any
great modifications of the Allied restrictions on neutral commerce, diplomatic controversies generally were not permitted to reach dangerous
levels — economic connections and the sympathy which many American
officials had for Great Britain and France mitigated the disputes. Furthermore, the British Foreign Secretary, Sir Edward Grey was keenly
aware of the danger to the Allied cause of a possible rupture between
America and Britain, and he handled Anglo-American controversies with
exemplary tact and caution in the early months of the war. By his efforts,
he managed to create a basis of understanding and friendship which
proved capable of surviving continued irritations and diplomatic
controversies.

16 · Lansing and Disputes with the Allies

I have already mentioned that in dealing with the British Government there was always in my mind the conviction that we would ultimately become an ally of Great Britain and that it would not do, therefore, to let our controversies reach a point where diplomatic correspondence gave place to action. There was another reason for prolonging discussion and avoiding too rigid an attitude, a reason which grew out of the same conviction, and of which I often thought as I studied the correspondence. On more than one occasion I felt concern lest we had gone too far when it looked as if the positions assumed by us were closing the door to further discussion.

If my conviction was right as to the United States' entry into the war, and I never doubted it after the sinking of the *Lusitania*, it was of the highest importance that we should not become a belligerent with our hands too tightly tied by what we had written. We would presumably wish to adopt some of the policies and practices, which the British had adopted, though certainly not all of them, for our object would be the same as theirs, and that was to break the power of Germany and destroy the morale of the German people by an economic isolation, which would cause them to lack the very necessaries of life. If we went too far in insisting that Great Britain must cease certain practices as violative of our neutral rights, our utterances would certainly be cited against us by other neutrals if we, as belligerents, attempted to do the same thing. While our conduct might be illegal, we would not be flagrantly inconsistent.

That reason was never lost sight of during the correspondence which passed between the two governments concerning the British restraints upon American trade. The notes that were sent were long and exhaustive treatises which opened up new subjects of discussion rather than closing those in controversy. Short and emphatic notes were dangerous. Everything was submerged in verbosity. It was done with deliberate purpose. It insured continuance of the controversies and left the questions unsettled, which was necessary in order to leave this country free to act and even to act illegally when it entered the war.

With increasing pressure from the American public and insistence by more and more senators, representatives and other prominent officials

16 From *War Memoirs of Robert Lansing, Secretary of State,* copyright, 1935, by The Bobbs-Merrill Company, Inc., reprinted by permission of the publishers. Pp. 128–129.

that the State Department do something drastic to relieve our commercial interests from British interference, and with my own conviction that the United States would ultimately be at war with Germany and ought, therefore, not to bring its controversies with the British Government to a climax by presenting a demand which would amount to an ultimatum, the situation was a difficult one. It required careful thought, patience and deliberation to work out a policy which would respond in a measure to American public opinion and at the same time conform to the conviction that our country could not afford in any circumstances to have an open rupture of our relations with Great Britain over illegal practices.

17 · Colonel House and Anglo-American Relations

November 28, 1915: I tried to impress upon Lansing [wrote House] the necessity of the United States making it clear to the Allies that we considered their cause our cause, and that we had no intention of permitting a military autocracy to dominate the world, if our strength could prevent it. We believed this was a fight between democracy and autocracy and we would stand with democracy. I pointed out that it was impossible to maintain cordial relations with Germany, not only for the reason that her system of government was different in its conception from ours, but also because so much hate against us had been engendered that it would be perhaps a generation or two before it could die out. Germany was being taught that her lack of success could be directly attributed to us. It was evident that the Government there was looking for some excuse for failure, and the easiest and best, in their opinion, seemed to be the United States' "unneutral attitude in regard to the shipment of munitions of war, and the lending of money to her enemies." I thought also that unless we did have a complete and satisfactory understanding with the Allies we would be wholly without friends when the war was ended, and our position would be not only perilous but might become hurtful from an economic viewpoint. . . .

---

17 Diary Entry in Seymour, *Intimate Papers of Colonel House,* II, 100–101.

18 · *Wilson Fears Parallels with the War of 1812*

September 30, 1914 [conference between Wilson and House]: When we were discussing the seizure of vessels by Great Britain, he read a page from his "History of the American People," telling how during Madison's Administration the War of 1812 was started in exactly the same way as this controversy is opening up. The passage said that Madison was compelled to go to war despite the fact that he was a peace-loving man and desired to do everything in his power to prevent it, but popular feeling made it impossible.

The President said: "Madison and I are the only two Princeton men that have become President. The circumstances of the War of 1812 and now run parallel. I sincerely hope they will not go further."

I told the British Ambassador about this conversation. He was greatly impressed, and said that in his cablegram to Sir Edward Grey he would call attention not only to the passage in the President's book, but to his comment to me upon it.

19 · *Sir Edward Grey Handles America with Caution*

The Navy acted and the Foreign Office had to find the argument to support the action; it was anxious work. British action provoked American argument; that was met by British counter-argument. British action preceded British argument; the risk was that action might follow American argument. In all this [Ambassador] Page's advice and suggestion were of the greatest value in warning us when to be careful or encouraging us when we could safely be firm.

One incident in particular remains in my memory. Page came to see me at the Foreign Office one day and produced a long despatch from

18 Diary Entry in Seymour, *Intimate Papers of Colonel House*, II, 303–304.
19 Viscount Grey of Fallodon, *Twenty-Five Years, 1892–1916* (New York: Hodder and Stoughton Co., 1925 — 2 vols.), II, 110–112, 115–117. Reprinted by permission of the Owner of the Copyright: Copyright 1925 R 1953.

Washington contesting our claim to act as we were doing in stopping contraband going to neutral ports. "I am instructed," he said, "to read this despatch to you." He read, and I listened. He then said: "I have now read the despatch, but I do not agree with it; let us consider how it should be answered!" On other occasions he would urge us to find means of avoiding provocation of American feeling; for instance, he urged us to find some way of acting other than by Orders in Council, which since 1812 had had such odious associations for the United States. He knew that these were only a matter of form, and that there was nothing in them intrinsically offensive to the United States, but the name was hateful in America. Unfortunately Orders in Council were formalities essential to make our action legal in British Courts of Law and we could not do without them.

The Germans were naturally active and ingenious in devising means to exploit and cultivate this ground, so fertile for quarrel between Britain and the United States; and they had plenty of clever agents and friends in America to help them. A ship would be chartered with contraband; the name of the ship and its intended voyage would be carefully revealed; American attention would be drawn to it; American feeling would be instigated to the point of readiness to resent British interference with it. The ship would then start; if we interfered with it, we ran the risk of provoking an outburst of opinion in America that might be formidable; if we allowed it to pass, we stultified our own action in other similar cases and admitted that our blockade was ineffective or nonexistent. The *Dacia*[1] was an example of this. Everybody knew what the *Dacia* was, when she was to sail, and where she was going. She was an open challenge to our blockade which we were bound to take up. Page suggested that the French Navy instead of the British should intercept the *Dacia*. This was done, and there was not a murmur in America. We used to hear it said, in days when Bryce was Ambassador at Washington, that he was the most popular European in America since Lafayette; but it was the memory of Lafayette that persisted through the war. France was the historical friend, and Britain the historical enemy.

It was possible, in notorious cases such as that of the *Dacia*, for French action to disarm American resentment and to counter German manœuvres; but, in the nature of things, the bulk of the blockade and contraband operations had to be carried out by the British Navy, which was not only the larger, but the best equipped for this purpose. The burden of defending it fell upon British diplomacy, i.e. the Foreign Office; the Board of Trade, which controlled British exports, and the Admiralty devised or executed the measures we took. The Secretary for Foreign Affairs was bombarded with the protests from neutrals that ensued. Much of his time was spent in reconciling neutral countries to what we

[1] The *Dacia* was purchased by American citizens in 1915 from the Hamburg-American Line and loaded with a shipment of cotton destined for Germany.

were doing, justifying British action, or promising enquiry, as the merits of each protest might seem to require. In the interest of the Allies, and of Britain in particular, it was desirable not to lose the good-will of neutrals; but the task of soothing and reconciling them was difficult and thankless. The stopping of contraband was bound to cause annoyance to neutral trade and shipping, and yet it had to be maintained. . . .

The question of cotton needs a little more explanation. It was important enough to be considered separately by the Cabinet in the early stage of the war. I thought it inadvisable to make it contraband. One reason has already been given, but there was more than that to be taken into account.

The cotton-growing States of America were hard hit in 1914 by the outbreak of the war. Their trade was temporarily disorganized, if not altogether suspended. That was not the fault of Britain; it was due to the war. But, if cotton were made contraband, this would be regarded as a fresh blow dealt mainly by Britain to an important industry of the United States, when it was already in distress. The attitude of the United States was going to be important and might be vital in the war; there were already materials enough for friction between us and the United States; the fomenting of these was the trump card of German diplomacy. My opinion was very decidedly that there was far more to be lost than to be gained by making cotton contraband in the first year of the war. The Cabinet took this view; it was right, even more right than we knew at the time.

After the war, when I went to America in 1919, an American of very high position in the business world, and friendly to us, volunteered the remark that it was very fortunate that we did not declare cotton contraband in 1914. I said that I had felt this at the time, but I was not quite sure what the consequence would have been; my fear was that the United States would begin convoying merchant ships possibly to enemy, certainly to neutral, ports; in this event we must have let the convoys pass, which means giving up our blockade and the stopping of supplies to Germany, for convoying, once begun, would not have been limited to cotton, but would have covered other things in which American trade was interested. Our only alternative would have been to stop the convoys by firing on the American ships of war that accompanied them; this meant war with the United States. My friend said that was not the danger to us that he thought the most likely. What he thought would have happened was an embargo on all export of munitions of war. Even as it was, there had been risk of this; the pacifist feeling in the United States was pressing for it; this section of opinion regarded the European war as a detestable thing in which American citizens should have no part, and which they should not help to keep alive by feeding any country engaged in it with munitions. All the pro-German element was pressing for an embargo, because the Allies needed American munitions and Germany did not; the anti-British element was strong on the same side. Had we exasperated the cotton States by making cotton contraband, this "block" of political influence would have gone to swell the body of opinion pressing for an embargo, and the thing which was already an appreciable risk might have become a certainty.

Another American friend, with unsurpassed knowledge of the feeling in executive and political circles at Washington at the time, has since told me that he thinks the United States would have resorted to convoy.

Later on, cotton was made contraband with a guarantee of a minimum price — that was when the trade had recovered and the cotton States were not in acute distress. The Germans at once found a substitute. Had we made it contraband in 1914 we should have run all the risk I have described, and gained nothing.

In all this discussion of contraband with the United States we were like men who had to steer a ship through an uncharted sea, perilous with shoals and rocks and treacherous currents. We kept on our course and came safely through, but we had to feel our way and often to go slow. It is to be hoped that those who think we ought to have gone straight ahead on higher speed may never have to make that voyage.

 III

THE CHALLENGE
OF THE U-BOAT

PART ONE

The Mining and Submarine Zones

Until the spring of 1915 American relations with Germany were generally uneventful. Previous controversies over neutral rights had been almost exclusively with the Entente Powers. With the launching of submarine warfare in February, 1915, the situation changed sharply. Although an earlier British announcement of the mining of the North Sea had not been protested — even though neutral ships and lives obviously were endangered — the declaration of the German submarine zone was. An American objection also was directed to the British government on February 10, 1915, against the use of neutral flags as protective cover for belligerent merchantmen — a *ruse de guerre* which Germany cited in defense of its submerged U-boat attacks. This protest, however, was not equal in severity to the "strict accountability" note to Germany.

1 · The British Foreign Office to the British Ambassador at Washington

November 3, 1914.

Please inform Government to which you are accredited that the Admiralty are issuing the following announcement:

During the last week the Germans have scattered mines indiscriminately in the open sea on main trade route from America to Liverpool via north of Ireland. Peaceful merchant ships have already been blown up with loss of life by this agency. The White Star liner *Olympic* escaped disaster by pure good luck and but for warnings given by British cruisers other British and neutral merchant and passenger vessels would have been destroyed.

These mines can not have been laid by any German ship of war. They have been laid by some merchant vessels flying neutral flag which have come along the trade route as if for purposes of peaceful commerce and while profiting to the full by immunity enjoyed by neutral merchant ships have wantonly and recklessly endangered the lives of all who travel on the sea regardless of whether they are friend or foe, civilian or military in character.

Mine laying under neutral flag and reconnaissance conducted by trawlers, hospital ships, and neutral vessels are the ordinary features of German naval warfare.

In these circumstances, having regard to the great interests entrusted to the British Navy, to the safety of peaceful commerce on high seas, and to the maintenance within limits of international law of trade between neutral countries, the Admiralty feel it necessary to adopt exceptional measures appropriate to the novel conditions under which this war is being waged.

They therefore give notice that the whole of the North Sea must be considered a military area. Within this area merchant shipping of all kinds, traders of all countries, fishing craft, and all other vessels will be exposed to the gravest dangers from mines which it has been necessary to lay and from warships searching vigilantly by night and day for suspicious craft.

All merchant and fishing vessels of every description are hereby warned of the dangers they encounter by entering this area except in strict accordance with Admiralty directions. Every effort will be made to convey this warning to neutral countries and to vessels on the sea, but from the 5th of November onwards the Admiralty announce that all ships

1 *Foreign Relations, 1914, Supplement,* p. 464.

passing a line drawn from the northern point of the Hebrides through Faroe Islands to Iceland do so at their own peril.

Ships of all countries wishing to trade to and from Norway, the Baltic, Denmark, and Holland are advised to come, if inward bound, by the English Channel and Straits of Dover. There they will be given sailing directions which will pass them safely so far as Great Britain is concerned up the east coast of England to Farn Island, whence safe route will, if possible, be given to Lindesnæs Lightship. From this point they should turn north or south according to their destination, keeping as near the coast as possible. Converse applies to vessels outward bound.

By strict adherence to these routes the commerce of all countries will be able to reach its destination in safety so far as Great Britain is concerned, but any straying even for a few miles from the course thus indicated may be followed by serious consequences.

BRITISH EMBASSY,
Washington, D.C.

2 · *The Minister in Norway to the Secretary of State*

AMERICAN LEGATION,
Christiania, November 6, 1914.

Referring to my cable of November 4, 5 p.m., the Minister for Foreign Affairs informed me Norwegian Government has sent a protest to the British Government against closing of the North Sea. Denmark and Sweden will do same. Norway depends on the United States for large amount of supplies. The Minister for Foreign Affairs expressed a hope that they will have the support of the United States and the United States Government will protest.

❊   ❊   ❊   ❊   ❊

The Secretary of State to the Minister in Norway

DEPARTMENT OF STATE,
Washington, November 10, 1914.

You may inform the Minister for Foreign Affairs that this Government does not see its way at the present time to joining other governments in protesting to the British Government against their announcement that ships entering the North Sea after November 5 do so at their own peril.

BRYAN

---

2 *Foreign Relations, 1914, Supplement,* pp. 465, 466.

3 · The Ambassador in Germany to the Secretary of State

BERLIN, *February 4, 1915.*

German Admiralty issues following proclamation: The waters surrounding Great Britain and Ireland including the whole English Channel are hereby declared to be comprised within the seat of war and that all enemy merchant vessels found in those waters after the eighteenth instant will be destroyed although it may not always be possible to save crews and passengers.

Neutral vessels expose themselves to danger within this zone of war since in view of the misuse of the neutral flag ordered by the British Government on January thirty-first and of the contingencies of maritime warfare it cannot always be avoided that neutral vessels suffer from attacks intended to strike enemy ships.

The navigation routes around the north of the Shetlands, in the eastern part of the North Sea and in a strip of at least thirty sea miles in width along the Dutch coast are not open to the danger zone. . . .

4 · The Secretary of State to the Ambassador in Germany

WASHINGTON, *February 10, 1915.*

Please address a note immediately to the Imperial German Government to the following effect:

The Government of the United States, having had its attention directed to the proclamation of the German Admiralty issued on the 4th of February, . . . feels it to be its duty to call the attention of the Imperial German Government, with sincere respect and the most friendly sentiments but very candidly and earnestly, to the very serious possibilities of the course of action apparently contemplated under that proclamation.

The Government of the United States views those possibilities with such grave concern that it feels it to be its privilege, and indeed its duty

---

3 *Foreign Relations, 1915, Supplement,* p. 94.
4 *Foreign Relations, 1915, Supplement,* pp. 98–100.

in the circumstances, to request the Imperial German Government to consider before action is taken the critical situation in respect of the relations between this country and Germany which might arise were the German naval forces, in carrying out the policy foreshadowed in the Admiralty's proclamation, to destroy any merchant vessel of the United States or cause the death of American citizens.

It is of course not necessary to remind the German Government that the sole right of a belligerent in dealing with neutral vessels on the high seas is limited to visit and search, unless a blockade is proclaimed and effectively maintained, which this Government does not understand to be proposed in this case. To declare or exercise a right to attack and destroy any vessel entering a prescribed area of the high seas without first certainly determining its belligerent nationality and the contraband character of its cargo would be an act so unprecedented in naval warfare that this Government is reluctant to believe that the Imperial Government of Germany in this case contemplates it as possible. The suspicion that enemy ships are using neutral flags improperly can create no just presumption that all ships traversing a prescribed area are subject to the same suspicion. It is to determine exactly such questions that this Government understands the right of visit and search to have been recognized.

This Government has carefully noted the explanatory statement issued by the Imperial German Government at the same time with the proclamation of the German Admiralty, and takes this occasion to remind the Imperial German Government very respectfully that the Government of the United States is open to none of the criticisms for unneutral action to which the German Government believe the governments of certain other neutral nations have laid themselves open; that the Government of the United States has not consented to or acquiesced in any measures which may have been taken by the other belligerent nations in the present war which operate to restrain neutral trade, but has, on the contrary, taken in all such matters a position which warrants it in holding those governments responsible in the proper way for any untoward effects upon American shipping which the accepted principles of international law do not justify; and that it, therefore, regards itself as free in the present instance to take with a clear conscience and upon accepted principles the position indicated in this note.

If the commanders of German vessels of war should act upon the presumption that the flag of the United States was not being used in good faith and should destroy on the high seas an American vessel or the lives of American citizens, it would be difficult for the Government of the United States to view the act in any other light than as an indefensible violation of neutral rights which it would be very hard indeed to reconcile with the friendly relations now so happily subsisting between the two Governments.

If such a deplorable situation should arise, the Imperial German Government can readily appreciate that the Government of the United States would be constrained to hold the Imperial German Government to a strict accountability for such acts of their naval authorities and to take any steps it might be necessary to take to safeguard American lives and property and to secure to American citizens the full enjoyment of their acknowledged rights on the high seas.

The Government of the United States, in view of these considerations, which it urges with the greatest respect and with the sincere purpose of making sure that no misunderstanding may arise and no circumstance occur that might even cloud the intercourse of the two Governments, expresses the confident hope and expectation that the Imperial German Government can and will give assurance that American citizens and their vessels will not be molested by the naval forces of Germany otherwise than by visit and search, though their vessels may be traversing the sea area delimited in the proclamation of the German Admiralty.

It is added for the information of the Imperial Government that representations have been made to His Britannic Majesty's Government in respect to the unwarranted use of the American flag for the protection of British ships.

BRYAN

PART TWO

The *Lusitania* Crisis

The sinking of the British liner *Falaba* on March 28, 1915, which caused the death of Leon C. Thrasher, an American citizen, first raised the question of how the "strict accountability" policy was to be implemented; while the subsequent torpedoing of the Cunard liner *Lusitania* on May 7, off the Irish coast, was to bring German-American relations to the verge of a rupture. The great liner, the pride of the British trans-Atlantic service, sank in eighteen minutes with the loss of 1198 men, women, and children, 128 of whom were Americans.

Although Washington sent no formal note of protest to Berlin on the *Falaba* sinking, a basic position of the American government soon emerged from the discussions of that incident between Wilson, Bryan, and Lansing and was applied in the case of the *Lusitania*. Despite his fervent objections, Bryan was unable to dissuade the President from taking a strong position on the issue in the first and second notes on the *Lusitania*. Although he had reluctantly signed the first note of May 13, Bryan feared that the diplomatic interchange would make war with Germany probable and declined to endorse the second note on June 9. The same day he resigned as Secretary of State and was succeeded by Robert Lansing.

The German reply of July 8 to the second American note still failed to satisfy Wilson's demands. Germany clearly was unwilling to abandon submarine warfare; on the other hand, the American government preferred to avoid a break in diplomatic relations if at all possible. Consequently President Wilson in effect retreated in his third note on July 21 (not reprinted here): the United States would accept U-boat warfare as long as the customary "rules of humanity" were followed and American lives were not lost. A relatively quiet period of negotiations for a more permanent adjustment in the relations between the two countries ensued, only to be halted when the next spectacular sinking occurred in mid-August.

5 · The Counselor for the Department of State to the Secretary of State

[WASHINGTON,] *April 2, 1915.*

DEAR MR. SECRETARY: The case of the death of an American citizen through the sinking of the British S. S. *Falaba* presents a question which will have to be decided and the decision will determine our policy in this case and in the event other Americans meet death in the same way.

I assume that, if the sinking of the *Falaba* had been the result of an attempt of the vessel to resist or to escape when summoned to stop or to surrender by a German submarine, there would be no ground of complaint for the loss of an American life as a result of the submarine's frustrating such attempt.

In that case the submarine would be exercising a belligerent right recognized by international law.

But the sinking of the *Falaba*, when no attempt is made to resist or escape, without giving the crew and passengers adequate time to leave the vessel is a different matter. It is a practice unwarranted by international usage.

Now the question is this: Ought we not to hold the German Government responsible for the death of an American through the act of their naval forces, when that act is in violation of the established rules of naval warfare?

An American taking passage on a belligerent merchant vessel is entitled to rely upon an enemy's war vessel conforming to the established rules of visit and search and of protection of non-combatants. He should not be exposed to greater dangers than the enforcement of the rules impose. If this is a correct statement, duty would appear to require a complaint and a demand for damages.

On the other hand, to enter complaint on account of the death of an American in these circumstances would compel this Government to denounce the sinking of merchant vessels in the manner referred to as a flagrant violation of international law. In fact it would be a denunciation of the German "war zone" plan, or at least of the method of carrying it out.

While as yet we are not fully advised as to the facts of the case I think that the policy of the Government should be determined in order

---

5 *Foreign Relations, Lansing Papers,* I, 365–366, 369–370.

that we may act promptly if action seems advisable and necessary, as delay in entering complaint and denunciation would be, in my opinion, a matter of just criticism.

I would like to be advised as to the policy of the Government in order that preparations may be made to act in case it is decided to act.

Faithfully yours,

ROBERT LANSING

❋   ❋   ❋   ❋   ❋

[WASHINGTON,] *April 5, 1915.*

DEAR MR. SECRETARY: In compliance with the President's note to you of the 3rd, I have drafted a memorandum for an instruction to Ambassador Gerard[1] in the Thrasher case.

The tone of the instruction is not conciliatory, and the language is plain almost to harshness. Probably it can be softened without weakening it.

I feel this: If it is decided to denounce the sinking of the *Falaba* as an act indefensible legally and morally, we will have to say so, and I do not see how we can say it in a pleasant way. We are dealing with a tragedy. It seems to me that we must assert our rights, condemn the violation and state the remedy which we expect. If we do this without evincing a firm determination to insist on compliance, the German Government will give little heed to the note and may even show contempt for its weakness.

Furthermore, American public opinion will never stand for a colorless or timid presentation of a case, in which an American has been killed by an atrocious act of lawlessness.

If the note is weak or uncertain, it had better not be sent. The situation does not seem to me to be one for compromise. We can not take the position that Thrasher should have kept out of the war zone. To do so would amount to an admission of Germany's right to perform lawless acts in that area. This would unquestionably arouse a storm of criticism, and I think that it would be justified.

On the other hand, the consequences of a strong, vigorous note may be most momentous.

In spite of the critical situation which may result I do not see how we can let the matter pass without protest.

As I said to you, I think that this case is pregnant with more sinister possibilities than any with which the Government has had to deal. After mature consideration from various points of view, I can not advise against a firm demand, and yet I feel the gravest anxiety as to the results of such a course. It by no means means war, but it means intense hostility and the charge of open support of the enemies of Germany. . . .

[LANSING]

---

[1] James W. Gerard, American Ambassador to Germany.

6 · The Secretary of State to President Wilson

WASHINGTON, *April 2, 1915*.

MY DEAR MR. PRESIDENT: I am enclosing a memorandum by Mr. Lansing in regard to the Thrasher case. . . .

It seems to me that the doctrine of contributory negligence has some bearing on this case — that is, the American who takes passage upon a British vessel knowing that this method of warfare will be employed, stands in a different position from that occupied by one who suffers without any fault of his own.

The first question raised is, What kind of a demand shall we make, if we make a demand? We can hardly insist that the presence of an American on a British ship shall operate to prevent attack unless we are prepared to condemn the methods employed as improper in warfare.

If we are to make a demand, shall we recognize the warfare as proper and ask indemnity for the loss of life? Can an American, by embarking upon a ship of the allies at such a time and under such conditions impose upon his Government an obligation to secure indemnity in case he suffers with others on the ship? I confess I have not yet been able to reach a conclusion which is entirely satisfactory to me, but I send this memorandum that you may revolve it in your mind as the question will probably arise.

W. J. BRYAN

✻ ✻ ✻ ✻ ✻

WASHINGTON, *April 19, 1915*.

MY DEAR MR. PRESIDENT: . . . There is no doubt as to the sentiment in Germany and the view they take is a natural one. 1st, They have warned Americans not to travel on British ships. Why do Americans take the risk? Not an unreasonable question. 2nd, If we allow the use of our flag, how can we complain, if in the confusion one of our boats is sunk by mistake? 3rd, Why be shocked at the drowning of a few people, if there is no objection to starving a nation? Of course Germany insists that by careful use she will have enough food, but if Great Britain cannot succeed in starving the noncombatants, why does she excite retaliation by threatening to do so?

If we are to prove our neutrality — and unless we do, we are likely to be drawn into the conflict by the growing feeling in Germany — it

---

6 *Foreign Relations, Lansing Papers*, I, 366, 11–12.

seems to me we must prevent the misuse of our flag and warn Americans not to use British vessels in the war zone unless we can bring pressure on Great Britain to withdraw threat to make bread or food contraband. . . .

With assurances [etc.]   W. J. BRYAN

7 · The Counselor for the Department of State to the Secretary of State

[WASHINGTON,] *May 9, 1915.*

DEAR MR. SECRETARY: I have been thinking over your suggestion that it might be considered that Americans, taking passage in a British vessel bound for a British port and passing through the German "war zone," did so, in a measure at least, at their own peril and, therefore, were not entitled to the full protection of this Government.

After carefully considering the suggestion I am convinced that this Government is in no position to adopt that view. To accept it would be to admit that the Government of the United States failed in its duty to its own citizens and permitted them to run risks without attempting to prevent them from doing so.

By its note to the German Government on February 10th this Government declared that it would hold Germany to a strict accountability for the loss of American lives and property within the "war zone." It did not discriminate as to the vessels carrying American citizens and property. If it intended to discriminate, it was its manifest duty to its own people to have said so, and to have issued a public warning to them to keep off British ships and to say to them "If you go, you go at your peril."

On the contrary, this Government has permitted in silence hundreds of American citizens to travel by British steamships crossing the "war zone." It has by its silence allowed them to believe that their Government approved and would stand behind them in case their legal rights were invaded.

I do not see how this Government can avoid responsibility now by asserting that an American in traveling by a British vessel took a risk, which he should not have taken. If it held that point of view it should have declared it at the time it protested against the "war zone."

The Government has even gone further than that. When the German Embassy published its "Warning"[1] (a most improper proceeding diplomatically) just prior to the sailing of the *Lusitania,* this Government continued silent. It did not even then advise Americans not to sail on British vessels. It continued to allow them to believe that the assertions in the note of February 10th were unconditional.

It is my opinion in view of the facts that it would cause general public condemnation and indignant criticism in this country, if the Government should attempt now to avoid vigorous action by asserting that the Americans drowned by the torpedoing of the *Lusitania* were blamable in having taken passage on that vessel. They had the right to rely on the note of February 10th, and they had the right to expect a warning from their Government if it considered that it could not support them if they took risks by going abroad on British vessels.

I think that it would be a serious mistake for this Government to take a position so untenable and so vulnerable to attack if it should be taken.

With great respect [etc.] Robert Lansing

❂ ❂ ❂ ❂ ❂

President Wilson's Reaction

Washington, *11 May, 1915.*

My Dear Mr. Secretary: Mr. Lansing's argument seems to me unanswerable. Even if it were just to take the position that a warning that an unlawful and outrageous thing would be done might operate as an exemption from responsibility on the part of those who issued it, so far as our citizens were concerned, it is now too late to take it. We defined our position at the outset and cannot alter it, — at any rate so far as it affects the past.

Faithfully Yours,

W. W.

8 · *The Secretary of State to President Wilson*

Washington [*May 12, 1915*].

My Dear Mr. President: . . .

But, my dear Mr. President, I join in this document [the May 13 protest

---

[1] The German Embassy published a warning in American newspapers, on May 1, against citizens embarking on Allied passenger vessels entering the war zone.

to Germany] with a heavy heart. I am as sure of your patriotic purpose as I am of my own, but after long consideration both careful and prayerful, I cannot bring myself to the belief that it is wise to relinquish the hope of playing the part of a friend to both sides in the role of peace maker and this note will, I fear, result in such relinquishment — a hope which requires for its realization the retention of the confidence of both sides. It will be popular in this country for a time at least, and possibly permanently, because public sentiment, already favorable to the Allies, has been perceptibly increased by the *Lusitania* tragedy, but there is peril in this very fact. Your position being the position of the government will be approved — that approval varying in emphasis in proportion to the intensity of the feeling against Germany. There being no intimation that the final accounting will be postponed until the war is over, the jingo element will not only predict but demand war (see enclosed editorial from *Washington Post* of this morning), and the line will be more distinctly drawn between those who sympathize with Germany and the rest of the people. Outside of the country the demand will be applauded by the Allies and the more they applaud the more Germany will be embittered, because we unsparingly denounce the retaliatory methods employed by her, without condemning the announced purpose of the Allies to starve the non-combatants of Germany and without complaining of the conduct of Great Britain in relying on passengers including men, women and children of the United States to give immunity to vessels carrying munitions of war — without even suggesting that she should convoy passenger ships as carefully as she does ships carrying horses and gasoline. This enumeration does not include a reference to Great Britain's indifference to the increased dangers thrown upon us by the misuse of our flag or to her unwarranted interference with our trade with neutral nations. Germany cannot but construe the strong statement of the case against her, coupled with silence as to the unjustifiable action of the Allies as evidence of partiality toward the latter — an impression which will be deepened in proportion to the loudness of the praise which the Allies bestow upon the statement of this government's position. The only way, as I see it, to prevent irreparable injury being done by the statement is to issue simultaneously a protest against the objectionable conduct of the Allies which will keep them from rejoicing and show Germany that we are defending our rights against aggression from both sides.

I am only giving you, my dear Mr. President, the situation as it appears to me — and praying all the while that I may be wholly mistaken and that your judgment may be vindicated by events.

[BRYAN]

9 · The Secretary of State to the Ambassador in Germany

WASHINGTON, May 13, 1915.

Please call on the Minister of Foreign Affairs and, after reading to him this communication, leave him with a copy:

In view of recent acts of the German authorities in violation of American rights on the high seas which culminated in the torpedoing and sinking of the British steamship *Lusitania* on May 7, 1915, by which over 100 American citizens lost their lives, it is clearly wise and desirable that the Government of the United States and the Imperial German Government should come to a clear and full understanding as to the grave situation which has resulted.

The sinking of the British passenger steamer *Falaba* by a German submarine on March 28, through which Leon C. Thrasher, an American citizen was drowned; the attack on April 28 on the American vessel *Cushing* by a German aeroplane; the torpedoing on May 1 of the American vessel *Gulflight* by a German submarine, as a result of which two or more American citizens met their death; and, finally, the torpedoing and sinking of the steamship *Lusitania,* constitute a series of events which the Government of the United States has observed with growing concern, distress, and amazement. . . .

The Government of the United States has been apprised that the Imperial German Government considered themselves to be obliged by the extraordinary circumstances of the present war and the measures adopted by their adversaries in seeking to cut Germany off from all commerce, to adopt methods of retaliation which go much beyond the ordinary methods of warfare at sea, in the proclamation of a war zone from which they have warned neutral ships to keep away. This Government has already taken occasion to inform the Imperial German Government that it can not admit the adoption of such measures or such a warning of danger to operate as in any degree an abbreviation of the rights of American shipmasters or of American citizens bound on lawful errands as passengers on merchant ships of belligerent nationality; and that it must hold the Imperial German Government to a strict accountability for any infringement of those rights, intentional or incidental. It does not understand the Imperial German Government to question those rights. It assumes, on the contrary, that the Imperial Government

---

9 *Foreign Relations, 1915, Supplement,* pp. 393–396.

accept, as of course, the rule that the lives of non-combatants, whether they be of neutral citizenship or citizens of one of the nations at war, can not lawfully or rightfully be put in jeopardy by the capture or destruction of an unarmed merchantman, and recognize also, as all other nations do, the obligation to take the usual precaution of visit and search to ascertain whether a suspected merchantman is in fact of belligerent nationality or is in fact carrying contraband of war under a neutral flag.

The Government of the United States, therefore, desires to call the attention of the Imperial German Government with the utmost earnestness to the fact that the objection to their present method of attack against the trade of their enemies lies in the practical impossibility of employing submarines in the destruction of commerce without disregarding those rules of fairness, reason, justice, and humanity, which all modern opinion regards as imperative. It is practically impossible for the officers of a submarine to visit a merchantman at sea and examine her papers and cargo. It is practically impossible for them to make a prize of her; and, if they can not put a prize crew on board of her, they can not sink her without leaving her crew and all on board of her to the mercy of the sea in her small boats. These facts it is understood the Imperial German Government frankly admit. We are informed that, in the instances of which we have spoken, time enough for even that poor measure of safety was not given, and in at least two of the cases cited, not so much as a warning was received. Manifestly submarines can not be used against merchantmen, as the last few weeks have shown, without an inevitable violation of many sacred principles of justice and humanity.

American citizens act within their indisputable rights in taking their ships and in traveling wherever their legitimate business calls them upon the high seas, and exercise those rights in what should be the well-justified confidence that their lives will not be endangered by acts done in clear violation of universally acknowledged international obligations, and certainly in the confidence that their own Government will sustain them in the exercise of their rights.

There was recently published in the newspapers of the United States, I regret to inform the Imperial German Government, a formal warning, purporting to come from the Imperial German Embassy at Washington, addressed to the people of the United States, and stating, in effect, that any citizen of the United States who exercised his right of free travel upon the seas would do so at his peril if his journey should take him within the zone of waters within which the Imperial German Navy was using submarines against the commerce of Great Britain and France, notwithstanding the respectful but very earnest protest of his Government, the Government of the United States. I do not refer to this for the purpose of calling the attention of the Imperial German Government at this time to the surprising irregularity of a communication from the Imperial German Embassy at Washington addressed to the people of the United States through the newspapers, but only for the purpose of pointing out that no warning that an unlawful and inhumane act will be committed can possibly be accepted as an excuse or palliation for that act or as an abatement of the responsibility for its commission.

Long acquainted as this Government has been with the character of the Imperial German Government and with the high principles of equity by which they have in the past been actuated and guided, the Government of the United States can not believe that the commanders of the vessels which committed these acts of lawlessness did so except under a misapprehension of the orders issued by the Imperial German naval authorities. It takes it for granted that, at least within the practical possibilities of every such case, the commanders even of submarines were expected to do nothing that would involve the lives of non-combatants or the safety of neutral ships, even at the cost of failing of their object of capture or destruction. It confidently expects, therefore, that the Imperial German Government will disavow the acts of which the Government of the United States complains, that they will make reparation so far as reparation is possible for injuries which are without measure, and that they will take immediate steps to prevent the recurrence of anything so obviously subversive of the principles of warfare for which the Imperial German Government have in the past so wisely and so firmly contended.

The Government and the people of the United States look to the Imperial German Government for just, prompt, and enlightened action in this vital matter with the greater confidence because the United States and Germany are bound together not only by special ties of friendship but also by the explicit stipulations of the treaty of 1828 between the United States and the Kingdom of Prussia.

Expressions of regret and offers of reparation in case of the destruction of neutral ships sunk by mistake, while they may satisfy international obligations, if no loss of life results, can not justify or excuse a practice, the natural and necessary effect of which is to subject neutral nations and neutral persons to new and immeasurable risks.

The Imperial German Government will not expect the Government of the United States to omit any word or any act necessary to the performance of its sacred duty of maintaining the rights of the United States and its citizens and of safeguarding their free exercise and enjoyment.

BRYAN

10 · *The Ambassador in Germany to the Secretary of State*

The following is the text of the reply of the German Government to the *Lusitania* note, which I am informed will be published here Monday:

BERLIN, *May 28, 1915.*

. . . The Imperial Government has subjected the statements of the Government of the United States to a careful examination and has the lively wish on its part also to contribute in a convincing and friendly manner to clear up any misunderstandings which may have entered into the relations of the two Governments through the events mentioned by the American Government.

With regard firstly to the cases of the American steamers *Cushing* and *Gulflight,* the American Embassy has already been informed that it is far from the German Government to have any intention of ordering attacks by submarines or flyers on neutral vessels in the zone which have not been guilty of any hostile act; on the contrary, the most explicit instructions have been repeatedly given the German armed forces to avoid attacking such vessels. If neutral vessels have come to grief through the German submarine war during the past few months, by mistake, it is a question of isolated and exceptional cases which are traceable to the misuse of flags by the British Government in connection with carelessness or suspicious actions on the part of [the] captains of the vessels. In all cases where a neutral vessel through no fault of its own has come to grief through the German submarine or flyers according to the facts as ascertained by the German Government, this Government has expressed its regret at the unfortunate occurrence and promised indemnification where the facts justified it. The German Government will treat the cases of the American steamers *Cushing* and *Gulflight* according to the same principles. An investigation of these cases is in progress. Its results will be communicated to the Embassy shortly. The investigation might, if thought desirable, be supplemented by an international commission of inquiry, pursuant to Title III of the Hague Convention of October 18, 1907, for the pacific settlement of international disputes.

In the case of the sinking of the English steamer *Falaba,* the com-

---

10 *Foreign Relations, 1915, Supplement,* pp. 419–421.

mander of the German submarine had the intention of allowing passengers and crew ample opportunity to save themselves. It was not until the captain disregarded the order to lay to and took to flight, sending up rocket signals for help, that the German commander ordered the crew and passengers by signals and megaphone to leave the ship within ten minutes. As a matter of fact he allowed them twenty-three minutes and did not fire the torpedo until suspicious steamers were hurrying to the aid of the *Falaba.*

With regard to the loss of life when the British passenger steamer *Lusitania* was sunk, the German Government has already expressed its deep regret to the neutral Governments concerned that nationals of those countries lost their lives on that occasion. The Imperial Government must state for the rest the impression that certain important facts most directly connected with the sinking of the *Lusitania* may have escaped the attention of the Government of the United States. It therefore considers it necessary in the interest of the clear and full understanding aimed at by either Government primarily to convince itself that the reports of the facts which are before the two Governments are complete and in agreement.

The Government of the United States proceeds on the assumption that the *Lusitania* is to be considered as an ordinary unarmed merchant vessel. The Imperial Government begs in this connection to point out that the *Lusitania* was one of the largest and fastest English commerce steamers, constructed with Government funds as auxiliary cruisers, and is expressly included in the navy list published by British Admiralty. It is moreover known to the Imperial Government from reliable information furnished by its officials and neutral passengers that for some time practically all the more valuable English merchant vessels have been provided with guns, ammunition, and other weapons, and reinforced with a crew specially practiced in manning guns. According to reports at hand here, the *Lusitania* when she left New York undoubtedly had guns on board which were mounted under decks and masked.

The Imperial Government furthermore has the honor to direct the particular attention of the American Government to the fact that the British Admiralty by a secret instruction of February of this year advised the British merchant marine not only to seek protection behind neutral flags and markings, but even when so disguised to attack German submarines by ramming them. High rewards have been offered by the British Government as a special incentive for the destruction of the submarines by merchant vessels, and such rewards have already been paid out. In view of these facts, which are satisfactorily known to it, the Imperial Government is unable to consider English merchant vessels any longer as "undefended territory" in the zone of maritime war designated by the Admiralty Staff of the Imperial German Navy, the German commanders are consequently no longer in a position to observe the rules of capture otherwise usual and with which they invariably complied before this. Lastly, the Imperial Government must specially point out that on her last trip the *Lusitania*, as on earlier occasions, had Candian troops and munitions on board, including no less than 5,400 cases of ammunition destined for the destruction of brave German soldiers who are fulfilling with self-sacrifice and devotion their duty in the service of the Fatherland. The German Government believes that it acts in just self-defense when it seeks to protect the lives of its soldiers by destroying ammunition destined for the enemy with the means of war at its command. The English steamship company must have been aware of the dangers to which passengers on board the *Lusitania* were exposed under the circumstances. In taking them on board in spite of this the company quite deliberately tried to use the lives of American citizens as protection for the ammunition carried, and violated the clear provisions of American laws which expressly prohibit, and provide punishment for, the carrying of passengers on ships which have explosives on board. The company thereby wantonly caused the death of so many passengers. According to the express report of the submarine commander concerned, which is further confirmed by all other reports, there can be doubt that the rapid sinking of the *Lusitania* was primarily due to the explosion of the cargo of ammunition caused by the torpedo. Otherwise, in all human probability, the passengers of the *Lusitania* would have been saved.

The Imperial Government holds the facts recited above to be of sufficient importance to recommend them to a careful examination by the American Government. The Imperial Government begs to reserve a final statement of its position with regard to the demands made in connection with the sinking of the *Lusitania* until a reply is received from the American Government. . . .

[FOREIGN MINISTER GOTTLIEB] VON JAGOW

11 · *Public Opinion and the Crisis*

Technically, remarks the New York *Sun*, the torpedoing of the great British liner *Lusitania* and the sacrifice of hundreds of non-combatants, including American citizens, "possesses neither more nor less significance" than the torpedoing of that other British passenger-ship, the *Falaba*, with the loss of one American life. . . . Yet the fact remains, the same paper goes on to say, that "no episode of the war has startled and aroused public opinion in this country in greater degree," and "the moral and intellectual effect is bound to be tremendous beyond measurement." " 'Das-

11 *The Literary Digest*, 50:1133–1134 (May 15, 1915).

tardly,'" it concludes, "is the word on millions of American lips." And ex-President Roosevelt, whose concern is instinctively with the human rather than the legal aspect of a problem, thinks it "inconceivable that we should refrain from taking action on this matter, for we owe it not only to humanity but to our own national self-respect." "This represents," he adds, "not merely piracy, but piracy on a vaster scale of murder than any old-time pirate ever practised." It is "the warfare which destroyed Louvain and Dinant, and hundreds of men, women and children in Belgium" applied to "our own fellow countrymen and country women."

The *Lusitania,* with 2,104 persons on board, including 187 Americans, was torpedoed without warning, at a few minutes after two o'clock on the afternoon of May 7, and went to the bottom in about twenty minutes. The attack took place only a few miles off the south coast of Ireland, just as she was rounding into St. George's Channel. So sudden was the disaster that the loss of life was enormous. On the day she left New York the papers of this city contained a notice, signed "Imperial German Embassy," warning transatlantic travelers that if they entered the "warzone" on "ships of Great Britain or her allies" they did so "at their own risk." Many prominent passengers on the *Lusitania* also received telegrams, signed with fictitious names, stating that the ship was to be torpedoed and advising them to cancel their passage; and others, on reaching the pier, were accosted by strangers who warned them to remain ashore.

The intensity of feeling aroused in American minds may be gaged by the fact that several leading papers hint at strong measures. The New York *Tribune* closes a vigorous editorial with the words: "The nation which remembered the sailors of the *Maine* will not forget the civilians of the *Lusitania!*" "From our Department of State," says the New York *Times,* "there must go to the Imperial Government at Berlin a demand that the Germans shall no longer make war like savages drunk with blood, that they shall cease to seek the attainment of their ends by the assassination of non-combatants and neutrals." In fact, "America is suddenly brought into the maelstrom of this gigantic war" by this "villainous blow," declares the Philadelphia *Press,* and "we have a right to expect that our Government will take some quick and decided action on this foul deed of enormous barbarity." America "can and must" demand "an immediate accounting," thinks the Boston *Herald,* and "now, if ever, is the time for the United States to speak for itself and for humanity — and would that there were a Hay, an Olney, or a Root to frame the momentous message." Even more insistent is the demand of the Memphis *Commercial Appeal,* which says:

> "The United States should notify Germany that the loss of American life and passenger-ships by torpedoing without taking off the passengers will be regarded as an act of war, and demand an answer. If the answer is not satisfactory Congress should be called in extra session to consider a declaration of war."

Condemnation of the act seems to be limited only by the restrictions of the English language. "If ever wholesale murder was premeditated, this slaughter on the high seas was," exclaims the New York *Herald,* which adds that "it is a time of gravity in American history unmatched since the Civil War." The New York *World* brands "the whole German submarine policy" as "a revival of piracy — piracy organized, systematized, and nationalized." As for the German defense:

> "The German authorities claim in extenuation that fair warning was given to Americans by the German Embassy in Washington that the *Lusitania* was to be torpedoed. Murder does not become innocent and innocuous because the victim has been warned in advance that the blow would be struck if he persisted in the exercise of his lawful rights."

The Chicago *Herald,* too, holds that "the idea that neutrals under such circumstances have cut loose from all protection of international law is untenable." The Springfield *Republican* fears more horrors are to come, for —

> "The very success of the attack on this splendid ship may unfortunately stiffen the Germans in their determination to make the most of their opportunities on the sea, utterly regardless of the murderous deterioration in the moral character of the warfare which submarine attacks on passenger-ships involve."
>
> "The base inhumanity of torpedoing such ships without warning tends to place the submarine on the level of the assassin, and from this point of view modern civilization will be unable to escape its fearful responsibility in reshaping the laws of war when the final accounting takes place in the great ultimate assize of the nations."

Yet the belief is felt by the Philadelphia *Record* that this event need not involve us in "insurmountable" difficulties with the German Government, and the Chicago *Tribune,* while not blinking the gravity of the case, appeals to the country with this calming and steadying counsel:

> "To the slaughter of the innocents in Belgium and in Poland has been added the slaughter of the innocents on the *Lusitania.* This last massacre violates all previous law of the seas. . . . . . .
>
> "Whether the American Government will acquiesce in this new German law of the seas is a question which will agitate all American hearts to-day and all days until the decision is announced.
>
> "We do not propose to weigh the value (if any) of the defense as compared with the evil of the deed. That is a function which belongs to our official Government, under the leadership of President Wilson, and which, in a crisis as grave as this one, should belong exclusively to our official Government.
>
> "It is not for any good American now to cloud its counsels with unsought advice or to attempt to force its decision.
>
> "We can only stand and wait, united in our determination to enforce the will of our Government, whatever that may be."

The German-American press emphasize the fact that the *Lusitania's* passengers had been amply warned, and argue that when they disregarded these warnings "they had only themselves to blame for what happened." Thus in the *New-Yorker Staats-Zeitung* we read:

"Whoever sails the seas in these war-times, taking passage under the British flag, assumes the risk attaching thereto. There can be no responsibility of the Government of the United States to protect British shipping in British waters. There is one way to safeguard American life, and that is by staying at home. Travel at sea is decidedly dangerous at the present time in the neighborhood of the English Channel.

"The submarine peril has been characterized in this country variously as a 'bluff,' a 'blunder,' and as further evidence of 'German savagery.' The sinking of the *Lusitania* will change the temper of this thought both in England and in the United States."

Noting that the *Lusitania's* cargo included a large quantity of ammunition, the New York *Herald* says:

"The manifest showed enormous quantities of war-material, among which were no fewer than 5,471 cases of ammunition, valued at $200,000. The fact is, the steamer might be considered not a passenger-ship but an army-supply ship. We are not quite certain whether the United States law permits a passenger-steamer to depart with such a highly dangerous cargo; at any rate, the Cunard Company seems not very solicitous about the security of its passengers. Suppose a fire had started near these ammunition-cases!"

George Sylvester Viereck, editor of *The Fatherland* (New York), argues that Secretary Bryan has been remiss in not warning Americans to avoid the "war-zone." He says:

"The United States Government warned Americans away from the Mexican war-zone, but not a word of warning has been officially uttered against Americans visiting the war-zone established by Germany around the British Isles. It is time for this Government to warn Americans that their lives are in constant danger aboard any British merchantman. If American ships are not good enough for American travelers, let them stay at home."

The *Lusitania* incident, adds Mr. Viereck, "will be a revelation to Americans and convince them that Germany is not bluffing in this war." Capt. Max Moeller, superintendent of the North German Lloyd, informs an interviewer that "it will be far-reaching and beneficial and show the world that Germans are good and thorough fighters."

12 · The Secretary of State to President Wilson

MY DEAR MR. PRESIDENT: I have gone over the note carefully and beg to submit the following suggestions. . . . In dealing with the *Lusitania*, it is, in my judgment, necessary to bear in mind that our only concern is with the protection of our people. We have not felt called upon to express an opinion on submarine warfare when other vessels not bearing Americans have been sunk. Whatever views we may have as to the moral character of the means employed by the belligerents, we do not feel it our duty to express opinions merely for the purpose of announcing our views. We could, of course, contribute something towards the formation of public opinion against the belligerent which employs methods which we might denounce and in favor of the belligerent which was the victim of the methods so denounced, but even the most biased among our citizens would hardly feel justified in asking us to make [take?] any position merely for the purpose of helping one side or the other.

It seems to me that, having stated our position without equivocation, we are not only justified but compelled by duty to do what we can to prevent our citizens incurring unnecessary risks. The precedents for this are abundant. . . . It seems to me that we cannot well justify a failure to warn American citizens against going into the danger zone on foreign ships — especially on ships which, by carrying ammunition, invite extraordinary risks. It is not sufficient to say that, according to international law, American citizens have a right to go anywhere and that the Government's protection will follow them no matter what risks they take. If the authorities of a city are justified in warning people off the streets of the city in which they reside, surely a nation is justified in warning its citizens off of the water highways which belong to no nation alone, but to all the nations in common. . . .

I believe that Germany is looking for a way out and that, having stated our position unequivocally on the subject of the use of submarines against merchantmen, we would be justified in taking all the precaution possible to prevent our citizens taking risks. If — not for the benefit of Germany but for the benefit of our own people — we announce that passenger ships will not hereafter be allowed to carry ammunition, I think Germany would be very likely to say that no passenger ship would

---

be attacked if assurances were given that it did not carry ammunition. This we could do without invoking any new legislation. In my judgment, you would be justified in going even further and saying that Congress would be asked for legislation authorizing the refusal of clearance to passenger ships carrying contraband. If such a rule was adopted, contraband would be carried on ships without passengers and thus the safety of passenger ships would be assured. But even if you do not feel justified in going so far as to advise the legislation suggested, forbidding the carrying of contraband on passenger ships, I believe the order in regard to ammunition would have a powerful influence upon Germany just at this time, and I feel sure that it would be approved in this country. A person would have to be very much biased in favor of the Allies to insist that ammunition intended for one of the belligerents should be safe-guarded in transit by the lives of American citizens or, for that matter, by the lives of citizens of any country.

I hope you will pardon the length of this note but I am sincerely anxious to render you any service I can in the solution of the difficult problem presented by the *Lusitania* disaster. I recognize, of course, that the responsibility rests upon you and that in the final decision your judgment and your conscience are the only guides upon which you are justified in relying. Those of us who have been honored by being selected as advisors are in duty bound to give you, when desired, the benefit of our judgment and conscience, but none of your associates realize more fully than I that we can only assist insofar as the reason[s] which support our conclusions appeal to you. I know of no other way of discharging the duty of an advisor than to outline the course that I would pursue if the responsibility for action were upon me. The earnestness with which I have spoken in the discussion of these questions measures the depth of my solicitude and the sincerity of my desire that your decisions may, by safeguarding our country's welfare, redound to your own personal credit and to the advantage of our party.

With assurances [etc.] W. J. BRYAN

13 · The Counselor for the Department of State to the Secretary of State

[WASHINGTON,] *June 3, 1915.*

DEAR MR. SECRETARY: I am submitting a memorandum on the allegations of facts contained in the German note of May 28th. If I had more time, it could be very much abbreviated.

It seems to me that only two of the allegations are relevant to the German defense, namely:

(1) That the *Lusitania* was armed, and

(2 That the commander of the submarine feared the *Lusitania* would ram him.

There is no evidence that the German Government had information that the vessel was armed or information sufficient to found a belief to that effect.

As to the second allegation, the danger of the *Lusitania,* a vessel of over 31000 tons burden, being able to maneuver so as to ram a small swift moving craft like a submarine is too remote to warrant serious consideration. That the commander actually feared being rammed I believe to be false.

The remaining allegations are irrelevant to the defense that the submarine was justified in torpedoing the *Lusitania* without visiting her and without putting her crew and passengers in a place of safety. If the vessel was laden with war supplies, if she flew a neutral flag, if she had Canadian soldiers on board, and if she violated several laws of the United States as to her cargo, these facts in no way affect the question.

While the memorandum reviews these facts, I think that it would be unwise to controvert or discuss them.

Faithfully yours,

ROBERT LANSING

14 · The Secretary of State ad interim to the Ambassador in Germany

WASHINGTON, *June 9, 1915.*

You are instructed to deliver textually the following note to the Minister of Foreign Affairs:

In compliance with your excellency's request I did not fail to transmit to my Government immediately upon their receipt your note of May 28 in reply to my note of May 15 [13], and your supplementary note of June 1, setting forth the conclusions so far as reached by the Imperial German Government concerning the attacks on the American steamers *Cushing* and *Gulflight.* I am now instructed by my Government to communicate the following in reply:

The Government of the United States notes with gratification the full recognition of the Imperial German Government, in discussing the cases of the *Cushing* and the *Gulflight,* of the principle of the freedom of all parts of the open sea to neutral ships and the frank willingness of the Imperial German Government to acknowledge and meet its liability where the fact of attack upon neutral ships "which have not been guilty of any hostile act" by German aircraft or vessels of war is satisfactorily established; and the Government of the United States will in due course lay before the Imperial German Government, as it requests, full information concerning the attack on the steamer *Cushing.*

With regard to the sinking of the steamer *Falaba,* by which an American citizen lost his life, the Government of the United States is surprised to find the Imperial German Government contending that an effort on the part of a merchantman to escape capture and secure assistance alters the obligation of the officer seeking to make the capture in respect of the safety of the lives of those on board the merchantman, although the vessel had ceased her attempt to escape when torpedoed. These are not new circumstances. They have been in the minds of statesmen and of international jurists throughout the development of naval warfare, and the Government of the United States does not understand that they have ever been held to alter the principles of humanity upon which it has insisted. Nothing but actual forcible resistance or continued efforts to escape by flight when ordered to stop for the purpose of visit on the part

14 *Foreign Relations, 1915, Supplement,* pp. 436–438.

of the merchantman has ever been held to forfeit the lives of her passengers or crew. The Government of the United States, however, does not understand that the Imperial German Government is seeking in this case to relieve itself of liability, but only intends to set forth the circumstances which led the commander of the submarine to allow himself to be hurried into the course which he took.

Your excellency's note, in discussing the loss of American lives resulting from the sinking of the steamship *Lusitania,* adverts at some length to certain information which the Imperial German Government has received with regard to the character and outfit of that vessel, and your excellency expresses the fear that this information may not have been brought to the attention of the Government of the United States. It is stated in the note that the *Lusitania* was undoubtedly equipped with masked guns, supplied with trained gunners and special ammunition, transporting troops from Canada, carrying a cargo not permitted under the laws of the United States to a vessel also carrying passengers, and serving, in virtual effect, as an auxiliary to the naval forces of Great Britain. Fortunately, these are matters concerning which the Government of the United States is in a position to give the Imperial German Government official information. Of the facts alleged in your excellency's note, if true, the Government of the United States would have been bound to take official cognizance in performing its recognized duty as a neutral power and in enforcing its national laws. It was its duty to see to it that the *Lusitania* was not armed for offensive action, that she was not serving as a transport, that she did not carry a cargo prohibited by the statutes of the United States, and that, if in fact she was a naval vessel of Great Britain, she should not receive clearance as a merchantman; and it performed that duty and enforced its statutes with scrupulous vigilance through its regularly constituted officials. It is able, therefore, to assure the Imperial German Government that it has been misinformed. If the Imperial German Government should deem itself to be in possession of convincing evidence that the officials of the Government of the United States did not perform these duties with thoroughness, the Government of the United States sincerely hopes that it will submit that evidence for consideration.

Whatever may be the contentions of the Imperial German Government regarding the carriage of contraband of war on board the *Lusitania* or regarding the explosion of that material by the torpedo, it need only be said that in the view of this Government these contentions are irrelevant to the question of the legality of the methods used by the German naval authorities in sinking the vessel.

But the sinking of passenger ships involves principles of humanity which throw into the background any special circumstances of detail that may be thought to affect the cases, principles which lift it, as the Imperial German Government will no doubt be quick to recognize and acknowledge, out of the class of ordinary subjects of diplomatic discussion or of international controversy. Whatever be the other facts regarding the *Lusitania*, the principal fact is that a great steamer, primarily and chiefly a conveyance for passengers, and carrying more than a thousand souls who had no part or lot in the conduct of the war, was torpedoed and sunk without so much as a challenge or a warning, and that men, women, and children were sent to their death in circumstances unparalleled in modern warfare. The fact that more than one hundred American citizens were among those who perished made it the duty of the Government of the United States to speak of these things and once more, with solemn emphasis, to call the attention of the Imperial German Government to the grave responsibility which the Government of the United States conceives that it has incurred in this tragic occurrence, and to the indisputable principle upon which that responsibility rests. The Government of the United States is contending for something much greater than mere rights of property or privileges of commerce. It is contending for nothing less high and sacred than the rights of humanity, which every Government honors itself in respecting and which no Government is justified in resigning on behalf of those under its care and authority. Only her actual resistance to capture or refusal to stop when ordered to do so for the purpose of visit could have afforded the commander of the submarine any justification for so much as putting the lives of those on board the ship in jeopardy. This principle the Government of the United States understands the explicit instructions issued on August 3, 1914, by the Imperial German Admiralty to its commanders at sea to have recognized and embodied, as do the naval codes of all other nations, and upon it every traveler and seaman had a right to depend. It is upon this principle of humanity as well as upon the law founded upon this principle that the United States must stand.

The Government of the United States is happy to observe that your excellency's note closes with the intimation that the Imperial German Government is willing, now as before, to accept the good offices of the United States in an attempt to come to an understanding with the Government of Great Britain by which the character and conditions of the war upon the sea may be changed. The Government of the United States would consider it a privilege thus to serve its friends and the world. It stands ready at any time to convey to either Government any intimation or suggestion the other may be willing to have it convey and cordially invites the Imperial German Government to make use of its services in this way at its convenience. The whole world is concerned in anything that may bring about even a partial accommodation of interests or in any way mitigate the terrors of the present distressing conflict.

In the meantime, whatever arrangement may happily be made between the parties to the war, and whatever may in the opinion of the Imperial German Government have been the provocation or the circumstantial justification for the past acts of its commanders at sea, the Government of the United States confidently looks to see the justice and humanity of the Government of Germany vindicated in all cases where Americans have been wronged or their rights as neutrals invaded.

The Government of the United States therefore very earnestly and very solemnly renews the representations of its note transmitted to the Imperial German Government on the 15th of May, and relies in these representations upon the principles of humanity, the universally recognized understandings of international law, and the ancient friendship of the German nation.

The Government of the United States can not admit that the proclamation of a war zone from which neutral ships have been warned to keep away may be made to operate as in any degree an abbreviation of the rights either of American shipmasters or of American citizens bound on lawful errands as passengers on merchant ships of belligerent nationality. It does not understand the Imperial German Government to question those rights. It understands it, also, to accept as established beyond question the principle that the lives of noncombatants can not lawfully or rightfully be put in jeopardy by the capture or destruction of an unresisting merchantman, and to recognize the obligation to take sufficient precaution to ascertain whether a suspected merchantman is in fact of belligerent nationality or is in fact carrying contraband of war under a neutral flag. The Government of the United States therefore deems it reasonable to expect that the Imperial German Government will adopt the measures necessary to put these principles into practice in respect of the safeguarding of American lives and American ships, and asks for assurances that this will be done.

LANSING

PART THREE

The *Arabic* Pledge

With the *Lusitania* case still unsettled, on August 19, 1915, the British White Star liner *Arabic* was sunk without warning by a German submarine with the loss of 44 lives, including two Americans. This incident further exacerbated relations between Washington and Berlin, and the American government was apparently prepared to sever diplomatic relations unless a satisfactory settlement was immediately offered. The German government, whose underseas fleet was still too small to offset the possible belligerency of the United States, was also apprehensive about the repercussions in Europe of such a break. Accordingly, she effected a partial retreat in the form of a pledge to cease U-boat attacks without warning against passenger vessels. The German Ambassador to the United States, Count Johann von Bernstorff, subsequently related his role in resolving the crisis.

15 · Bernstorff and the *Arabic* Crisis

The risk that the United States might join in the War was for the first time brought within the bounds of possibility by the torpedoing of the *Lusitania*. The deaths of over a hundred Americans, and among them many women and children, produced an agitation in the United States of which, even to-day, there is no real conception in Germany. In the first days after the fateful event President Wilson himself seemed to have under-estimated the prevailing indignation; otherwise, he would probably not have taken up the attitude he did in his famous speech. On May 10, 1915, at Philadelphia, he testified to his pacific sentiments and said: "The example of America must be a special example, the example of America must be the example not merely of peace because it will not fight, but of peace because peace is the healing and elevating influence of the world, and strife is not. There is such a thing as a man being too proud to fight. There is such a thing as a nation being so right that it does not need to convince others by force that it is right." This speech increased the outburst of indignation throughout the country. "Too proud to fight" became the term of abuse flung by the Jingo and Entente party against Wilson. Almost unanimously public opinion demanded the severance of diplomatic relations with Germany. Under the pressure of this primitive emotion the President thought it necessary to offer a further and official interpretation of what he had said. On May 13th he sent the first well-known sharply-worded note to Berlin. In Germany the U-Boat war was regarded as a justifiable reprisal against the English blockade. On the other hand, it was maintained in the United States that the Neutrals — apart from the case of an effective blockade — were justified in travelling where they pleased, without risk to their lives, while the German U-Boats were only authorised to hold up merchant ships for the purpose of search. The American demand made the U-Boat war impossible, which was in fact the intention of the American Government. The conflict between the two points of view seemed unbridgeable, and would inevitably have led, in the persistent excitement, to the breach of diplomatic relations, unless it were possible to gain time, during which the waves of indignation might die down. Telegraphic communication between the German Government and the Washington Embassy could only be established by devious ways and was thus extraordinarily slow. I had to take decisions on my own responsibility and conduct business with rapidity. It was immediately clear to me that a breach of diplomatic

---

15 Johann H. von Bernstorff, *Memoirs of Count Bernstorff* (New York: Random House, 1936), 141–145.

relations would mean war. . . . The main point, therefore, was to preserve diplomatic relations under all circumstances. In any case, however, my efforts at that time were reasonable, in case the breach could be ultimately avoided. Now, when the issue is known to us, it may be urged that it would have been better if the United States had entered the War at that time. The final catastrophe would then have come earlier, and have fallen upon the German people, when it was not yet demoralised and shattered by a four years' war and blockade. At that time I had a well-founded hope of being able to bring about a peace through the mediation of America, and I accordingly wanted to gain time at any cost. Without awaiting instructions from Berlin I exercised my privileges as Ambassador and asked for an audience of the President. As I discovered later, on the very day of my visit to the President, all preparations had been made for a breach of relations and the consequent war. I had a long private interview with the President, whom I found much shaken and most heartily anxious to avoid war. We both agreed that time must be gained. . . . In the meantime the exchange of sharp-toned Notes between Washington and Berlin went on, without leading to any understanding. But the excitement in the United States gradually died down, and the first crisis was overcome.

Since the above-mentioned interview with Wilson I had been firmly convinced that he would never initiate a war with Germany. Otherwise it was extremely difficult to see why the President fell in with my proposals on that occasion, instead of breaking off relations. If he had taken the last course, he would have had public opinion behind him to a far greater extent than was the case in 1917. There would have been little objection, except on the part of Secretary of State Bryan, who resigned from his post, because the exchange of Notes was too ominous of war to square with his pacific views. In the course of that exchange of Notes the American Government so far modified its position, as to describe the U-Boat war as admissible if, before the ship were sunk, the crews and passengers were given an opportunity to save their lives. But in the last [3rd] *Lusitania* Note of July 21st, 1915, the German Government was categorically requested to express its disapproval of the act, and was informed that a repetition would be regarded as a "deliberately unfriendly action." Days after the despatch of that Note, the new Secretary of State Lansing asked me to come and see him, and told me that the American Government could see no other way out. If Americans again lost their lives through the torpedoing of a merchant ship, war could not be avoided. The United States Government would write no further Notes, which would indeed be useless, but he asked me to undertake the further negotiations. As I wanted to avoid war, I would perhaps find a way out. From that day forward the American Government agreed to allow me to send despatches in cipher to my Government in Berlin, through the State Department and the American Embassy. While I was consulting my Government regarding a solution the passenger steamer *Arabic* was sunk on August 19th, and a number of Americans were drowned. I at once announced in Washington, without awaiting instructions, that we would on our side offer satisfaction. It thus proved possible to allay the fresh agitation before it had become unmanageable. Fortunately, before the *Arabic* was torpedoed, instructions had been issued to the U-Boat commanders to the effect that liners were not to be torpedoed without previous warning, and provisions made for the safety of the noncombatants, unless the vessel had tried to escape or offered resistance. On September 1st I was requested to make these instructions known to the American Government. It was not until October 5th that I could finally bury the *Arabic* incident, the formula for the proposed satisfaction not having met the requirements of both sides before that date. To avoid a breach I was forced, on my own responsibility, to go further than was desired in Berlin, where the naval authorities would not disavow the action in question. I was not much affected by a subsequent remonstrance from home, as I was conscious of having on my own authority prevented war. The second crisis was thus fortunately overcome.

16 · *The German Ambassador to the Secretary of State*

WASHINGTON, *October 5, 1915.*

MY DEAR MR. SECRETARY: Prompted by the desire to reach a satisfactory agreement with regard to the *Arabic* incident, my Government has given me the following instructions:

The orders issued by His Majesty the Emperor to the commanders of the German submarines — of which I notified you on a previous occasion — have been made so stringent that the recurrence of incidents similar to the *Arabic* case is considered out of the question.

According to the report of Commander Schneider of the submarine that sank the *Arabic*, and his affidavit as well as those of his men, Commander Schneider was convinced that the *Arabic* intended to ram the submarine. On the other hand, the Imperial Government does not doubt the good faith of the affidavits of the British officers of the *Arabic*, according to which the *Arabic* did not intend to ram the submarine. The attack

---

16 *Foreign Relations, 1915, Supplement,* p. 560.

of the submarine, therefore, was undertaken against the instructions issued to the commander. The Imperial Government regrets and disavows this act and has notified Commander Schneider accordingly.

Under these circumstances my Government is prepared to pay an indemnity for the American lives which, to its deep regret, have been lost on the *Arabic.* I am authorized to negotiate with you about the amount of this indemnity.

I remain [etc.]

J. V. BERNSTORFF

PART FOUR

The Problem of
Armed Merchantmen

The defensive arming of merchantmen was an ancient practice, seemingly of little significance in an age of steel warships — hence the American government recognized its legality in a circular issued in 1914 largely as a matter of routine. But the advent of the submarine, frail and vulnerable to even light gunfire, drastically altered the situation. The German government argued plausibly that so-called defensive arms were really offensive in relation to the U-boat and compelled submerged attacks without warning or safety provisions for the crew and passengers of enemy merchantmen. The failure of the American government's effort at a *modus vivendi* to solve the dilemma — proposed by Secretary Lansing on January 18, 1916, but rejected by the Allies as too favorable to Germany — allowed the German *Kriegsmarine* to use the issue as an excuse for the renewal of ruthless underseas warfare.

In Germany the pressures for an intensified use of the underseas weapon steadily increased. The German Admiralty, eager to demonstrate the value of its Navy, extolled the potential of the U-boat if only the restrictions hampering its use could be removed. The conservative and center political parties eventually rallied to the cause, envisioning the new weapon as the sole means of ending the costly land warfare and achieving a decisive victory by starving Great Britain into submission. The Army generals, who were increasingly the real masters of Germany and who had seen whole army corps melt away in the holocausts of the Western Front, were also attracted by the U-boat's possibilities.

In the following selection, Admiral Alfred von Tirpitz argued for completely unrestricted submarine warfare. He was successfully resisted for the time being by the Chancellor, Theobald von Bethmann-Hollweg, who feared the disastrous results of an American entry into the war if unrestricted warfare was adopted and questioned the efficacy of the submarine in any case. A cautious man, a compromiser by nature, and subject to heavy pressure by Germany's military leaders, the Chancellor attempted to follow the ambiguous policy of placating the military by permitting the use of the submarine weapon, while at the same time making periodic concessions to the United States just sufficient in scope and number to avert war between the two nations.

17 · The Armed-Ship Circular of 1914

DEPARTMENT OF STATE,
Washington, September 19, 1914.

THE STATUS OF ARMED MERCHANT VESSELS

A. A merchant vessel of belligerent nationality may carry an armament and ammunition for the sole purpose of defense without acquiring the character of a ship of war.

B. The presence of an armament and ammunition on board a merchant vessel creates a presumption that the armament is for offensive purposes, but the owners or agents may overcome this presumption by evidence showing that the vessel carries armament solely for defense.

C. Evidence necessary to establish the fact that the armament is solely for defense and will not be used offensively, whether the armament be mounted or stowed below, must be presented in each case independently at an official investigation. The result of the investigation must show conclusively that the armament is not intended for, and will not be used in, offensive operations. Indications that the armament will not be used offensively are:

1. That the caliber of the guns carried does not exceed six inches.
2. That the guns and small arms carried are few in number.
3. That no guns are mounted on the forward part of the vessel.
4. That the quantity of ammunition carried is small.
5. That the vessel is manned by its usual crew, and the officers are the same as those on board before war was declared.
6. That the vessel intends to and actually does clear for a port lying in its usual trade route, or a port indicating its purpose to continue in the same trade in which it was engaged before war was declared.
7. That the vessel takes on board fuel and supplies sufficient only to carry it to its port of destination, or the same quantity substantially which it has been accustomed to take for a voyage before war was declared.
8. That the cargo of the vessel consists of articles of commerce unsuited for the use of a ship of war in operations against an enemy.
9. That the vessel carries passengers who are as a whole unfitted to enter the military or naval service of the belligerent whose flag the vessel flies, or of any of its allies, and particularly if the passenger list includes women and children.
10. That the speed of the ship is slow.

---

17 *Foreign Relations, 1914, Supplement,* pp. 611–612.

D. Port authorities, on the arrival in a port of the United States of an armed vessel of belligerent nationality, claiming to be a merchant vessel, should immediately investigate and report to Washington on the foregoing indications as to the intended use of the armament, in order that it may be determined whether the evidence is sufficient to remove the presumption that the vessel is, and should be treated as, a ship of war. Clearance will not be granted until authorized from Washington, and the master will be so informed upon arrival.

E. The conversion of a merchant vessel into a ship of war is a question of fact which is to be established by direct or circumstantial evidence of intention to use the vessel as a ship of war.

18 · *The Secretary of State to President Wilson*

WASHINGTON, *January 2, 1916.*

MY DEAR MR. PRESIDENT: The enclosed copies of telegrams telling of the sinking of the British steamship *Persia* on December 30th about three hundred miles northwest of Alexandria do not, in my opinion, seriously affect the *Ancona* case[1], since the evidence of torpedoing is inconclusive, the nationality of the submarine, if one was the cause, is unknown, and it is stated that the *Persia* carried an armament.

The fact that the vessel was carrying a 4.7 gun raises a question which, .it seems to me, we ought to settle.

Three or four days ago I forwarded to the Italian Ambassador at his request the statement in regard to armed merchant vessels, which we issued in September, 1914. I had discussed the question some four or five weeks before with Mr. Barclay of the British Embassy and told him that, in view of the development of submarines as commerce destroyers, which had been unknown when our statement was issued, I felt that the arming of merchant vessels with any gun, of sufficient calibre to attack a submarine, would make it very difficult, if not impossible, to insist that a submarine should expose itself to attack by coming to the surface and hailing a vessel so armed; and that, while the armament might be termed "defensive", it was capable of being used offensively against a submarine and so, I thought, that a merchant ship carrying a gun or guns would

---

[1] The *Ancona*, an Italian liner, was sunk on November 7, 1915, by a submarine flying the Austrian flag. The Austro-Hungarian government complied with American demands and disavowed the act.

18 *Foreign Relations, Lansing Papers*, I, 332–333.

have to be considered and treated as a vessel of war if it entered our ports. . . .

Since we issued the statement of September, 1914, formally, it appears to me advisable to issue a new statement setting forth the new conditions resulting from the successful employment of submarines in interrupting and destroying commercial vessels, the impossibility of a submarine's communicating with an armed merchant ship without exposing itself to the gravest danger of being sunk by gunfire because of its weakness defensively, the unreasonableness of requiring a submarine to run the danger of being almost certainly destroyed by giving warning to a vessel carrying an armament, and that, therefore, merchant vessels should refrain from mounting guns large enough to sink a submarine, and that, if they do, they become vessels of war and liable to treatment as such by both belligerents and neutrals.

The chief difficulty with the situation seems to me to lie in this: If some merchant vessels carry arms and others do not, how can a submarine determine this fact without exposing itself to great risk of being sunk? Unless the Entente Allies positively agree not to arm any of their merchant vessels and notify the Central Powers to that effect, is there not strong reason why a submarine should not warn a vessel before launching an attack?

You will recall the case of the *Baralong* where a German submarine was bombarding a vessel from which the crew had escaped in boats, when a tramp steamer approached flying the American flag. The submarine remained on the surface and awaited the steamer, which on nearing the submarine lowered the American flag, hoisted the British colors, and with a gun mounted on the stern (a defensive armament according to our early definition) opened fire and sank the German vessel killing all the crew. The British Government would urge that this was merely a *ruse de guerre* and entirely allowable, and so it would have been under old conditions, but under the new conditions it presents a strong argument in favor of submarine attack without warning.

Not only, therefore, should we, in my judgment, rewrite our statement as to the status of armed merchant vessels but show that if any vessels of that class is armed, all merchant vessels are in danger of sudden attack without warning. As to the use of the American flag on any merchant ship converted into an armed vessel it might be well also to make representations to the British Government.

In view of the sinking of the *Persia* it would seem to be opportune and advisable to act in this matter, if it is decided to act, as expeditiously as possible.

Faithfully yours,

ROBERT LANSING

19 · The Secretary of State to the British Ambassador

WASHINGTON, *January 18, 1916.*

MY DEAR MR. AMBASSADOR: It is a matter of the deepest interest to my Government to bring to an end, if possible, the dangers to life which attend the use of submarines as at present employed in destroying enemy commerce on the high seas, since on any merchant vessel of belligerent nationality there may be citizens of the United States who have taken passage or are members of the crew, in the exercise of their recognized rights as neutrals. I assume that your excellency's Government are equally solicitous to protect their nationals from the exceptional hazards which are presented by their passage on a merchant vessel through those portions of the high seas in which undersea craft of their enemy are operating.

While I am fully alive to the appalling loss of life among noncombatants, regardless of age or sex, which has resulted from the present method of destroying merchant vessels without removing the persons on board to places of safety, and while I view that practice as contrary to those humane principles which should control belligerents in the conduct of their naval operations, I do not feel that a belligerent should be deprived of the proper use of submarines in the interruption of enemy commerce since those instruments of war have proven their effectiveness in this particular branch of warfare on the high seas.

In order to bring submarine warfare within the general rules of international law and the principles of humanity without destroying its efficiency in the destruction of commerce, I believe that a formula may be found which, though it may require slight modifications of the practice generally followed by nations prior to the employment of submarines, will appeal to the sense of justice and fairness of all the belligerents in the present war.

Your excellency will understand that in seeking a formula or rule of this nature I approach it of necessity from the point of view of a neutral, but I believe that it will be equally efficacious in preserving the lives of all non-combatants on merchant vessels of belligerent nationality.

My comments on this subject are predicated on the following propositions:

---

19 *Papers Relating to the Foreign Relations of the United States, 1916, Supplement* (Washington: G.P.O., 1929), pp. 146–148.

1. A non-combatant has a right to traverse the high seas in a merchant vessel entitled to fly a belligerent flag and to rely upon the observance of the rules of international law and principles of humanity if the vessel is approached by a naval vessel of another belligerent.

2. A merchant vessel of enemy nationality should not be attacked without being ordered to stop.

3. An enemy merchant vessel, when ordered to do so by a belligerent submarine, should immediately stop.

4. Such vessel should not be attacked after being ordered to stop unless it attempts to flee or to resist, and in case it ceases to flee or resist, the attack should discontinue.

5. In the event that it is impossible to place a prize crew on board of an enemy merchant vessel or convoy it into port, the vessel may be sunk, provided the crew and passengers have been removed to a place of safety.

In complying with the foregoing propositions which, in my opinion, embody the principal rules, the strict observance of which will insure the life of a non-combatant on a merchant vessel which is intercepted by a submarine, I am not unmindful of the obstacles which would be met by undersea craft as commerce destroyers.

Prior to the year 1915 belligerent operations against enemy commerce on the high seas had been conducted with cruisers carrying heavy armaments. Under these conditions international law appeared to permit a merchant vessel to carry an armament for defensive purposes without losing its character as a private commercial vessel. This right seems to have been predicated on the superior defensive strength of ships of war, and the limitation of armament to have been dependent on the fact that it could not be used effectively in offense against enemy naval vessels, while it could defend the merchantman against the generally inferior armament of piratical ships and privateers.

The use of the submarine, however, has changed these relations. Comparison of the defensive strength of a cruiser and a submarine shows that the latter, relying for protection on its power to submerge, is almost defenseless in point of construction. Even a merchant ship carrying a small caliber gun would be able to use it effectively for offense against a submarine. Moreover, pirates and sea rovers have been swept from the main trade channels of the seas, and privateering has been abolished. Consequently, the placing of guns on merchantmen at the present day of submarine warfare can be explained only on the ground of a purpose to render merchantmen superior in force to submarines and to prevent warning and visit and search by them. Any armament, therefore, on a merchant vessel would seem to have the character of an offensive armament.

If a submarine is required to stop and search a merchant vessel on the high seas and, in case it is found that she is of enemy character and that conditions necessitate her destruction, to remove to a place of safety all persons on board, it would not seem just or reasonable that the submarine should be compelled, while complying with these requirements, to expose itself to almost certain destruction by the guns on board the merchant vessel.

It would, therefore, appear to be a reasonable and reciprocally just arrangement if it could be agreed by the opposing belligerents that submarines should be caused to adhere strictly to the rules of international law in the matter of stopping and searching merchant vessels, determining their belligerent nationality, and removing the crews and passengers to places of safety before sinking the vessels as prizes of war, and that merchant vessels of belligerent nationality should be prohibited and prevented from carrying any armament whatsoever.

In presenting this formula as a basis for conditional declarations by the belligerent governments, I do so in the full conviction that your Government will consider primarily the humane purpose of saving the lives of innocent people rather than the insistence upon a doubtful legal right which may be denied on account of new conditions.

I would be pleased if you would be good enough to bring this suggestion to the attention of your Government and inform me of their views upon the subject and whether they would be willing to make such a declaration conditioned upon their enemies' making a similar declaration.

A communication similar to this one has been addressed to the Ambassadors of France, Russia, and Italy and the Minister of Belgium at this capital.

I should add that my Government is impressed with the reasonableness of the argument that a merchant vessel carrying an armament of any sort, in view of the character of submarine warfare and the defensive weakness of undersea craft, should be held to be an auxiliary cruiser and so treated by a neutral as well as by a belligerent government, and is seriously considering instructing its officials accordingly.

ROBERT LANSING

20 · The Ambassador in Great Britain to the Secretary of State

LONDON, *January 25, 1916.*

Sir Edward Grey sent for me this afternoon to talk about the Administration's proposals about submarine warfare and about forbidding any merchantman from carrying a gun astern for defensive use. I was obliged to tell him that I knew nothing about such proposals. He seemed disappointed [and] he showed me a telegram on the subject from Spring Rice, not omitting Sir Edward's telegram of to-day in reply.

I have only once before seen Sir Edward so grave and disappointed, and that was when he informed me that the British had sent the German Government an ultimatum. After he discovered that I had not been informed of the subject he seemed disposed to say little. He did say, however, that he indulged the hope that the Department had not foreseen the results of the proposal which was wholly in favor of the Germans theoretically and practically [and] wholly against the Allies. Then he asked me for House's address because, as I gathered, he had talked with him at my table so frankly and freely about the relations of our two Governments that he thought he ought to inform House that he [did not] then know that this proposal would come.[1] He spoke as one speaks of a great calamity. He said that he would not mention the subject in his speech in the House of Commons to-morrow because the announcement that such a proposal had been made by the United States would cause a storm that would drive every other subject out of the mind of the House and of the country. He is the best friend that we have in the Government and his surprise and dismay are overwhelming.

Sir Edward is too courteous to expose himself, but the Government and British opinion will regard this change by us of an accepted practice made while the war is in progress as a complete German victory over us in the submarine controversy. [The] engendered bitterness against us will be intense in the Allied countries and such influence as we might have had with the Allied Governments will be lost. If this proposal be persisted in, the Administration will forfeit the confidence [and] good will of England and France. Can we gain enormously by it to offset this loss? . . .

It has been rumored here in well-informed circles for several weeks, and I believe it is true, that the British Government have been construct-

---

[1] Colonel House was then in Europe on a special peace mission for President Wilson.

ing extra munition works in England and Canada which can on short notice be manned and used to make as many munitions as the United States now supplies. The reason given for this expensive preparation is the fear of Bernstorff's success in his efforts to cause the Administration to embarrass the Allies. If necessary, orders placed in the United States could now be stopped within a month without diminishing the total supply. If no merchantman may carry a defensive gun into an American port, [this] change may precipitate a cutting off of American orders, not from any wish to cut them off, but from fear that other embarrassing acts by us may follow.

PAGE

21 · *The British Ambassador to the Secretary of State*

WASHINGTON, *March 23, 1916.*

MY DEAR MR. SECRETARY: I did not fail to communicate to my Government copy of your unofficial letter of the 18th January relative to submarine warfare.

My Government has given the matter its careful consideration in consultation with the Allied Governments and, in obedience to my instructions, I beg to communicate the accompanying memorandum embodying its views.

I am [etc.]   CECIL SPRING RICE

MEMORANDUM

Upon perusal of the personal letter addressed under date of January 18 last, by the Honourable Secretary of State of the United States to the Ambassador of England at Washington, the Government of His Britannic Majesty could not but appreciate the lofty sentiments by which Mr. Lansing was inspired on submitting to the countries concerned certain considerations touching the defensive armament of merchant vessels. But the enemy's lack of good faith, evidenced in too many instances to permit of their being regarded as isolated accidents, justifies the most serious doubt as to the possibility of putting into practice the suggestions thus formulated.

From a strictly legal standpoint, it must be admitted that the arming of merchant vessels for defence is their acknowledged right. It was established in some countries by long usage, in other countries it was expressly sanctioned by the legislator, such being the case in the United States in particular.

It being so, it seems obvious that any request that a belligerent forego lawful means of protection from the enemy's unlawful attacks, places upon him, whoever he may be, who formulates the proposition, the duty and responsibility of compelling that enemy to desist from such attacks, for the said enemy would otherwise be encouraged rather to persist in that course. Now, the suggestions above referred to do not provide any immediately efficacious sanction. . . .

Great Britain is unable to agree that, upon a non-guaranteed German promise, human life may be surrendered defenseless to the mercy of an enemy who, in circumstances of this kind as in many others, has shown himself to be both faithless and lawless. . . .

22 · The Ambassador in Germany to the Secretary of State

BERLIN, *February 10, 1916.*

The following is translation of memorandum of the Imperial German Government on the treatment of armed merchantmen:

I

1. Even before the outbreak of the present war the British Government had given English shipping companies the opportunity to arm their merchant vessels with guns. On March 26, 1913, Winston Churchill, then First Lord of the Admiralty, made the declaration in the British Parliament . . . that the Admiralty had called upon the shipowners to arm a number of first-class liners for protection against danger menaced in certain cases by fast auxiliary cruisers of other powers; the liners were not, however, to assume the character of auxiliary cruisers themselves. The Government desired to place at the disposal of the shipowners the necessary guns, sufficient ammunition, and suitable personnel for the training of the gun crews.

2. The English shipowners have readily responded to the call of the Admiralty. Thus Sir Owen Philipps, president of the Royal Mail Steam Packet Company, was able to inform the stockholders of his company

---

22 *Foreign Relations, 1916, Supplement,* pp. 163–165.

in May 1913, that the larger steamers of the company were equipped with guns; furthermore, the British Admiralty published in January 1914 a list according to which 29 steamers of various English lines carried guns aft. . . .

II

1. With regard to the legal character of armed merchantmen in international law, the British Government has taken the position in respect of it own merchantmen that such vessels retain the character of peaceable merchant vessels as long as they carry arms for defensive purposes only. In accordance with this, the British Ambassador at Washington, in a note dated August 25, 1914 . . . gave the American Government the fullest assurances that British merchant vessels were never armed for purposes of attack, but solely for defense, and that they consequently never fire unless first fired upon. On the other hand, the British Government set up the principle for armed vessels of other flags that they are to be treated as war vessels. No. 1 of Order 1 of the prize court rules, promulgated by the order in council of August 5, 1914, expressly provides "ship of war shall include armed ship."

2. The German Government has no doubt that a merchantman assumes a warlike character by armament with guns, regardless of whether the guns are intended to serve for defense or attack. It considers any warlike activity of an enemy merchantman contrary to international law, although it accords consideration to the opposite view by treating the crew of such a vessel not as pirates but as belligerents. The details of its position are set forth in the memorandum on the treatment of armed merchantmen in neutral ports . . . communicated to the American Government in October 1914, the contents of which were likewise communicated to other neutral powers.

3. Some of the neutral powers have accepted the position of the British Government and therefore permitted armed merchantmen of the belligerent powers to stay in their ports and shipyards without the restrictions which they had imposed on ships of war through their neutrality regulations. Some, however, have taken the contrary view and subjected armed merchantmen of belligerents to the neutrality rules applicable to ships of war.

III

1. During the course of the war the armament of English merchantmen has been more and more generally carried out. From reports of the German naval forces numerous cases became known in which English merchantmen not only offered armed resistance to the German war vessels, but proceeded to attack them on their own initiative, and in so doing they frequently even made use of false flags. A list of such cases is found in Exhibit 4, which from the nature of the matter can include

only a part of the attacks which were actually made. It is also shown by this list that the practice described is not limited to English merchantmen, but is imitated by the merchantmen of England's allies.

2. The explanation of the action of the armed English merchantmen described is contained in Exhibits 5 to 12, which are photographic reproductions of confidential instructions of the British Admiralty found by German naval forces on captured ships. These instructions regulate in detail artillery attack by English merchantmen on German submarines. They contain exact regulations touching the reception, treatment, activity, and control of the British gun crews taken on board merchantmen; for example, they are not to wear uniform in neutral ports and thus plainly belong to the British navy. Above all, it is shown by these instructions that these armed vessels are not to await any action of maritime war on the part of the German submarines, but are to attack them forthwith. In this respect the following regulations are particularly instructive:

(a) The instructions for guidance in the use, care, and maintenance of armament in defensively armed merchant ships . . . provide in the section headed "Action," in paragraph 4: "It is not advisable to open fire at a range greater than 800 yards unless the enemy has already opened fire." From this it is the duty of the merchantman in principle to open fire without regard to the attitude of the submarine.

(b) The instructions regarding submarines applicable to vessels carrying a defensive armament . . . prescribe under No. 3: "If a submarine is obviously pursuing a ship by day and it is evident to the master that she has hostile intentions, the ship pursued should open fire in self-defense, notwithstanding the submarine may not have committed a definite hostile act such as firing a gun or torpedo." From this also the mere appearance of a submarine in the wake of the merchantman affords sufficient occasion for an armed attack.

In all these orders, which do not apply merely to the zone of maritime war around England, but are unrestricted as regards their validity . . . the greatest emphasis is laid on secrecy, plainly in order that the action of merchantmen, in absolute contradiction of international law and the British assurances . . . might remain concealed from the enemy as well as the neutrals.

3. It is thus made plain that the armed English merchantmen have official instructions to attack the German submarines treacherously wherever they come near them; that is, orders to conduct relentless warfare against them. Since England's rules of maritime war are adopted by her allies without question, the proof must be taken as demonstrated in respect of the armed merchantmen of the other enemy countries also.

IV

In the circumstances set forth above, enemy merchantmen armed with guns no longer have any right to be considered as peaceable vessels of commerce. Therefore the German naval forces will receive orders, within a short period, paying consideration to the interests of the neutrals, to treat such vessels as belligerents.

The German Government brings this state of things to the knowledge of the neutral powers in order that they may warn their nationals against continuing to entrust their persons or property to armed merchantmen of the powers at war with the German Empire.

BERLIN, *February 8, 1916.*

23 · *Secretary of State of the Imperial Marine Service v. Tirpitz to Imperial Chancelor v. Bethmann-Hollweg*

BERLIN, *February 13, 1916.*

I have the honor to submit to your Excellency in all respect, the enclosed memorial. It includes in the form of a general survey the answers submitted by me to the latest inquiries of your Excellency. . . .

v. TIRPITZ.

[ENCLOSURE]

Can England be forced to sue for peace by means of a U-boat war? I. The most important and surest means which can be adopted to bring England to her knees is the use of our U-boats at the present time. We shall not be able to defeat England by a war on land alone. The unrestricted carrying out of the U-boat war, supported by our other naval craft and by our air fleet — all under a unified and determined leadership — is of the most decisive importance in obtaining the desired result. England will be cut to the heart by the destruction by U-boats of

---

23 Reprinted with the permission of the Carnegie Endowment for International Peace, from *Official German Documents Relating to the World War* (New York & London: Carnegie Endowment for International Peace, 1923 — 2 vols.), II, 1122 — 1128, 1130–1139. These reports of the first and second subcommittees of the committee appointed by the National Constituent Assembly in 1919 to inquire into the responsibility for the war contain stenographic notes of the hearings together with attached documents. One scholar has found the English translations of this source collection to be not entirely accurate. — see Karl E. Birnbaum, *Peace Moves and U-Boat Warfare* (Stockholm, 1958), f.n., p. 352.

every ship which approaches the English coast. The ocean's commerce is the very elixir of life for England, its interruption for any length of time a deadly danger, its permanent interruption absolutely fatal within a short time. Every attack upon England's transoceanic communication is therefore a blow in the direction of the termination of the war. The more the losses take place with merciless regularity at the very gates of the island kingdom, the more powerful will be the material and moral effect on the English people. In spite of its former resources, England will not be able to make a successful defense against the attacks of submarines directed against its transoceanic commerce, provided they are well planned. That is precisely why a timely U-boat war is the most dangerous and, if vigorously carried on, the form of warfare which will unconditionally decide the war to England's disadvantage.

II. The prerequisites of a successful carrying out of an unrestricted U-boat war are military and economic. In both respects they are noticeably more favorable than in February, 1915. . . .

III. In order to get the correct view of America's attitude in the U-boat question, it is necessary to go back over its development during the course of the war.

From the very beginning, the attitude of the United States toward us has not been a friendly one. The close racial feeling which bound the greater part of the population to England, together with the combinations of English and American economic forces which have constantly resulted in more and more intimate relations in this direction, necessarily resulted in the antagonism referred to. In spite of this, there existed in the beginning, at least so far as the government was concerned, a certain objection against openly taking sides with either party. If from the date of the February note onward, we could have afforded to pay no attention at all to the objections urged by the United States against the U-boat war, the unrestricted conduct of this war would not, in my opinion, have led to a break with the United States. In view of the restrictions imposed upon the conduct of the U-boat war and of the enormous deliveries of ammunition and war material of every kind which was made possible thereby, the whole economic life of the United States, and the American policy as well, came to be connected with the British cause in a manner quite different from that existing at the beginning of the war. America is directly interested in the fate of England's economic existence, and, as a logical consequence, in England's intention to crush Germany. As a result, the conviction on the part of Americans of the growing dangers involved in Japan's hostile attitude, and that sooner or later differences with Japan will be bound to ensue, has become stronger as the war has run its course. Understandings unquestionably exist today, if not between the two governments, at least, in any case, between the leaders of the trusts in England and America, whose purpose is to give Japan a very definite setback by means of the combined forces of England and the United States after the war. But this is possible only if England can be absolutely secured against any danger emanating from Europe, that is, if Germany is overpowered. It follows that the United States, whether they desire to be so or not, are directly interested in our defeat, and have become a direct enemy of Germany.

If the United States intends to push this position to its logical conclusion and to let matters come to a break with us, the resulting circumstances would suffer no material change, provided this break were limited to a refusal to maintain diplomatic relations. But if the United States should go as far as to declare war against us, then the problem of shipping space would occupy a prominent place among those questions on which we would have to pass in connection with the then newly created situation. The assistance in men and material with which the United States would then be in a position to provide England and our other opponents would, as a practical proposition, be measured by the amount of tonnage for commercial purposes actually at their disposal.

The attempt on the part of the United States to increase this tonnage to any appreciable extent through a retaliatory seizure of the German commercial tonnage within their reach would, in the first place, be confronted with quite substantial obstacles and, in the second place, be useless in any case.

The gross tonnage of German steamers now in the United States [interned by the war] amounts to 440,000 tons, according to my estimate. There are about 116,850 gross tons in the American colonies. . . .

But assuming that, in spite of all this, the United States should succeed in placing the German merchant ships in their service, the personal interests of the country would make it necessary for these ships to be held for their own purposes. So that an advantage to England or a lightening of England's burdens would not result from this situation.

Were America, after a break with us, to provide financial support in ever-increasing volume to England and our opponents, the only result for the latter would be that they would become more and more dependent upon the United States. And moreover, the practical effect of such financial support would, for the most part, take the form of possibly providing them with increased shipments of war material of all kinds which were not obtainable in their own country, and of supplying them with those articles essential to their economic life. But this possibility can only become an established fact if the shipments in question can actually be delivered. For instance, an increase in Italy's financial resources for the purpose of obtaining coal does not actually bring coal to the country. And so an increased financial support of our opponents by America would, in the last analysis, for its effective working out, be inseparably and mainly dependent upon the problem of tonnage. . . .

V. With regard to supplementing the tremendous results of the war on land, we have the following:

1. The entrance of America into the list of our opponents would be of no definite assistance to England.

2. It is only by making the fullest use of all of our instrumentalities adapted to warfare on the sea, amongst which the U-boats will play an important part by shutting England off from all intercourse by sea, that it will be possible to bring about England's defeat.

BERLIN, *February 8, 1916.*

❖   ❖   ❖   ❖   ❖

Memorial of Imperial Chancelor v. Bethmann-Hollweg

BERLIN, *February 29, 1916.*

The announcement of the U-boat war carried on in conformity with the desires of the Admiralty Staff, that is, torpedoing freight steamers and passenger steamers without distinction and without warning, whether sailing under a neutral or hostile flag, would certainly result in the entrance of the United States into the war on the side of our enemies.

. . . the navy expects that, as the result of its policy, England will be eliminated as a belligerent within a period of from six to eight months. The Supreme High Command has announced its opinion to the effect that, since Austria-Hungary's power of endurance will hardly extend beyond the year 1916, every available means ought to be used to bring the war to an end before that time.

Assuming that these premises are correct, the issue to be decided is whether or not we should adopt the policy of unrestricted U-boat warfare; and hence the following questions must be considered:

1. Is it certain that the new U-boat war will bring about a shrinkage in the cargo capacity of the English fleet as it now exists, by approximating 4 million tons, within the period set out above . . . ?

2. Can we assume with certainty that the hoped-for losses to the English merchant marine will force England to sue for peace?

3. What results will the expected entrance of the neutrals, and in particular that of the United States, have upon the war? . . .

That the break with America will come if we announce and carry on the U-boat war in accordance with the plans now under consideration, is beyond question, in view of the attitude which the Union has maintained up to this time and the stand that she takes on the question of armed merchant ships. Negotiations with the United States with regard to the details of carrying on such a war by us are out of the question, because no decision would be reached concerning them, if at all, until months would have passed. We would have to reject the protests which we have every reason to expect from America as the result of our announcement. The moment that we rejected them would be the moment of the break.

The break with America will have the following results:

1. The cause of our enemies will receive a new and enormous moral support through America's public entrance into the enemy's camp. The confidence in a victorious termination of the war would be revived, and the will to endure would be strengthened. Strong points of difference existing in inner circles of the Entente, as is now publicly known, would vanish in a flash, and the hope that even now predominates with regard to the attitude of France and Russia — that a war of exhaustion will be carried through, will be realized almost to the point of certainty if the one existing world Power that still remains neutral unites its interests with theirs.

2. The irritation of the neutral States against the arbitrary attitude of England is on the constant increase, but it will be dissipated at that moment when England, certain of American support, needs no longer exercise restraint in applying its oppressive measures.

3. The impression which the entrance of the United States into the war would be bound to make upon our allies is a matter entitled to the most earnest consideration. Baron Burian has stated again and again that we should not so conduct the U-boat war in the Mediterranean as to bring about a break with the United States. He has now even gone so far as to postpone the war against armed enemy merchant vessels as the result of American protests. Unless we can prove to the exclusion of all doubt on the part of the Vienna Cabinet that we can look forward to the overthrow of England, we shall have to consider as an element of our calculations the fact that they will object to the resumption of a U-boat war of such a nature as to bring about a break with the United States — a war which we as faithful allies would have to announce previously to Vienna. At the very least, Austria's war spirit, which is beginning to be sated after the overthrow of Serbia and Montenegro, and which even today gives evidence of a strong pro-English feeling, will not be heightened as the result of a break with the United States.

The Turkish Minister, too, has already expressed his earnest solicitude about the possible results of a break with the United States.

These objections naturally apply to Bulgaria as well.

Even the moral effects of the break with the United States upon our allies, and our opponents the neutrals, must not be underestimated. The longer the war lasts, so much clearer does it become that he will win the war who keeps his nerves under best control. History teaches us that in coalition wars which can not be brought to a termination by decisive strokes of the military arm, the end is usually brought about by differences between the allies themselves. It is a dangerous gamble to disregard these differences if one is not assured of success.

Then, again, the morale in Germany is not to be judged merely by the articles of the pan-German press. The overwhelming preponderance of our enemies has prevented us up to the present time from bringing the war to a triumphant termination. People will ask whether the increase of the number of our enemies could not have been avoided, and the entrance of the United States into the war will have a discouraging and depressing effect in broad circles of the German people.

The break with America will have the following practical consequences:

1. The attempts made by the Allies up to the present time to obtain money from the United States have only had a very mediocre result. If America breaks with us, then, driven on as a matter of prestige and in deference to its own material interests, it will exert all of its resources to the end that the war shall be rapidly terminated in favor of the Entente. All of its financial resources will be put at the disposal of the Entente, and England will gladly include in the bargain the results of its financial dependence on the United States which, as it is, has already come to pass, if she can only succeed in cementing together the entire Anglo-Saxon world in one military brotherhood, united for the purpose of our destruction. Even if money alone can not determine the outcome of the war, the financial aid proffered by the United States will constitute a very material increase of our opponents' resources.

The assertion which is made so often, that financial assistance afforded by America will avail England nothing if England is cut off from the outer world through the U-boat war, and as a result would be unable to make any use of American gold, is based upon the premise that England will be separated from the rest of the world as if by an iron curtain as the result of the U-boat war. This assumption is inaccurate and is not entertained by the Admiralty Staff. . . .

3. Military assistance on the part of the United States gives our military authorities very little concern; but it can scarcely be doubted that participation by the United States in this war would necessarily bring about the supplying of our opponents with further war material, particularly of such a kind as that on which the United States, at least outwardly up to this time and on grounds of international law, has imposed limitations, such, for instance, as the direct delivery of U-boats. Moreover, no one who is acquainted with American conditions will entertain any doubt that the American sporting spirit, based upon its English prototype, would result in bringing over to our opponents volunteer contingents which one can surely venture to estimate at a few hundred thousands.

4. (Comments about the European neutrals follow). . . .

So the question comes down to this, whether our position is so desperate that we are bound to play a win-all lose-all game in which our existence as a world Power and our whole future as a nation would be at stake, whereas the chances of winning, that is, the prospect of crushing England by next fall, are uncertain. This question is to be answered unqualifiedly in the negative.

The Supreme High Command of the Army denies the possibility of bringing the war to an end through crushing blows delivered by our land forces. That body entertains the belief that a termination of the war is in any event only possible after England or we ourselves have been crushed to the ground. No human being can state with absolute certainty that this point of view is erroneous. . . . But just as impossible is it for us to deny, with the certainty of being correct, the possibility of ending the war even without the application of the unrestricted U-boat warfare in the course of the year 1916. It is certainly reasonable to argue that our military successes in the west, the failure of the great and long-heralded enemy offensives in the spring, the increasing financial straits of the Entente, and the absence of all prospects of starving us out in the current year, will so increase the general recognition of the fact in England that the prolongation of the war is a bad business, even from the standpoint of British interests, as to make England desist from attempting to carry on the war to the point of our exhaustion. We are cutting ourselves off from the benefits of all these possibilities if, through the adoption of unrestricted U-boat warfare, we drive the United States, and with the United States still other neutral Powers, into making war upon us. Only then will a state of affairs come into being, for which we alone are responsible, on account of which there will be no alternative but to fight the war through to the bitter end, come what may. Therefore there devolves upon us the task of carrying on the U-boat war in such a way as to make it possible to avoid the break with the United States. In this case, we shall be able to list as pure profit all the injuries which we inflict upon England. That these injuries are not inconsiderable is evidenced by the results of the restricted U-boat war carried on since the summer of 1915. The increased number of U-boats which are now at our disposal would increase results many times over. . . .

PART FIVE

The *Sussex* Pledge

German U-boat commanders were apparently unable, or unwilling, to distinguish between armed and unarmed enemy merchant vessels. The torpedoing of the unarmed French channel steamer *Sussex*, on March 24, 1916, resulted in an American ultimatum and a categorical German promise not to sink any type of enemy merchant ship without warning and safety provisions for crews and passengers. Chancellor Bethmann-Hollweg was able to placate his remonstrating admirals and temporarily, at least, to convince the Kaiser that the European situation was too precarious to risk an American entry into the war. The issue was so sharply drawn after the *Sussex* pledge that a renewal of ruthless underseas warfare would leave President Wilson no alternative but to sever diplomatic relations with the German government.

24 · The Secretary of State to the Ambassador in Germany

WASHINGTON, April 18, 1916.

You are instructed to deliver to the Secretary of Foreign Affairs a communication reading as follows. . . .

Information now in the possession of the Government of the United States fully establishes the facts in the case of the *Sussex*, and the inferences which my Government has drawn from that information it regards as confirmed by the circumstances set forth in your excellency's note of the 10th instant. On the 24th of March 1916, at about 2.50 o'clock in the afternoon, the unarmed steamer *Sussex*, with 325 or more passengers on board, among whom were a number of American citizens, was torpedoed while crossing from Folkstone to Dieppe. The *Sussex* had never been armed; was a vessel known to be habitually used only for the conveyance of passengers across the English Channel; and was not following the route taken by troopships or supply ships. About 80 of her passengers, non-combatants of all ages and sexes, including citizens of the United States, were killed or injured.

A careful, detailed, and scrupulously impartial investigation by naval and military officers of the United States has conclusively established the fact that the *Sussex* was torpedoed without warning or summons to surrender and that the torpedo by which she was struck was of German manufacture. In the view of the Government of the United States these facts from the first made the conclusion that the torpedo was fired by a German submarine unavoidable. It now considers that conclusion substantiated by the statements of your excellency's note. A full statement of the facts upon which the Government of the United States has based its conclusion is enclosed.

The Government of the United States, after having given careful consideration to the note of the Imperial Government of the 10th of April, regrets to state that the impression made upon it by the statements and proposals contained in that note is that the Imperial Government has failed to appreciate the gravity of the situation which has resulted, not alone from the attack on the *Sussex*, but from the whole method and character of submarine warfare as disclosed by the unrestrained practice of the commanders of German undersea craft during the past twelve-month and more in the indiscriminate destruction of merchant vessels of all sorts, nationalities, and destinations. If the sinking of the *Sussex*

---

24 *Foreign Relations, 1916, Supplement,* pp. 232–234.

had been an isolated case, the Government of the United States might find it possible to hope that the officer who was responsible for that act had wilfully violated his orders or had been criminally negligent in taking none of the precautions they prescribed, and that the ends of justice might be satisfied by imposing upon him an adequate punishment, coupled with a formal disavowal of the act and payment of a suitable indemnity by the Imperial Government. But, though the attack upon the *Sussex* was manifestly indefensible and caused a loss of life so tragical as to make it stand forth as one of the most terrible examples of the inhumanity of submarine warfare as the commanders of German vessels are conducting it, it unhappily does not stand alone.

On the contrary, the Government of the United States is forced by recent events to conclude that it is only one instance, even though one of the most extreme and most distressing instances, of the deliberate method and spirit of indiscriminate destruction of merchant vessels of all sorts, nationalities, and destinations which have become more and more unmistakable as the activity of German undersea vessels of war has in recent months been quickened and extended.

The Imperial Government will recall that when, in February 1915, it announced its intention of treating the waters surrounding Great Britain and Ireland as embraced within the seat of war and of destroying all merchant ships owned by its enemies that might be found within that zone of danger, and warned all vessels, neutral as well as belligerent, to keep out of the waters thus proscribed or to enter them at their peril, the Government of the United States earnestly protested. It took the position that such a policy could not be pursued without constant gross and palpable violations of the accepted law of nations, particularly if submarine craft were to be employed as its instruments, inasmuch as the rules prescribed by that law, rules founded on the principles of humanity and established for the protection of the lives of non-combatants at sea, could not in the nature of the case be observed by such vessels. It based its protest on the ground that persons of neutral nationality and vessels of neutral ownership would be exposed to extreme and intolerable risks; and that no right to close any part of the high seas could lawfully be asserted by the Imperial Government in the circumstances then existing. The law of nations in these matters, upon which the Government of the United States based that protest, is not of recent origin or founded upon merely arbitrary principles set up by convention. It is based, on the contrary, upon manifest principles of humanity and has long been established with the approval and by the express assent of all civilized nations.

The Imperial Government, notwithstanding, persisted in carrying out the policy announced, expressing the hope that the dangers involved, at any rate to neutral vessels, would be reduced to a minimum by the instructions which it had issued to the commanders of its submarines, and assuring the Government of the United States that it would take every

possible precaution both to respect the rights of neutrals and to safeguard the lives of non-combatants.

In pursuance of this policy of submarine warfare against the commerce
of its adversaries, thus announced and thus entered upon in despite of
the solemn protest of the Government of the United States, the commanders of the Imperial Government's undersea vessels have carried on
practices of such ruthless destruction which have made it more and more
evident as the months have gone by that the Imperial Government has
found it impracticable to put any such restraints upon them as it had
hoped and promised to put. Again and again the Imperial Government
has given its solemn assurances to the Government of the United States
that at least passenger ships would not be thus dealt with, and yet it has
repeatedly permitted its undersea commanders to disregard those assurances with entire impunity. As recently as February last it gave notice
that it would regard all armed merchantmen owned by its enemies
as part of the armed naval forces of its adversaries and deal with them
as with men-of-war, thus, at least by implication, pledging itself to give
warning to vessels which were not armed and to accord security of life
to their passengers and crews; but even this limitation its submarine
commanders have recklessly ignored.

Vessels of neutral ownership, even vessels of neutral ownership bound
from neutral port to neutral port, have been destroyed along with vessels
of belligerent ownership in constantly increasing numbers. Sometimes
the merchantmen attacked have been warned and summoned to surrender before being fired on or torpedoed; sometimes their passengers
and crews have been vouchsafed the poor security of being allowed to
take to the ship's boats before the ship was sent to the bottom. But again
and again no warning has been given, no escape even to the ship's boats
allowed to those on board. Great liners like the *Lusitania* and *Arabic*
and mere passenger boats like the *Sussex* have been attacked without a
moment's warning, often before they have even become aware that they
were in the presence of an armed ship of the enemy, and the lives of
non-combatants, passengers, and crew have been destroyed wholesale
and in a manner which the Government of the United States can not but
regard as wanton and without the slightest color of justification. No limit
of any kind has in fact been set to their indiscriminate pursuit and destruction of merchantmen of all kinds and nationalities within the waters
which the Imperial Government has chosen to designate as lying within
the seat of war. The roll of Americans who have lost their lives upon
ships thus attacked and destroyed has grown month by month until the
ominous toll has mounted into the hundreds.

The Government of the United States has been very patient. At every
stage of this distressing experience of tragedy after tragedy it has sought
to be governed by the most thoughtful consideration of the extraordinary
circumstances of an unprecedented war and to be guided by sentiments

of very genuine friendship for the people and Government of Germany. It has accepted the successive explanations and assurances of the Imperial Government as, of course, given in entire sincerity and good faith, and has hoped, even against hope, that it would prove to be possible for the Imperial Government so to order and control the acts of its naval commanders as to square its policy with the recognized principles of humanity as embodied in the law of nations. It has made every allowance for unprecedented conditions and has been willing to wait until the facts became unmistakable and were susceptible of only one interpretation.

It now owes it to a just regard for its own rights to say to the Imperial Government that that time has come. It has become painfully evident to it that the position which it took at the very outset is inevitable, namely, the use of submarines for the destruction of an enemy's commerce is, of necessity, because of the very character of the vessels employed and the very methods of attack which their employment of course involves, utterly incompatible with the principles of humanity, the long-established and incontrovertible rights of neutrals, and the sacred immunities of non-combatants.

If it is still the purpose of the Imperial Government to prosecute relentless and indiscriminate warfare against vessels of commerce by the use of submarines without regard to what the Government of the United States must consider the sacred and indisputable rules of international law and the universally recognized dictates of humanity, the Government of the United States is at last forced to the conclusion that there is but one course it can pursue. Unless the Imperial Government should now immediately declare and effect an abandonment of its present methods of submarine warfare against passenger and freight-carrying vessels, the Government of the United States can have no choice but to sever diplomatic relations with the German Empire altogether. This action the Government of the United States contemplates with the greatest reluctance but feels constrained to take in behalf of humanity and the rights of neutral nations.

LANSING

25 · The Ambassador in Germany to the Secretary of State

BERLIN, May 4, 1916.

Following is the text of the note handed to me both in German and English at 5.30 this afternoon by Secretary of State for Foreign Affairs:

FOREIGN OFFICE, BERLIN, May 4, 1916.

. . . In connection with the case of the *Sussex*, the Government of the United States has made a series of statements, gist of which is the assertion that this incident is to be considered as one instance for [of] the deliberate method of indiscriminate destruction of vessels of all sorts, nationalities, and destinations by German submarine commanders. The German Government must emphatically repudiate this assertion. The German Government, however, thinks it of little avail to enter into details in the present stage of affairs, more particularly as the Government of the United States has omitted to substantiate this assertion by reference to concrete facts. The German Government will only state that it has imposed far-reaching restraints upon the use of the submarine weapon solely in consideration of the interests of neutrals, in spite of the fact that these restrictions are necessarily of advantage to Germany's enemies; no such consideration has ever been shown to the neutrals by Great Britain and her allies.

The German submarine forces have had, in fact, orders to conduct submarine warfare in accordance with the general principles of visit and search and destruction of merchant vessels as recognized by international law, the sole exception being the conduct of warfare against the enemy trade carried on enemy freight ships that are encountered in the war zone surrounding Great Britain; with regard to these no assurances have ever been given to the Government of the United States; no such assurance was contained in the declaration of February 8, 1916. The German Government can not admit any doubt that these orders have been given and are executed in good faith. Errors have actually occurred; they can in no kind of warfare be avoided altogether, and allowances must be made in the conduct of naval warfare against an enemy resorting to all kinds of ruses, whether permissible or illicit. But, apart from the possibility of errors, naval warfare, just like warfare on land, implies unavoidable dangers for neutral persons and goods entering the fighting zone. Even in cases where naval action was confined to their ordinary forms of cruiser warfare, neutral persons and goods have repeatedly come to grief. The German Government has repeatedly and explicitly pointed out the dangers from mines that have led to the loss of numerous ships. The German Government has made several proposals to the Government of the United States in order to reduce to a minimum for American travelers and goods the inherent dangers of naval warfare. Unfortunately the Government of the United States has decided not to accept these proposals; had it accepted, the Government of the United States would have been instrumental in preventing the greater part of the accidents that American citizens have met with in the meantime. The German Government still stands by its offer to come to an agreement along these lines.

As the German Government has repeatedly declared, it can not dispense with the use of the submarine weapon in the conduct of warfare against enemy trade. The German Government, however, has now decided to make a further concession in adapting the methods of submarine warfare to the interests of the neutrals; in reaching this decision the German Government has been actuated by considerations which are above the level of the disputed question.

The German Government attaches no less importance to the sacred principles of humanity than the Government of the United States. Again, it fully takes into account that both Governments have for many years cooperated in developing international law in conformity with these principles, the ultimate object of which has been always to confine warfare on sea and on land to the armed forces of the belligerents and to safeguard, as far as possible, non-combatants against the horrors of war.

But, although those considerations are of great weight, they alone would not, under the present circumstances, have determined the attitude of the German Government.

For, in answer to the appeal made by the United States Government on behalf of the sacred principles of humanity and international law, the German Government must repeat once more with all emphasis that it was not the German but the British Government which, ignoring all the accepted rules of international law, has extended this terrible war to the lives and property of non-combatants, having no regard whatever for the interests and rights of the neutrals and non-combatants that through this method of warfare have been severely injured.

In self-defense against the illegal conduct of British warfare, while fighting a bitter struggle for her national existence, Germany had to resort to the hard but effective weapon of submarine warfare. As matters stand, the German Government can not but reiterate its regret that the sentiments of humanity which the Government of the United States extends with such fervor to the unhappy victims of submarine warfare are not extended with the same warmth of feeling to the many millions of women and children who, according to the avowed intentions of the British Government, shall be starved and who, by their sufferings, shall force the victorious armies of the Central powers into ignominious capitulation. The German Government, in agreement with the German people, fails to understand this discrimination, all the more as it has repeatedly and explicitly declared itself ready to use the submarine weapon in strict conformity with the rules of international law as recognized before the outbreak of the war, if Great Britain were likewise ready to adapt her conduct of warfare to these rules. The several attempts made by the Government of the United States to prevail upon the British Government to act accordingly have failed because of the flat refusal on the part of the British Government. Moreover, Great Britain has ever since again and again violated international law, surpassing all bounds in outraging neutral rights. The latest measure adopted by Great Britain, declaring German bunker coal as contraband and establishing conditions under which alone English bunker coal shall be supplied to neutrals, is nothing but an unheard of attempt, by way of exaction, to force neutral tonnage into the service of the British trade war.

The German people knows that the Government of the United States has the power to confine this war to the armed forces of the belligerent countries in the interest of humanity and the maintenance of international law. The Government of the United States would have been certain of attaining this end had it been determined to insist against Great Britain on its incontestable rights to the freedom of the seas. But, as matters stand, the German people is under the impression that the Government of the United States, while demanding that Germany, struggling for her existence, shall restrain the use of an effective weapon, and while making the compliance with these demands a condition for the maintenance of relations with Germany, confines itself to protests against the illegal methods adopted by Germany's enemies. Moreover, the German people knows to what a considerable extent its enemies are supplied with all kinds of war material from the United States.

It will therefore be understood that the appeal made by the Government of the United States to the sentiments of humanity and to the principles of international law can not, under the circumstances, meet with the same hearty response from the German people which such an appeal is otherwise always certain to find here. If the German Government, nevertheless, has resolved to go to the utmost limit of concessions, it has not alone been guided by the friendship connecting the two great nations for over a hundred years, but it also has thought of the great doom which threatens the entire civilized world should this cruel and sanguinary war be extended and prolonged.

The German Government, conscious of Germany's strength, has twice within the last few months announced before the world its readiness to make peace on a basis safeguarding Germany's vital interests, thus indicating that it is not Germany's fault if peace is still withheld from the nations of Europe.

The German Government feels all the more justified to declare that the responsibility could not be borne before the forum of mankind and history if, after 21 months' duration of the war, the submarine question under discussion between the German Government and the Government of the United States were to take a turn seriously threatening the maintenance of peace between the two nations.

As far as it lies with the German Government, it wishes to prevent things from taking such a course. The German Government, moreover, is prepared to do its utmost to confine the operations of war for the rest of the duration to the fighting forces of the belligerents, thereby also insuring the freedom of the seas, as principle upon which the German Government believes, now as before, to be in agreement with the Government of the United States.

The German Government, guided by this idea, notifies the Government of the United States that the German naval forces have received the following orders: In accordance with the general principles of visit and search and destruction of merchant vessels recognized by international law, such vessels, both within and without the area declared as naval war zone, shall not be sunk without warning and without saving human lives, unless these ships attempt to escape or offer resistance.

But neutrals can not expect that Germany, forced to fight for her existence, shall, for the sake of neutral interest, restrict the use of an effective weapon if her enemy is permitted to continue to apply at will methods of warfare violating the rules of international law. Such a demand would be incompatible with the characters of neutrality, and the German Government is convinced that the Government of the United States does not think of making such a demand, knowing that the Government of the United States has repeatedly declared that it is determined to restore the principle of the freedom of the seas, from whatever quarter it has been violated.

Accordingly, the German Government is confident that, in consequence of the new orders issued to its naval forces, the Government of the United States will now consider all impediments removed which may have been in the way of a mutual cooperation towards the restoration of the freedom of the seas during the war, as suggested in the note of July 23, 1915, and it does not doubt that the Government of the United States will now demand and insist that the British Government shall forthwith observe the rules of international law universally recognized before the war, as they are laid down in the notes presented by the Government of the United States to the British Government on December 28, 1914, and November 5, 1915. Should the steps taken by the Government of the United States not attain the object it desires, to have the laws of humanity followed by all belligerent nations, the German Government would then be facing a new situation in which it must reserve itself complete liberty of decision.

The undersigned avails himself of this occasion to renew to the American Ambassador the assurances of his highest consideration.

[Von Jagow]
Secretary of State

 IV

AMERICA ENTERS
THE WAR

PART ONE

An Abortive Scheme
for Mediation

As the result of an extended correspondence with Sir
Edward Grey, Colonel House persuaded President Wilson to send him on
a special peace mission to Europe early in 1916. A succession of submarine
crises seemed to portend an early American entry into the war against Germany. Apparently House envisioned the resultant House-Grey Memorandum as an instrument, if attempts at an understanding with Germany
failed, to bring the United States into the struggle on broader grounds
than American resentment against submarine warfare. Wilson, on the
other hand, seems to have seized upon the mediatory aspects of the
agreement and hoped to make use of its provisions to avoid American
involvement. The agreement was never invoked, however, despite subsequent American efforts. The Allied Powers, sensing that an American
entry into the conflict was inevitable, were reluctant to implement the
agreement; moreover, the British Government — committed to a policy
of total victory — preferred not to enter peace negotiations until Germany
had been decisively defeated.

1 · The House-Grey Memorandum

October 8, 1915: I outlined very briefly [House noted] a plan which has occurred to me and which seems of much value. I thought we had lost our opportunity to break with Germany, and it looked as if she had a better chance than ever of winning, and if she did win our turn would come next; and we were not only unprepared, but there would be no one to help us stand the first shock. Therefore, we should do something decisive now — something that would either end the war in a way to abolish militarism or that would bring us in with the Allies to help them do it. My suggestion is to ask the Allies, unofficially, to let me know whether or not it would be agreeable to them to have us demand that hostilities cease. We would put it upon the high ground that the neutral world was suffering along with the belligerents and that we had rights as well as they, and that peace parleys should begin upon the broad basis of both military and naval disarmament. . . .

If the Allies understood our purpose, we could be as severe in our language concerning them as we were with the Central Powers. The Allies, after some hesitation, could accept our offer or demand and, if the Central Powers accepted, we would then have accomplished a master-stroke of diplomacy. If the Central Powers refused to acquiesce, we could then push our insistence to a point where diplomatic relations would first be broken off, and later the whole force of our Government — and perhaps the force of every neutral — might be brought against them.

The President was startled by this plan. He seemed to acquiesce by silence. I had not time to push it further, for our entire conversation did not last longer than twenty minutes.

❋   ❋   ❋   ❋   ❋

October 11, 1915: Frank Polk[1] took lunch with me. I told him something of the plan I had outlined to the President, concerning our enforcing peace before the Allies reached a position where they could not be of assistance in the event we had war with the Central Powers. I am looking at the matter from the American viewpoint and also from the broader viewpoint of humanity in general. It will not do for the United States to let the Allies go down and leave Germany the dominant military factor in the world. We would certainly be the next object of attack, and the Monroe Doctrine would be less indeed than "a scrap of paper." . . . Polk thought the idea was good from every standpoint, and he hoped the President would finally put it through. . . .

[1] Polk was then Counselor in the State Department.

1 Seymour, *The Intimate Papers of Colonel House*, II, 84–86.

2 · Memorandum of Sir Edward Grey

(*Confidential*)

Colonel House told me that President Wilson was ready, on hearing from France and England that the moment was opportune, to propose that a Conference should be summoned to put an end to the war. Should the Allies accept this proposal, and should Germany refuse it, the United States would probably enter the war against Germany.

Colonel House expressed the opinion that, if such a Conference met, it would secure peace on terms not unfavourable to the Allies; and, if it failed to secure peace, the United States would [probably]¹ leave the Conference as a belligerent on the side of the Allies, if Germany was unreasonable. Colonel House expressed an opinion decidedly favourable to the restoration of Belgium, the transfer of Alsace and Lorraine to France, and the acquisition by Russia of an outlet to the sea, though he thought that the loss of territory incurred by Germany in one place would have to be compensated to her by concessions to her in other places outside Europe. If the Allies delayed accepting the offer of President Wilson, and if, later on, the course of the war was so unfavourable to them that the intervention of the United States would not be effective, the United States would probably disinterest themselves in Europe and look to their own protection in their own way.

I said that I felt the statement, coming from the President of the United States, to be a matter of such importance that I must inform the Prime Minister and my colleagues; but that I could say nothing until it had received their consideration. The British Government could, under no circumstances, accept or make any proposal except in consultation and agreement with the Allies. . . .

(Intd.) E. G.

Foreign Office
22 *February* 1916

---

¹ Inserted by President Wilson, to correspond with the 'probably' three lines above and eight lines below. . . .

2 Seymour, *The Intimate Papers of Colonel House*, II, 201–202.

PART TWO

Wilson's Peace Overtures

President Wilson gave much thought to the peace which should end the war. It should be a peace among equals, he believed, from which no side would emerge as a conqueror; if such a settlement could be capped by an international collective security organization, to which the United States would belong, an era of justice, stability, security, and progress would be assured for the entire world. In a May, 1916, address to the League to Enforce Peace, a citizens' organization dedicated to the elimination of war and aggression, Wilson indicated the approach which was to culminate in 1919 in the drafting of the Covenant of the League of Nations. After the presidential election of 1916, in which great popular sentiment for continued neutrality was indicated, Wilson made two major efforts to mediate the war before the United States could be forced in by a renewal of submarine warfare. On December 18, 1916, he requested statements of war aims from the belligerents, and on January 22, 1917, he addressed the Senate in an appeal for a peace based on justice and collective security within a new international organization. Wilson's efforts failed, since neither side was willing to abandon hopes of gain for the mere restoration of the prewar status-quo.

3 · Wilson's Address Before the League to Enforce Peace

May 27, 1916

When the invitation to be here to-night came to me I was glad to accept it — not because it offered me an opportunity to discuss the program of the league — that you will, I am sure, not expect of me — but because the desire of the whole world now turns eagerly, more and more eagerly, toward the hope of peace; and there is just reason why we should take our part in counsel upon this great theme. It is right that I, as spokesman of our Government, should attempt to give expression to what I believe to be the thought and purpose of the people of the United States in this vital matter.

This great war that broke so suddenly upon the world two years ago, and which has swept within its flame so great a part of the civilized world, has affected us very profoundly, and we are not only at liberty, it is perhaps our duty, to speak very frankly of it and of the great interests of civilization which it affects.

Rights of Nation Affected. With its causes and its objects we are not concerned. The obscure fountains from which its stupendous flood has burst forth we are not interested to search for or explore. But so great a flood, spread far and wide to every quarter of the globe, has of necessity engulfed many a fair province of right that lies very near to us.

Our own rights as a nation, the liberties, the privileges, and the property of our people have been profoundly affected. We are not mere disconnected lookers-on. . . .

We are participants, whether we would or not, in the life of the world. The interests of all nations are our own also. We are partners with the rest. What affects mankind is inevitably our affair as well as the affair of the nations of Europe and of Asia. . . .

We believe these fundamental things: First, that every people has a right to choose the sovereignty under which they shall live. Like other nations, we have ourselves no doubt once and again offended against that principle when for a little while controlled by selfish passion, as our franker historians have been honorable enough to admit; but it has become more and more our rule of life and action. Second, that the small States of the world have a right to enjoy the same respect for their sovereignty and for their territorial integrity that great and power-

---

3 *Congressional Record*, Vol. 53, 64th Cong., 1st sess., p. 8854.

ful nations expect and insist upon. And, third, that the world has a right to be free from every disturbance of its peace that has its origin in aggression and disregard of the rights of peoples and nations.

So sincerely do we believe in these things that I am sure that I speak the mind and wish of the people of America when I say that the United States is willing to become a partner in any feasible association of nations formed in order to realize these objects and make them secure against violation.

There is nothing that the United States wants for itself that any other nation has. We are willing, on the contrary, to limit ourselves along with them to a prescribed course of duty and respect for the rights of others which will check any selfish passion of our own, as it will check any aggressive impulse of theirs.

If it should ever be our privilege to suggest or initiate a movement for peace among the nations now at war, I am sure that the people of the United States would wish their Government to move along these lines:

First, such a settlement with regard to their own immediate interests as the belligerents may agree upon. We have nothing material of any kind to ask for ourselves, and are quite aware that we are in no sense or degree parties to the present quarrel. Our interest is only in peace and its future guarantees.

Second, an universal association of the nations to maintain the inviolate security of the highway of the seas for the common and unhindered use of all the nations of the world, and to prevent any war begun either contrary to treaty covenants or without warning and full submission of the causes to the opinion of the world — a virtual guarantee of territorial integrity and political independence.

But I did not come here, let me repeat, to discuss a program. I came only to avow a creed and give expression to the confidence I feel that the world is even now upon the eve of a great consummation, when some common force will be brought into existence which shall safeguard right as the first and most fundamental interest of all peoples and all Governments, when coercion shall be summoned not to the service of political ambition or selfish hostility, but to the service of a common order, a common justice, and a common peace.

God grant that the dawn of that day of frank dealing and of settled peace, concord, and cooperation may be near at hand!

4 · The Secretary of State to the Ambassadors and Ministers in Belligerent Countries

WASHINGTON, December 18, 1916.

The President directs me to send you the following communication to be presented immediately to the Minister of Foreign Affairs of the government to which you are accredited, and he requests that you present it with the utmost earnestness of support. He wishes the impression clearly conveyed that it would be very hard for the Government of the United States to understand a negative reply. After yourself reading it to the Minister of Foreign Affairs and making the oral representations suggested, please leave a copy of this paper with him:

The President of the United States has instructed me to suggest to (substitute name of government to which you are accredited) a course of action with regard to the present war which he hopes that the (substitute name of government to which you are accredited) will take under consideration as suggested in the most friendly spirit and as coming not only from a friend but also as coming from the representative of a neutral nation whose interests have been most seriously affected by the war and whose concern for its early conclusion arises out of a manifest necessity to determine how best to safeguard those interests if the war is to continue. . . .

The President suggests that an early occasion be sought to call out from all the nations now at war such an avowal of their respective views as to the terms upon which the war might be concluded and the arrangements which would be deemed satisfactory as a guaranty against its renewal or the kindling of any similar conflict in the future as would make it possible frankly to compare them. He is indifferent as to the means taken to accomplish this. He would be happy himself to serve or even to take the initiative in its accomplishment in any way that might prove acceptable, but he has no desire to determine the method or the instrumentality. One way will be as acceptable to him as another if only the great object he has in mind be attained.

He takes the liberty of calling attention to the fact that the objects which the statesmen of the belligerents on both sides have in mind in

---

4 *Foreign Relations, 1916, Supplement,* pp. 97–99. The German government had made a bid on December 12, 1916, for the immediate opening of peace negotiations. Since the existing war map strongly favored Germany, and a peace settlement then would undoubtedly have reflected that fact, the Allied Powers evinced no enthusiasm and rejected the overture.

this war are virtually the same, as stated in general terms to their own people and to the world. Each side desires to make the rights and privileges of weak peoples and small states as secure against aggression or denial in the future as the rights and privileges of the great and powerful states now at war. Each wishes itself to be made secure in the future, along with all other nations and peoples, against the recurrence of wars like this and against aggression or selfish interference of any kind. Each would be jealous of the formation of any more rival leagues to preserve an uncertain balance of power amidst multiplying suspicions; but each is ready to consider the formation of a league of nations to insure peace and justice throughout the world. Before that final step can be taken, however, each deems it necessary first to settle the issues of the present war upon terms which will certainly safeguard the independence, the territorial integrity, and the political and commercial freedom of the nations involved.

In the measures to be taken to secure the future peace of the world the people and Government of the United States are as vitally and as directly interested as the Governments now at war. Their interest, moreover, in the means to be adopted to relieve the smaller and weaker peoples of the world of the peril of wrong and violence is as quick and ardent as that of any other people or government. They stand ready, and even eager, to cooperate in the accomplishment of these ends, when the war is over, with every influence and resource at their command. But the war must first be concluded. The terms upon which it is to be concluded they are not at liberty to suggest; but the President does feel that it is his right and his duty to point out their intimate interest in its conclusion, lest it should presently be too late to accomplish the greater things which lie beyond its conclusion, lest the situation of neutral nations, now exceedingly hard to endure, be rendered altogether intolerable, and lest, more than all, an injury be done civilization itself which can never be atoned for or repaired.

The President, therefore, feels altogether justified in suggesting an immediate opportunity for a comparison of views as to the terms which must precede those ultimate arrangements for the peace of the world, which all desire and in which the neutral nations, as well as those at war, are ready to play their full responsible part. If the contest must continue to proceed towards undefined ends by slow attrition until the one group of belligerents or the other is exhausted, if million after million of human lives must continue to be offered up until on the one side or the other there are no more to offer, if resentments must be kindled that can never cool and despairs engendered from which there can be no recovery, hopes of peace and of the willing concert of free peoples will be rendered vain and idle.

The life of the entire world has been profoundly affected. Every part of the great family of mankind has felt the burden and terror of this unprecedented contest of arms. No nation in the civilized world can be said in truth to stand outside its influence or to be safe against its disturbing effects. And yet the concrete objects for which it is being waged have never been definitively stated.

The leaders of the several belligerents have, as has been said, stated those objects in general terms. But, stated in general terms, they seem the same on both sides. Never yet have the authoritative spokesmen of either side avowed the precise objects which would, if attained, satisfy them and their people that the war had been fought out. The world has been left to conjecture what definitive results, what actual exchange of guaranties, what political or territorial changes or readjustments, what stage of military success even would bring the war to an end.

It may be that peace is nearer than we know; that the terms which the belligerents on the one side and on the other would deem it necessary to insist upon are not so irreconcilable as some have feared; that an interchange of views would clear the way at least for conference and make the permanent concord of the nations a hope of the immediate future, a concert of nations immediately practicable.

The President is not proposing peace; he is not even offering mediation. He is merely proposing that soundings be taken in order that we may learn, the neutral nations with the belligerent, how near the haven of peace may be for which all mankind longs with an intense and increasing longing. He believes that the spirit in which he speaks and the objects which he seeks will be understood by all concerned, and he confidently hopes for a response which will bring a new light into the affairs of the world.

LANSING

5 · The Ambassador in Great Britain to the Secretary of State

LONDON, December 22, 1916.

Your circular 18th. The dominant tone in public and private comment on the President's suggestion is surprise and sorrowful consternation, and all public comment so far is visibly restrained. The Foreign Office gave the British press a hint last night to maintain its comments cautiously and not to question the President's sincerity. Beneath open comment is a deep feeling of disappointment and in many quarters even of anger. The only section of opinion that is pleased is the small group of pacifists.

---

5 Foreign Relations, 1916, Supplement, pp. 108–109.

The President's suggestion itself would have provoked little or no criticism if it had been made at another time. But his remarks accompanying his suggestion are interpreted as placing the Allies and the Central powers on the same moral level. The Westminster *Gazette* this afternoon, alone among all the London dailies, explains that such an interpretation is not warranted by a careful reading of the note.

The opinion even in the least excitable and most friendly circles is that the note was a mistake because they judge it ill-timed and because they interpret it to show a misunderstanding of the aims of the Allies. The British feel that this is a holy and defensive war which must be fought to a decisive conclusion to save free government in the world from a military tyranny, and that even to suggest ending it indecisively is a blow at free government. . . .

[Lord] Northcliffe tells me that his papers, the *Times* and the *Daily Mail*, are saying and will continue to say as little as possible, but that "the people are as mad as hell." I am told that Mr. Asquith[1] when asked about the note replied sadly, "Don't talk to me about it. It is most disheartening." A luncheon guest at the palace yesterday informed me that the King wept while he expressed his surprise and depression.

It is perhaps too soon to venture an opinion about the permanent effect of the note on British feeling towards our Government; but there is reason to fear that it will for a long time cause a deep, even if silent, resentment because, as the British interpret it, it seems to them to mean that the President fails to understand the motives and high necessities, the aims and the sacrifices of the Allies who regard themselves as fighting, now with good hope, to save the world from a despotic inundation. . . .

PAGE

6 · *The Ambassador in France to the Secretary of State*

PARIS, *January 10, 1917.*

Translation of French note as follows:

The Allied Governments have received the note which was delivered to them in the name of the Government of the United States on the 19th of December, 1916. They have studied it with the care imposed

[1] Herbert Asquith, recently resigned as British Prime Minister.

6 *Papers Relating to the Foreign Relations of the United States, 1917, Supplement 1* (Washington: G.P.O., 1931), pp. 6–9.

upon them both by the exact realization which they have of the gravity of the hour and by the sincere friendship which attaches them to the American people.

In general way they wish to declare that they pay tribute to the elevation of the sentiment with which the American note is inspired and that they associate themselves with all their hopes with the project for the creation of a league of nations to insure peace and justice throughout the world. They recognize all the advantages for the cause of humanity and civilization which the institution of international agreements, destined to avoid violent conflicts between nations, would present; agreements which must imply the sanctions necessary to insure their execution and thus to prevent an apparent security from only facilitating new aggressions. But a discussion of future arrangements destined to insure an enduring peace presupposes a satisfactory settlement of the actual conflict; the Allies have as profound a desire as the Government of the United States to terminate as soon as possible a war for which the Central Empires are responsible and which inflicts such cruel sufferings upon humanity. But they believe that it is impossible at the present moment to attain a peace which will assure them reparation, restitution, and such guaranties to which they are entitled by the aggression for which the responsibility rests with the Central powers and of which the principle itself tended to ruin the security of Europe; a peace which would on the other hand permit the establishment of the future of European nations on a solid basis. The Allied nations are conscious that they are not fighting for selfish interests, but above all to safeguard the independence of peoples, of right, and of humanity. . . .

The Allied Governments believe that they must protest in the most friendly but in the most specific manner against the assimilation established in the American note between the two groups of belligerents; this assimilation, based upon public declarations by the Central powers, is in direct opposition to the evidence, both as regards responsibility for the past and as concerns guaranties for the future; President Wilson in mentioning it certainly had no intention of associating himself with it.

If there is an historical fact established at the present date, it is the wilful aggression of Germany and Austria-Hungary to insure their hegemony over Europe and their economic domination over the world. Germany proved by her declaration of war, by the immediate violation of Belgium and Luxemburg, and by her manner of conducting the war, her simulating contempt for all principles of humanity and all respect for small states; as the conflict developed the attitude of the Central powers and their allies has been a continual defiance of humanity and civilization. . . .

President Wilson desires more: he desires that the belligerent powers openly affirm the objects which they seek by continuing the war; the Allies experience no difficulty in replying to this request. Their objects in the war are well known; they have been formulated on many occasions by the chiefs of their divers governments. Their objects in the war will not be made known in detail with all the equitable compensations and indemnities for damages suffered until the hour of negotiations. But the civilized world knows that they imply in all necessity and in the first instance the restoration of Belgium, of Serbia, and of Montenegro, and the indemnities which are due them; the evacuation of the invaded territories of France, of Russia, and of Roumania with just reparation; the reorganization of Europe, guaranteed by a stable régime and founded as much upon respect of nationalities and full security and liberty, economic development, which all nations, great or small, possess, as upon territorial conventions and international agreements suitable to guarantee territorial and maritime frontiers against unjustified attacks; the restitution of provinces or territories wrested in the past from the Allies by force or against the will of their populations, the liberation of Italians, of Slavs, of Roumanians and of Czecho-Slovaks from foreign domination; the enfranchisement of populations subject to the bloody tyranny of the Turks; the expulsion from Europe of the Ottoman Empire decidedly [foreign] to western civilization. The intentions of His Majesty the Emperor of Russia regarding Poland have been clearly indicated in the proclamation which he has just addressed to his armies. It goes without saying that if the Allies wish to liberate Europe from the brutal covetousness of Prussian militarism, it never has been their design, as has been alleged, to encompass the extermination of the German peoples and their political disappearance. That which they desire above all is to insure a peace upon the principles of liberty and justice, upon the inviolable fidelity to international obligation with which the Government of the United States has never ceased to be inspired.

United in the pursuits of this supreme object the Allies are determined, individually and collectively, to act with all their power and to consent to all sacrifices to bring to a victorious close a conflict upon which they are convinced not only their own safety and prosperity depend but also the future of civilization itself.

7 · Address of the President of the United States to the Senate, January 22, 1917

GENTLEMEN OF THE SENATE: On the 18th of December last I addressed an identic note to the governments of the nations now at war requesting them to state, more definitely than they had yet been stated by either group of belligerents, the terms upon which they would deem it possible to make peace. I spoke on behalf of humanity and of the rights of all neutral nations like our own, many of whose most vital interests the war puts in constant jeopardy. The Central powers united in a reply which stated merely that they were ready to meet their antagonists in conference to discuss terms of peace. The Entente powers have replied much more definitely and have stated, in general terms, indeed, but with sufficient definiteness to imply details, the arrangements, guarantees, and acts of reparation which they deem to be the indispensable conditions of a satisfactory settlement. We are that much nearer a definite discussion of the peace which shall end the present war. We are that much nearer the discussion of the international concert which must thereafter hold the world at peace. In every discussion of the peace that must end this war it is taken for granted that that peace must be followed by some definite concert of power which will make it virtually impossible that any such catastrophe should ever overwhelm us again. Every lover of mankind, every sane and thoughtful man, must take that for granted.

I have sought this opportunity to address you because I thought that I owed it to you, as the council associated with me in the final determination of our international obligations, to disclose to you without reserve the thought and purpose that have been taking form in my mind in regard to the duty of our Government in the days to come when it will be necessary to lay afresh and upon a new plan the foundations of peace among the nations.

It is inconceivable that the people of the United States should play no part in that great enterprise. To take part in such a service will be the opportunity for which they have sought to prepare themselves by the very principles and purposes of their polity and the approved practices of their Government ever since the days when they set up a new nation in the high and honourable hope that it might in all that it was and did show mankind the way to liberty. They can not in honour

---

7 *Foreign Relations, 1917, Supplement 1,* pp. 24–29.

withhold the service to which they are now about to be challenged. They do not wish to withhold it. But they owe it to themselves and to the other nations of the world to state the conditions under which they will feel free to render it. . . .

The present war must first be ended; but we owe it to candour and to a just regard for the opinion of mankind to say that, so far as our participation in guarantees of future peace is concerned, it makes a great deal of difference in what way and upon what terms it is ended. The treaties and agreements which bring it to an end must embody terms which will create a peace that is worth guaranteeing and preserving, a peace that will win the approval of mankind, not merely a peace that will serve the several interests and immediate aims of the nations engaged. We shall have no voice in determining what those terms shall be, but we shall, I feel sure, have a voice in determining whether they shall be made lasting or not by the guarantees of a universal covenant; and our judgment upon what is fundamental and essential as a condition precedent to permanency should be spoken now, not afterwards when it may be too late.

No covenant of cooperative peace that does not include the peoples of the New World can suffice to keep the future safe against war; and yet there is only one sort of peace that the peoples of America could join in guaranteeing. The elements of that peace must be elements that engage the confidence and satisfy the principles of the American governments, elements consistent with their political faith and with the practical convictions which the peoples of America have once for all embraced and undertaken to defend.

I do not mean to say that any American government would throw any obstacle in the way of any terms of peace the governments now at war might agree upon, or seek to upset them when made, whatever they might be. I only take it for granted that mere terms of peace between the belligerents will not satisfy even the belligerents themselves. Mere agreements may not make peace secure. It will be absolutely necessary that a force be created as a guarantor of the permanency of the settlement so much greater than the force of any nation now engaged or any alliance hitherto formed or projected that no nation, no probable combination of nations, could face or withstand it. If the peace presently to be made is to endure, it must be a peace made secure by the organized major force of mankind.

The terms of the immediate peace agreed upon will determine whether it is a peace for which such a guarantee can be secured. The question upon which the whole future peace and policy of the world depends is this: Is the present war a struggle for a just and secure peace, or only for a new balance of power? If it be only a struggle for a new balance of power, who will guarantee, who can guarantee, the stable equilibrium of the new arrangement? Only a tranquil Europe can be a stable Europe. There must be, not a balance of power, but a community of power; not organized rivalries, but an organized common peace.

Fortunately we have received very explicit assurances on this point. The statesmen of both of the groups of nations now arrayed against one another have said, in terms that could not be misinterpreted, that it was no part of the purpose they had in mind to crush their antagonists. But the implications of these assurances may not be equally clear to all — may not be the same on both sides of the water. I think it will be serviceable if I attempt to set forth what we understand them to be.

They imply, first of all, that it must be a peace without victory. It is not pleasant to say this. I beg that I may be permitted to put my own interpretation upon it and that it may be understood that no other interpretation was in my thought. I am seeking only to face realities and to face them without soft concealments. Victory would mean peace forced upon the loser, a victor's terms imposed upon the vanquished. It would be accepted in humiliation, under duress, at an intolerable sacrifice, and would leave a sting, a resentment, a bitter memory upon which terms of peace would rest, not permanently, but only as upon quicksand. Only a peace between equals can last, only a peace the very principle of which is equality and a common participation in a common benefit. The right state of mind, the right feeling between nations, is as necessary for a lasting peace as is the just settlement of vexed questions of territory or of racial and national allegiance.

The equality of nations upon which peace must be founded if it is to last must be an equality of rights; the guarantees exchanged must neither recognize nor imply a difference between big nations and small, between those that are powerful and those that are weak. Right must be based upon the common strength, not upon the individual strength, of the nations upon whose concert peace will depend. Equality of territory or of resources there of course cannot be; nor any other sort of equality not gained in the ordinary peaceful and legitimate development of the peoples themselves. But no one asks or expects anything more than an equality of rights. Mankind is looking now for freedom of life, not for equipoises of power.

And there is a deeper thing involved than even equality of right among organized nations. No peace can last, or ought to last, which does not recognize and accept the principle that governments derive all their just powers from the consent of the governed, and that no right anywhere exists to hand peoples about from sovereignty to sovereignty as if they were property. I take it for granted, for instance, if I may venture upon a single example, that statesmen everywhere are agreed that there should be a united, independent, and autonomous Poland, and that henceforth inviolable security of life, of worship, and of industrial and social development should be guaranteed to all peoples who have lived hitherto under the power of governments devoted to a faith and purpose hostile to their own.

I speak of this, not because of any desire to exalt an abstract political principle which has always been held very dear by those who have sought to build up liberty in America, but for the same reason that I have spoken of the other conditions of peace which seem to me clearly indispensable — because I wish frankly to uncover realities. Any peace which does not recognize and accept this principle will inevitably be upset. It will not rest upon the affections or the convictions of mankind. The ferment of spirit of whole populations will fight subtly and constantly against it, and all the world will sympathize. The world can be at peace only if its life is stable, and there can be no stability where the will is in rebellion, where there is not tranquility of spirit and a sense of justice, of freedom, and of right.

So far as practicable, moreover, every great people now struggling towards a full development of its resources and of its powers should be assured a direct outlet to the great highways of the sea. Where this can not be done by the cession of territory, it can no doubt be done by the neutralization of direct rights of way under the general guarantee which will assure the peace itself. With a right comity of arrangement no nation need be shut away from free access to the open paths of the world's commerce.

And the paths of the sea must alike in law and in fact be free. The freedom of the seas is the *sine qua non* of peace, equality, and cooperation. No doubt a somewhat radical reconsideration of many of the rules of international practice hitherto thought to be established may be necessary in order to make the seas indeed free and common in practically all circumstances for the use of mankind, but the motive for such changes is convincing and compelling. There can be no trust or intimacy between the peoples of the world without them. The free, constant, unthreatened intercourse of nations is an essential part of the process of peace and of development. It need not be difficult either to define or to secure the freedom of the seas if the governments of the world sincerely desire to come to an agreement concerning it.

It is a problem closely connected with the limitation of naval armaments and the cooperation of the navies of the world in keeping the seas at once free and safe, and the question of limiting naval armaments opens the wider and perhaps more difficult question of the limitation of armies and of all programmes of military preparation. Difficult and delicate as these questions are, they must be faced with the utmost candour and decided in a spirit of real accommodation if peace is to come with healing in its wings, and come to stay. Peace cannot be had without concession and sacrifice. There can be no sense of safety and equality among the nations if great preponderating armaments are henceforth to continue here and there to be built up and maintained. The statesmen of the world must plan for peace and nations must adjust and accommodate their policy to it as they have planned for war and made ready for pitiless contest and rivalry. The question of armaments, whether on land or sea, is the most immediately and intensely practical question connected with the future fortunes of nations and of mankind.

I have spoken upon these great matters without reserve and with the utmost explicitness because it has seemed to me to be necessary if the world's yearning desire for peace was anywhere to find free voice and utterance. Perhaps I am the only person in high authority amongst all the peoples of the world who is at liberty to speak and hold nothing back. I am speaking as an individual, and yet I am speaking also, of course, as the responsible head of a great government, and I feel confident that I have said what the people of the United States would wish me to say. May I not add that I hope and believe that I am in effect speaking for liberals and friends of humanity in every nation and of every programme of liberty? I would fain believe that I am speaking for the silent mass of mankind everywhere who have as yet had no place or opportunity to speak their real hearts out concerning the death and ruin they see to have come already upon the persons and the homes they hold most dear.

And in holding out the expectation that the people and Government of the United States will join the other civilized nations of the world in guaranteeing the permanence of peace upon such terms as I have named I speak with the greater boldness and confidence because it is clear to every man who can think that there is in this promise no breach in either our traditions or our policy as a nation, but a fulfilment, rather, of all that we have professed or striven for.

I am proposing, as it were, that the nations should with one accord adopt the doctrine of President Monroe as the doctrine of the world: that no nation should seek to extend its polity over any other nation or people, but that every people should be left free to determine its own polity, its own way of development, unhindered, unthreatened, unafraid, the little along with the great and powerful.

I am proposing that all nations henceforth avoid entangling alliances which would draw them into competitions of power, catch them in a net of intrigue and selfish rivalry, and disturb their own affairs with influences intruded from without. There is no entangling alliance in a concert of power. When all unite to act in the same sense and with the same purpose, all act in the common interest and are free to live their own lives under a common protection.

I am proposing government by the consent of the governed; that freedom of the seas which in international conference after conference representatives of the United States have urged with the eloquence of those who are the convinced disciples of liberty; and that moderation of armaments which makes of armies and navies a power for order merely, not an instrument of aggression or of selfish violence.

These are American principles, American policies. We could stand for no others. And they are also the principles and policies of forward-looking men and women everywhere, of every modern nation, of every enlightened community. They are the principles of mankind and must prevail.

8 · The German Ambassador to Colonel House

WASHINGTON, *January 31, 1917.*

MY DEAR COLONEL HOUSE: I have received a telegram from Berlin, according to which I am to express to the President the thanks of the Imperial Government for his communication made through you. The Imperial Government has complete confidence in the President and hopes that he will reciprocate such confidence. As proof I am to inform you in confidence that the Imperial Government will be very glad to accept the services kindly offered by the President for the purpose of bringing about a peace conference between the belligerents. My Government, however, is not prepared to publish any peace terms at present, because our enemies have published such terms which aim at the dishonor and destruction of Germany and her allies. My Government considers that as long as our enemies openly proclaim such terms, it would show weakness, which does not exist, on our part if we publish our terms and we would in so doing only prolong the war. However, to show President Wilson our confidence, my Government through me desires to inform him personally of the terms under which we would have been prepared to enter into negotiations, if our enemies had accepted our offer of December 12.

Restitution of the part of Upper Alsace occupied by the French;
Gaining of a frontier which would protect Germany and Poland economically and strategically against Russia;
Restitution of colonies in form of an agreement which would give Germany colonies adequate to her population and economic interest;
Restitution of those parts of France occupied by Germany under reservation of strategical and economic changes of the frontier and financial compensations;

---

8 *Foreign Relations, 1917, Supplement 1,* pp. 34–36.

Restoration of Belgium under special guaranty for the safety of Germany which would have to be decided on by negotiations with Belgium;

Economic and financial mutual compensation on the basis of the exchange of territories conquered and to be restituted at the conclusion of peace;

Compensation for the German business concerns and private persons who suffered by the war; abandonment of all economic agreements and measures which would form an obstacle to normal commerce and intercourse after the conclusion of peace, and instead of such agreements reasonable treaties of commerce;

The freedom of the seas.

The peace terms of our allies run on the same lines.

My Government further agrees, after the war has terminated, to enter into the proposed second international conference on the basis of the President's message to the Senate. . . .

PART THREE

The Decision for Unrestricted Submarine Warfare

The failure to open peace negotiations at a time which the Central Powers considered to be favorable to their interests, and the apparent stalemate in land warfare, caused the German government to seek a military solution through unrestricted submarine warfare. The question was debated in the summer of 1916, but the final decision was not taken until January 9, 1917, at the Pless conference. Chancellor Bethmann-Hollweg was still opposed to a measure which he thought would bring the United States into the war against Germany and would probably ensure the ultimate defeat of the Central Powers. He was virtually powerless, however, to continue his resistance. The prevailing sentiment of the German press and within the Reichstag was strongly in favor of unrestricted underseas warfare, while the Kaiser was increasingly under the influence of the German High Command. When Field Marshal Paul von Hindenburg and General Erich Ludendorff agreed with the admirals that only full use of the U-boat promised an end to the costly, seemingly inconclusive land war by a decisive victory over England, Bethmann felt compelled to capitulate. Any other course probably would have meant his immediate removal from office.

After the failure of his peace overtures, President Wilson apparently contemplated a diplomatic retreat from his previous position on the submarine. He realized that continuation of the war would further weaken neutral rights and he seems to have been prepared to accept ruthless U-boat warfare against armed merchantmen and perhaps against all enemy vessels except passenger liners. The German announcement on January 31, 1917 of unrestricted warfare against *all* shipping, neutral as well as belligerent, however, left him no choice but to break diplomatic relations on February 3.

9 · Conference with Regard to the Adoption of the Unrestricted U-Boat War

PLESS CASTLE, *August 31, 1916.*

Admiral v. HOLTZENDORFF[1], after reading an official comment concerning the present determination of the U-boat question, said: According to the general military situation, we are placed in a situation of defense; the continuation of the war on the part of our opponents is completely dependent upon England's attitude; it is therefore necessary for us to prevent England, by the use of all means in our power, from continuing to carry on the war, and the destruction of England's ocean commerce will accomplish this purpose; the last memorial of the Admiralty Staff sets out plainly what the result of this destruction would be.

The reaction of the United States and the remaining neutral Powers is used as an argument against carrying on the unrestricted U-boat warfare; that in such case the entire shipping space of the world would be made available to England; that Russia's incapacity to carry out a third winter campaign and its necessity for peace are also arguments against the taking up of the U-boat war at an early date.

In the meanwhile, time is working against us; the blockade of Germany is becoming more and more oppressive; as the result of a good harvest we will be less dependent upon imports, and, speaking from the military standpoint, we can maintain an effective defensive.

So far as the neutrals are concerned, Holland will attack the first one to put foot upon her territory; the entrance of Denmark into the war is very improbable; England will not be able to gain in freight space; no freight space will be placed at its disposal by any action of the United States; nor is this likely to be the case with regard to the South American States, since they themselves are suffering from a shortage of tonnage; the tonnage of those of our ships which are in the possession of the enemy is negligible; it is within our power to break England's determination to carry on the war to the end of the year; to put off commencing the U-boat war would put off the results in question; in this connection the question must be well considered as to whether our allies will be able to hold out any longer; if we renounce the use of the U-boat weapon we may have reason to believe that this means *finis Germaniae.*

Secretary of State v. JAGOW: Unrestricted U-boat war would in any

[1] Admiral Henning von Holtzendorff, Chief of the Admiralty Staff.

9 Excerpts, *Official German Documents,* II, 1154–1163, 1317–1321.

172

event mean the breaking of diplomatic relations with the United States, and, if American lives are lost, would finally lead to war; if the last neutral world Power were to take the side of the Entente, the smaller neutral States would be left with no choice other than to work with us or against us. (Here follow comments about the European neutral Powers.) If we take up unrestricted U-boat warfare, the attitude of all neutral Powers will be changed against us and we shall have to calculate upon establishing new fronts. Germany will in such case be looked upon as a mad dog against whom the hand of every man will be raised for the purpose of finally bringing about peace. . . .

Secretary of State [Karl] HELFFERICH[2]: It is to be admitted that the situation both here and in England for launching a U-boat war is more favorable now than it was a year ago or in the spring, because at that time the mere blockade on the part of the neutrals would have been sufficient to starve us. Our harvest is notably better than it was last year, but at the same time we shall be pinched, and every importation would be welcome by us. . . .

The reactions of the U-boat war from the political and economic standpoint must not be underestimated. Everybody is perfectly convinced that a break with the United States and a war with the United States would be unavoidable. The assumption that the hostile attitude of the United States can not reach a higher pitch so far as we are concerned, is erroneous. Up to the present time, the Allies have received from the United States in the way of loans $1,250,000,000. In the case of war, America will stand ready with all of its reserves available for the cause of the Allies, which will then become the cause of the United States. America will desire to win the war as quickly as possible and will summon all its energies for putting this wish into execution. Acting in cooperation with England, the very strongest kind of pressure can be exerted upon the neutral Powers to join the Entente. Since Denmark and Holland are dependent upon imports by water, they will be utterly unable to oppose it. We have no means of exerting pressure to avoid this result. Our need for iron is now so urgent that we are already at the point at which we can release no more. Holland can obtain from England, with limitations, whatever she needs in the way of coal. I see nothing but catastrophe following the application of the U-boat weapon at this time. A method which will lead us out of one serious situation only into the toils of another more serious, is not practical if we are not able to adopt counter-measures for the purpose of rendering the otherwise disadvantageous result ineffectual. . . .

Imperial Chancelor v. BETHMANN-HOLLWEG notes a reservation with regard to the report of his views contained in the written comment which was read by Admiral v. Holtzendorff, and continues as follows: I take the stand that the decision of the U-boat question must depend very greatly on the estimate of the military situation made by the Supreme

[2] for the Treasury.

High Command. According to the view of Field Marshal v. Hindenburg, with whom I have had a preliminary conference, no decision, either *pro* or *con*, can be reached as long as the military situation resulting from the participation of Roumania is not clear. According to my personal opinion the declaration of a U-boat war would be looked upon as an act of desperation both by the hostile and neutral world, as well as by a great portion of our own people. It would be very inadvisable to label such an undertaking from the very outset as an act of desperation.

If we combine the results of the statements made yesterday and today, no one will doubt that we shall be able to rely upon the destruction of, roughly speaking, 4 million tons of British shipping within from four to six months. The Admiralty Staff is of the opinion that England will then be ready to conclude peace. This opinion is considered by other gentlemen, for instance, by Secretary of State Helfferich, as of doubtful correctness, and nobody can prove that the hoped-for success will really come about. I, too, believe that this is merely an assumption. It is certain that a complete blockade from and to England can not be carried out, because U-boats can undertake nothing in the night time. We can lay down no iron ring around England, and, moreover, our blockade can be broken by the accompaniment of transports by war-ships. I have understood Admiral v. Holtzendorff to say that intercourse to and from Holland and Denmark can be stopped. Will it be possible to do this if, at the same time, we are carrying on an intensive U-boat war against the English coast?

We must realize that the break with the United States will certainly follow the launching of the U-boat war. (Here follow comments concerning European neutral Powers.)

I believe that a decision with regard to the launching of the U-boat war without an understanding with our allies is out of the question. We must calculate, in this connection, on the contingency that Turkey will be alienated from us. . . . Nor can we involve Austria-Hungary in a war with the remaining neutral Powers without asking her opinion in the matter. If the Roumanian war were to turn out unfavorably for us, the U-boat war would avail us nothing; if Austria-Hungary falls to pieces, I do not know whether we shall be able to put up any further opposition. For these reasons, a final decision seems to me to be possible only after a clearing up of the military situation. . . .

✻ ✻ ✻ ✻ ✻

Report of the conference between Imperial Chancelor v. Bethmann-Hollweg, General Field Marshal v. Hindenburg, and General Ludendorff, at Pless, January 9, 1917

The CHANCELOR: If His Majesty commands that a ruthless U-boat war shall be launched, the Chancelor will endeavor to succeed in keeping America "out of it." For this purpose, certain concessions already taken up previously with the Admiralty Staff would have to be made. But we will have to calculate upon America's entrance into the war against us.

The Chancelor feels more assurance about the attitude of the European neutrals. Our peace note has brought good results. Holland and Denmark will not enter the war, at least not as long as they do not see that the U-boat war brings us no success.

With regard to Switzerland, we shall have to bear in mind the possibility that the Entente will bring pressure to bear on Switzerland if food becomes scarce in that country, to make it possible for French armies to march through or even for Switzerland to join the cause of the Entente.

Denmark will possibly lay up its shipping.

The Chancelor requests that the military measures which are to be taken with regard to the neutral boundaries, and particularly with regard to the Danish boundary, be such as not to carry the implication of excessive menace.

General LUDENDORFF: The purpose is just to detail a few regiments of cavalry to the borders.

CHANCELOR: The determination to launch the unrestricted U-boat war depends, then, upon the results which we may expect. Admiral v. Holtzendorff assumes that we will have England on her knees by the next harvest. The experiences of the U-boats during the last few months, the increased number of U-boats, and England's bad economic situation, will at least increase our chances of success.

On the whole, the prospects for the unrestricted U-boat war are very favorable.

Of course, it must be admitted that those prospects are not capable of being demonstrated by proof.

We should be perfectly certain that, so far as the military situation is concerned, great military strokes are insufficient as such to win the war.

The U-boat war is the "last card." A very serious decision. "But if the military authorities consider the U-boat war essential, I am not in a position to contradict them."

FIELD MARSHAL: We are ready to meet all eventualities and to meet America, Denmark, Holland, and Switzerland too.

The restricted U-boat war on commerce will only bring about a slight increase in the results reached up to this time. We need the most energetic, ruthless methods which can be adopted. For this reason, we need the ruthless U-boat war to start from February 1, 1917.

The war must be brought to an end rapidly, although we would be able to hold out still longer, but haste is needed on account of our allies.

CHANCELOR: It may be imagined that the U-boat war might postpone the end of hostilities.

General LUDENDORFF: The U-boat war will also bring our armies into a different and a better situation. Through the lack of wood needed for mining purposes and for lack of coal, the production of ammunition is hard-pressed. It means that there will be some relief for the western front. We must spare the troops a second battle of the Somme. That this relief will come about will be proved by our own situation and the effects of our transportation crisis.

And, too, Russia's power of initiative will be detrimentally affected by the lack of ammunition which will result from shortage in tonnage. The Siberian railroad alone will not be sufficient for Russia's needs.

CHANCELOR: America's assistance, in case she enters the war, will consist in the delivery of food supplies to England, financial support, delivery of airplanes and the dispatching of corps of volunteers.

FIELD MARSHAL: We can take care of that. The opportunity for the U-boat war is such that it can perhaps never become as favorable again; we can carry it on and we must carry it on.

CHANCELOR: Of course, if success beckons, we must follow.

FIELD MARSHAL: We would reproach ourselves later if we let the opportunity pass by.

CHANCELOR: The situation is certainly better than it was in September.

GENERAL LUDENDORFF: The measures of security taken against the neutrals will have nothing about them in the nature of a challenge; they will be purely defensive measures.

CHANCELOR: And suppose Switzerland came into the war, or that the French were to come through Switzerland.

FIELD MARSHAL: That would not be unfavorable from a military standpoint.

10 · *The German Ambassador to the Secretary of State*

WASHINGTON, *January 31, 1917.*

MR. SECRETARY OF STATE: . . . Enclosing two memoranda regarding the details of the contemplated military measures at sea, I remain [etc.]

J. BERNSTORFF

MEMORANDUM

After bluntly refusing Germany's peace offer, the Entente powers stated in their note addressed to the American Government that they

---

10 *Foreign Relations, 1917, Supplement 1*, pp. 97–102.

are determined to continue the war in order to deprive Germany of German provinces in the West and the East, to destroy Austria- Hungary, and to annihilate Turkey. In waging war with such aims, the Entente allies are violating all rules of international law, as they prevent the legitimate trade of neutrals with the Central powers, and of the neutrals among themselves. Germany has, so far, not made unrestricted use of the weapon which she possesses in her submarines. Since the Entente powers, however, have made it impossible to come to an understanding based upon equality of rights of all nations, as proposed by the Central powers, and have instead declared only such a peace to be possible which shall be dictated by the Entente allies and shall result in the destruction and humiliation of the Central powers, Germany is unable further to forego the full use of her submarines. The Imperial Government, therefore, does not doubt that the Government of the United States will understand the situation thus forced upon Germany by the Entente allies' brutal methods of war and by their determination to destroy the Central powers, and that the Government of the United States will further realize that the now openly disclosed intentions of the Entente allies give back to Germany the freedom of action which she reserved in her note addressed to the Government of the United States on May 4, 1916.

Under these circumstances Germany will meet the illegal measures of her enemies by forcibly preventing after February 1, 1917, in a zone around Great Britain, France, Italy, and in the eastern Mediterranean all navigation, that of neutrals included, from and to England and from and to France, etc., etc. All ships met within that zone will be sunk.

The Imperial Government is confident that this measure will result in a speedy termination of the war and in the restoration of peace which the Government of the United States has so much at heart. Like the Government of the United States, Germany and her allies had hoped to reach this goal by negotiations. Now that the war, through the fault of Germany's enemies, has to be continued, the Imperial Government feels sure that the Government of the United States will understand the necessity of adopting such measures as are destined to bring about a speedy end of the horrible and useless bloodshed. The Imperial Government hopes all the more for such an understanding of her position, as the neutrals have under the pressure of the Entente powers, suffered great losses, being forced by them either to give up their entire trade or to limit it according to conditions arbitrarily determined by Germany's enemies in violation of international law.

MEMORANDUM

From February 1, 1917, all sea traffic will be stopped with every available weapon and without further notice in the following blockade zones around Great Britain, France, Italy, and in the Eastern Mediterranean. . . .

Sailing of regular American passenger steamers may continue un-disturbed after February 1, 1917, if —

(*a*) the port of destination is Falmouth.

(*b*) sailing to or coming from that port course is taken via the Scilly Islands and a point 50°N. 20° W.

(*c*) the steamers are marked in the following way which must not be allowed to other vessels in American ports: On ships' hull and superstructure 3 vertical stripes 1 meter wide each to be painted alternately white and red. Each mast should show a large flag checkered white and red, and the stern the American national flag.

   Care should be taken that, during dark, national flag and painted marks are easily recognizable from a distance and that the boats are well lighted throughout.

(*d*) one steamer a week sails in each direction with arrival at Falmouth on Sunday and departure from Falmouth on Wednesday.

(*e*) the United States Government guarantees that no contraband (according to German contraband list) is carried by those steamers.

II · *Address of the President of the United States to Congress, February 3, 1917*

GENTLEMEN OF THE CONGRESS: The Imperial German Government on the 31st of January announced to this Government and to the governments of other neutral nations that on and after the 1st day of February, the present month, it would adopt a policy with regard to the use of submarines against all shipping seeking to pass through certain designated areas of the high seas to which it is clearly my duty to call your attention. . . .

   I think that you will agree with me that, in view of this declaration, which suddenly and without prior intimation of any kind deliberately withdraws the solemn assurance given in the Imperial Government's note of the 4th of May, 1916, this Government has no alternative consistent with the dignity and honour of the United States but to take the course

11 *Foreign Relations, 1917, Supplement 1*, pp. 109–112.

which, in its note of the 18th of April, 1916, it announced that it would take in the event that the German Government did not declare and effect an abandonment of the methods of submarine warfare which it was then employing and to which it now purposes again to resort.

I have, therefore, directed the Secretary of State to announce to his excellency the German Ambassador that all diplomatic relations between the United States and the German Empire are severed, and that the American Ambassador at Berlin will immediately be withdrawn; and, in accordance with this decision, to hand to his excellency his passports.

Notwithstanding this unexpected action of the German Government, this sudden and deeply deplorable renunciation of its assurances given this Government at one of the most critical moments of tension in the relations of the two Governments, I refuse to believe that it is the intention of the German authorities to do in fact what they have warned us they will feel at liberty to do. I can not bring myself to believe that they will indeed pay no regard to the ancient friendship between their people and our own or to the solemn obligations which have been exchanged between them and destroy American ships and take the lives of American citizens in the wilful prosecution of the ruthless naval programme they have announced their intention to adopt. Only actual overt acts on their part can make me believe it even now.

If this inveterate confidence on my part in the sobriety and prudent foresight of their purpose should unhappily prove unfounded; if American ships and American lives should in fact be sacrificed by their naval commanders in heedless contravention of the just and reasonable understandings of international law and the obvious dictates of humanity, I shall take the liberty of coming again before the Congress, to ask that authority be given me to use any means that may be necessary for the protection of our seamen and our people in the prosecution of their peaceful and legitimate errands on the high seas. I can do nothing less. I take it for granted that all neutral governments will take the same course.

We do not desire any hostile conflict with the Imperial German Government. We are the sincere friends of the German people and earnestly desire to remain at peace with the Government which speaks for them. We shall not believe that they are hostile to us unless and until we are obliged to believe it; and we purpose nothing more than the reasonable defense of the undoubted rights of our people. We wish to serve no selfish ends. We seek merely to stand true alike in thought and in action to the immemorial principles of our people which I sought to express in my address to the Senate only two weeks ago — seek merely to vindicate our right to liberty and justice and an unmolested life. These are the bases of peace, not war. God grant we may not be challenged to defend them by acts of wilful injustice on the part of the Government of Germany!

PART FOUR

Transition to War

From February 3 to April 2, 1917, there was a gradual transition in Washington from peace to belligerency. As his message to Congress on the severance of relations with Germany had indicated, President Wilson hoped that Germany would not implement its threat of unrestricted submarine warfare. Even when "actual overt acts" occurred, he seems to have considered armed neutrality or a limited form of defensive naval war as acceptable alternatives to full belligerency. Finally he decided, however, that nothing less than formal entry into the war would suffice to vindicate American rights and honor and ensure the government a significant role in the eventual peacemaking.

The publication in America of the British-intercepted and decoded Zimmermann Telegram and the sinking of three unarmed American ships in mid-March were important events in Wilson's decision to request Congress to declare a state of war with Germany and in the readiness of the American people to approve belligerency. The Zimmermann Telegram, with its proposal by the German Foreign Secretary of a German-Mexican alliance against the United States, had actually been sent in code to the German minister in Mexico City through the facilities of the American State Department. Its release to the press created a sensation in America and seemed to reveal the true nature of Germany's hostile intentions. After the submarine attacks on American ships, Lansing and the other members of the Cabinet urged the President to request Congress to declare war (Lansing's Memorandum of the Cabinet meeting on March 20, 1917). President Wilson concurred, but only with great reluctance and mental anguish as the recollections of the reporter Frank Cobb reveal.

12 · The Ambassador in Great Britain to the Secretary of State

LONDON, *February 24, 1917.*

For the President and the Secretary of State. Balfour[1] has handed me the text of a cipher telegram from [Arthur] Zimmermann, German Secretary of State for Foreign Affairs, to the German Minister to Mexico, which was sent via Washington and relayed to Bernstorff on January 19. You can probably obtain a copy of the text relayed by Bernstorff from the cable office in Washington. The first group is the number of the telegram, 130, and the second is 13042, indicating the number of the code used. The last group but two is 97556, which is Zimmermann's signature. I shall send you by mail a copy of the cipher text and of the decode into German and meanwhile I give you the English translation as follows:

> We intend to begin on the 1st of February unrestricted submarine warfare. We shall endeavor in spite of this to keep the United States of America neutral. In the event of this not succeeding, we make Mexico a proposal of alliance on the following basis: make war together, make peace together, generous financial support and an understanding on our part that Mexico is to reconquer the lost territory in Texas, New Mexico, and Arizona. The settlement in detail is left to you. You will inform the President [of Mexico] of the above most secretly as soon as the outbreak of war with the United States of America is certain and add the suggestion that he should, on his own initiative, invite Japan to immediate adherence and at the same time mediate between Japan and ourselves. Please call the President's attention to the fact that the ruthless employment of our submarines now offers the prospect of compelling England in a few months to make peace. Signed, Zimmermann.

The receipt of this information has so greatly exercised the British Government that they have lost no time in communicating it to me to transmit to you, in order that our Government may be able without delay to make such disposition as may be necessary in view of the threatened invasion of our territory.

---

[1] Arthur J. Balfour had recently replaced Grey as Foreign Secretary.

13 · The Secretary of State to President Wilson

WASHINGTON, March 19, 1917.

MY DEAR MR. PRESIDENT: After considering carefully our conversation this morning I wish to say that I am in entire agreement with you that the recent attacks by submarines on American vessels[1] do not materially affect the international situation so far as constituting a reason for declaring that a state of war exists between this country and Germany. I think that these incidents, however, show very plainly that the German Government intends to carry out its announced policy without regard to consequences and to make no exception in the case of American vessels. It will, therefore, be only a question of time before we are forced to recognize these outrages as hostile acts which will amount to an announcement that a state of war exists.

I firmly believe that war will come within a short time whatever we may do, because the German Government seems to be relentless in pursuing its methods of warfare against neutral ships. It will not be many days, if past experience indicates the future, before an engagement will take place between one of our guarded steamships and a submarine. Whether that event will cause Germany to declare war or will cause us to recognize a state of war I do not know, but I do not think that we can successfully maintain the fiction that peace exists.

With the conviction that war is bound to come — and I have come to this conviction with the greatest reluctance and with an earnest desire to avoid it — the question seems to me to be whether or not the greatest good will be accomplished by waiting until some other events have taken place before we enter the conflict, or by entering now.

The advantage of delay would seem to be that in some future submarine attack on an American vessel the armed guard would with gun fire sink or drive off the submarine and by so doing induce the German Government to declare war upon us. If there is any other advantage I have been unable to imagine it. I am also convinced in my own mind that the German Government will not declare war in any circumstances. Why should it? It will prefer to continue to wage war on us, as it is today, and at the same time keep our hands tied by our admitted neutrality. It can do everything practical to injure us and prevent us from doing many things to injure Germany. It would seem most unreasonable

---

[1] The *Illinois*, *City of Memphis*, and *Vigilencia*.

to expect the German Government to increase its difficulties by declaring the United States an enemy.

The advantages of our immediate participation in the war appear to me to [be] based largely upon the premise that war is inevitable. Of course if that premise is wrong what I say is open to question. I should add two other premises, the truth of which seem to me well established. They are that the Entente Allies represent the principle of Democracy, and the Central Powers, the principle of Autocracy, and that it is for the welfare of mankind and for the establishment of peace in the world that Democracy should succeed.

In the first place it would encourage and strengthen the new democratic government of Russia,[2] which we ought to encourage and with which we ought to sympathize. If we delay, conditions may change and the opportune moment when our friendship would be useful may be lost. I believe that the Russian Government founded on its hatred of absolutism and therefore of the German Government would be materially benefited by feeling that this republic was arrayed against the same enemy of liberalism.

In the second place it would put heart into the democratic element in Germany, who are already beginning to speak boldly and show their teeth at their rulers. Possibly delay would not affect to a very great degree the movement, but I believe it would hasten the time when the German people assert themselves and repudiate the military oligarchy in control of the Empire.

In the third place it would give moral support to the Entente Powers already encouraged by recent military successes and add to the discouragement of the Teutonic Allies, which would result in the advancement of Democracy and in shortening the war. The present seems to be an especially propitious time to exert this influence on the conflict.

In the fourth place the American people, feeling, I am sure, that war is bound to come, are becoming restive and bitterly critical of what they believe to be an attempt to avoid the unavoidable. If there is a possibility of keeping out of the war, this attitude of the public mind would affect me not at all, but convinced as I am that we will in spite of all we may do become participants, I can see no object in adopting a course which will deprive us of a certain measure of enthusiastic support which speedy action will bring.

In the fifth place, I believe that our future influence in world affairs, in which we can no longer refuse to play our part, will be materially increased by prompt, vigorous and definite action in favor of Democracy and against Absolutism. This would be first shown in the peace negotiations and in the general readjustment of international relations. It is my belief that the longer we delay in declaring against the military absolutism

2 The Czarist government had been overthrown in the March 1917 Revolution and a provisional republican regime was in control.

which menaces the rule of liberty and justice in the world, so much the less will be our influence in the days when Germany will need a merciful and unselfish foe.

I have written my views with great frankness, as I am sure you would wish me to do, and I trust that you will understand my views are in no way influenced by any bitterness of feeling toward Germany or by any conscious emotion awakened by recent events. I have tried to view the situation coldly, dispassionately and justly.

    Faithfully yours,

                                                          ROBERT LANSING

14 · *Memorandum of the Cabinet Meeting, 2:30–5 p.m. Tuesday, March 20, 1917*

The Cabinet Meeting of today I consider the most momentous and, therefore, the most historic of any of those which have been held since I became Secretary of State, since it involved, unless a miracle occurs, the question of war with Germany and the abandonment of the policy of neutrality which has been pursued for two years and a half. . . .

The corridors of the State Department and Executive Office swarmed with press correspondents seeking to get some inkling of what would be done from passing officials. It was through these eager crowds of newsgatherers that I forced my way at half-past two Tuesday afternoon under a bombardment of questions, to which I made no reply, and entered the Cabinet room where all the other members had arrived.

Three minutes later the President came in and passed to his place at the head of the table shaking hands with each member and smiling as genially and composedly as if nothing of importance was to be considered. Composure is a marked characteristic of the President. Nothing ruffles the calmness of his manner or address. It has a sobering effect on all who sit with him in council. Excitement would seem very much out of place at the Cabinet table with Woodrow Wilson presiding.

. . . the President said that he desired advice from the Cabinet on our relations with Germany and the course which should be pursued. He began with a review of his actions up to the present time pointing out

---

14 Private Memoranda, Papers of Robert Lansing.

that he had said to Congress on February 3rd that, while the announced policy of Germany had compelled the severance of diplomatic relations, he could not bring himself to believe that the German Government would carry it out against American vessels, but that, if an "overt act" occurred, he would come before them again and ask means to protect Americans on the high seas even though he thought he possessed the constitutional power to act without Congress. He said that the situation compelled him to do this on February 23rd and Congress had desired to adopt the measures, which he sought, but had been prevented, and that he had then acted on his own authority and placed armed guards on American vessels intending to proceed to the German barred zone.

He went on to say that he did not see from a practical point of view what else could be done to safeguard American vessels more than had already been done unless we declared war or declared that a state of war existed, which was the same thing; and that the power to do this lay with Congress.

He said that the two questions as to which he wished to be advised were —

Should he summon Congress to meet at an earlier date than April 16th, for which he had already issued a call?

Second. What should he lay before Congress when it did assemble?

He then spoke in general terms of the political situations in the belligerent countries, particularly in Russia where the revolution against the autocracy had been successful, and in Germany where the liberal element in the Prussian Diet was grumbling loudly against their rulers. He also spoke of the situation in this country, of the indignation and bitterness in the East and the apparent apathy of the Middle West.

After the President had finished McAdoo[1] was the first to speak. He said that war seemed to him a certainty and he could see no reason for delay in saying so and acting accordingly; that we might just as well face the issue and come out squarely in opposition to Germany, whose Government represented every evil in history; that, if we did not do so at once, the American people would compel action and we would be in the position of being pushed forward instead of leading, which would be humiliating and unwise. He further said that he believed that we could best aid the Allies against Germany by standing back of their credit, by underwriting their loans, and that they were sorely in need of such aid. He felt, however, that we could do little else, and doubted whether we could furnish men.

McAdoo spoke with great positiveness in advocating an immediate call of Congress. His voice was low and his utterance deliberate, but he gave the impression of great earnestness.

Houston,[2] who followed, said that he agreed with McAdoo that it

[1] Secretary of the Treasury.
[2] David F. Houston, Secretary of Agriculture.

would create a most unfortunate, if not disastrous, impression on the American public as well as in Europe if we waited any longer to take a firm stand now that Germany had shown her hand. He said that he doubted whether we should plan to do more than to use our navy and to give financial aid to the Allies; that to equip an army of any size would divert the production of our industrial plants and so cut off from the Allies much needed supplies; and he thought that we ought to be very careful about interfering with their efficiency. He concluded by urging the President to summon Congress at once because he felt that a state of war already existed and should be declared.

Redfield[3] followed Houston with his usual certainty of manner and vigor of expression. He was for declaring war and doing everything possible to aid in bringing the Kaiser to his knees. He made no points which particularly impressed me; and, as he had so often shown his strong pro-Ally sentiments, I was sure his words made little impression upon the President.

Baker[4] was the next to express an opinion and he did so with the wonderful clearness of diction of which he is master. He said that he considered the state of affairs called for drastic action with as little delay as possible, and that he believed Congress should meet before April 16th. He said that the recent German outrages showed that the Germans did not intend to modify in the least degree their policy of inhumanity and lawlessness, and that such acts could mean only one thing, and that was war.

Since we were now forced into the struggle he favored entering it with all our vigor. He advocated preparing an army at once to be sent to Europe in case the Allies became straightened in the number of their men. He said that he believed the very knowledge of our preparations would force the Central Powers to realize that their cause was hopeless. He went on to discuss the details of raising, equipping and training a large force.

I followed Baker and can very naturally remember what I said better and more fully than I can the remarks of others.

I began with the statement that in my opinion an actual state of war existed today between this country and Germany, but that, as the acknowledgment of such a state officially amounted to a declaration of war, I doubted the wisdom as well as the constitutional power of the President to announce such fact or to act upon it; that I thought that the facts should be laid before Congress and that they should be asked to declare the existence of a state of war and to enact the laws necessary to meet the exigencies of the case. I pointed out that many things could be done under our present statutes which seriously menaced our national safety and that the Executive was powerless to prevent their being done.

[3] William C. Redfield, Secretary of Commerce.
[4] Newton D. Baker, Secretary of War.

I referred in some detail to the exodus of Germans from this country to Mexico and Cuba since we severed diplomatic relations, to the activities of German agents here, to the transferrence of funds by Germans to Latin American countries, to the uncensored use of the telegraph and the mails, &c.

For the foregoing reasons I said that I felt that there should be no delay in calling Congress together and securing these necessary powers.

In addition to these reasons which so vitally affected our domestic situation I said that the revolution in Russia, which appeared to be successful, had removed the one objection to affirming that the European War was a war between Democracy and Absolutism; that the only hope of a permanent peace between all nations depended upon the establishment of democratic institutions throughout the world; that no League of Peace would be of value if a powerful autocracy was a member, and that no League of Peace would be necessary if all nations were democratic; and that in going into the war at this time we could do more to advance the cause of Democracy than if we failed to show sympathy with the democratic powers in their struggle against the autocratic government of Germany.

I said that the present time seemed to me especially propitious for action by us because it would have a great moral influence in Russia, because it would encourage the democratic movement in Germany, because it would put new spirit in the Allies already flushed with recent military successes, and because it would put an end to the charges of vacillation and hesitation, which were becoming general and bring the people solidly behind the President. . . .

The President said that he did not see how he could speak of a war for Democracy or of Russia's revolution in addressing Congress. I replied that I did not perceive any objection but in any event I was sure that he could do so indirectly by attacking the character of the autocratic government of Germany as manifested by its deeds of inhumanity, by its broken promises, and by its plots and conspiracies against this country.

To this the President only answered, "Possibly."

Whether the President was impressed with the idea of a general indictment of the German Government I do not know. I felt strongly that to go to war solely because American ships had been sunk and Americans killed would cause debate, and that the sounder basis was the duty of this and every other democratic nation to suppress an autocratic government like the German because of its atrocious character and because it was a menace to the national safety of this country and of all other countries with liberal systems of government. Such an arraignment would appeal to every liberty-loving man the world over. This I said during the discussion, but just when I do not remember.

When I had finished, Secretary Wilson[5] in his usual slow but emphatic

5 William B. Wilson, Secretary of Labor.

way said: "Mr. President, I think we must recognize the fact that Germany has made war upon this country and, therefore, I am for calling Congress together as soon as possible. I have reached this conviction with very great reluctance, but having reached it I feel that we should enter the war with the determination to employ all our resources to put an end to Prussian rule over Germany which menaces human liberty and peace all over the world. I do not believe we should employ half-measures or do it half-heartedly." . . .

Gregory,[6] who had been listening with much attention although on account of his deafness I am sure only heard his neighbors at the table, gave it as his opinion that it was useless to delay longer, that the possibility of peace with Germany was a thing of the past, and that he was in favor of assembling Congress as soon as possible, of enacting all necessary legislation, and of pursuing as aggressive action toward Germany as we were able. He went on to speak of German intrigues here, of the departure of German reservists and of the helplessness of his Department under existing laws. He said that every day's delay increased the danger and Congress ought to be called on to act at once.

After Gregory had given his views the President said, "We have not yet heard from Burleson and Daniels."

Burleson[7] spoke up immediately and said: "Mr. President, I am in favor of calling Congress together and declaring war; and when we do that I want it to be understood that we are in the war to the end, that we will do everything we can to aid the Allies and weaken Germany with money, munitions, ships, and men, so that those Prussians will realize that, when they made war on this country, they woke up a giant which will surely defeat them. I would authorize the issue of five billions in bonds and go the limit." He stopped a moment and then added, "There are many personal reasons why I regret this step, but there is no other way. It must be carried through to the bitter end."

The President then turned his head toward Daniels who sat opposite Burleson and said: "Well, Daniels?" Daniels[8] hesitated a moment as if weighing his words and then spoke in a voice which was low and trembled with emotion. His eyes were suffused with tears. He said that he saw no other course than to enter the war, that do what we would it seemed bound to come, and that, therefore, he was in favor of summoning Congress as soon as possible and getting their support for active measures against Germany.

Burleson had at previous meetings resisted an aggressive policy toward Germany, and he had, as late as the Cabinet meeting on Friday, the 16th, advocated very earnestly taking a radical stand against Great Britain on account of detention of the mails. Whenever I had called

---

6 Thomas W. Gregory, Attorney-General.
7 Albert S. Burleson, Postmaster-General.
8 Josephus Daniels, Secretary of the Navy.

attention to the illegal acts of Germany he would speak of British wrong-doings. I felt sure that he did this to cause a diversion of attention from the German violations of law. Possibly I misjudged him, and there was no such motive. His words at this meeting indicated hostility to Germany and a desire for drastic action, so I may have been mistaken.

As for Daniels his pacifist tendencies and personal devotion to Mr. Bryan and his ideas were well known. It was, therefore, a surprise to us all when he announced himself to be in favor of war. I could not but wonder whether he spoke from conviction or because he lacked strength of mind to stand out against the united opinion of his colleagues. I prefer to believe the former reason, though I am not sure.

The President said, as Daniels ceased speaking: "Everybody has spoken but you, Lane."

Lane[9] answered that he had nothing to add to what had been said by the other members of the Cabinet, with whom he entirely agreed as to the necessity of summoning Congress, declaring war and obtaining powers. He reviewed some of the things which had been said but contributed no new thought. He emphasized particularly the intensity of public indignation against the Germans and said that he felt that the people would force us to act even if we were unwilling to do so. . . .

When at last every Cabinet officer had spoken and all had expressed the opinion that war was inevitable and that Congress ought to be called in extraordinary session as soon as possible, the President in his cool, unemotional way said: "Well, gentlemen, I think that there is no doubt as to what your advice is. I thank you."

The President, during the discussion or at the close, gave no sign what course he would adopt. However as we were leaving the room he called back Burleson and me and asked our views as to the time of calling a session if he so decided. After some discussion we agreed that to prepare the necessary legislation for submission to Congress would take over a week and that, therefore, Monday, April 2nd, would be the earliest day Congress could conveniently be summoned. I asked the President if he would issue a proclamation that afternoon so it would appear in the morning papers on Wednesday. He replied smilingly: "Oh, I think I will sleep on it."

Thus ended a Cabinet meeting the influence of which may change the course of history and determine the destinies of the United States and possibly of the world. The possible results are almost inconceivably great. I am sure that every member of the Cabinet felt the vital importance of the occasion and spoke with a full realization of the grave responsibility which rested upon him as he advised the President to adopt a course which if followed can only mean open and vigorous war against the Kaiser and his Government. The solemnity of the occasion as one after another spoke was increasingly impressive and showed in

[9] Franklin K. Lane, Secretary of the Interior.

every man's face as he rose from the council table and prepared to leave the room. Lane, Houston and Redfield, however, did not hide their gratification, and I believe we all felt a deep sense of relief that not a dissenting voice had been raised to break the unanimity of opinion that there should be no further parley or delay. The ten councillors of the President had spoken as one, and he — well, no one could be sure that he would echo the same opinion and act accordingly.

15 · *Wilson's Travail*

The night before he asked Congress for a declaration of war against Germany he sent for me. . . .

I'd never seen him so worn down. He looked as if he hadn't slept, and he said he hadn't. He said he was probably going before Congress the next day to ask a declaration of war, and he'd never been so uncertain about anything in his life as about that decision. For nights, he said, he'd been lying awake going over the whole situation; over the provocation given by Germany, over the probable feeling in the United States, over the consequences to the settlement and to the world at large if we entered the melee. . . .

He said he couldn't see any alternative, that he had tried every way he knew to avoid war. "I think I know what war means," he said, and he added that if there were any possibility of avoiding war he wanted to try it. "What else can I do?" he asked. "Is there anything else I can do?"

I told him his hand had been forced by Germany, that so far as I could see we couldn't keep out.

. . . He said war would overturn the world we had known; that so long as we remained out there was a preponderance of neutrality, but that if we joined with the Allies the world would be off the peace basis. . . .

It would mean that we should lose our heads along with the rest and stop weighing right and wrong. It would mean that a majority of people in this hemisphere would go war-mad, quit thinking and devote their energies to destruction. The President said a declaration of war would mean that Germany would be beaten and so badly beaten that there would be a dictated peace, a victorious peace. . . .

---

15 Reprinted by permission from *Cobb of "The World"* (Frank I. Cobb) by John L. Heaton (New York: E. P. Dutton & Co., Inc., 1924, 1931), pp. 268–269. Frank Cobb was a well-known reporter for the *New York World*. Cobb actually had seen Wilson not on April 1, as his account indicates, but earlier in mid-March.

16 · Address of the President of the United States Delivered at a Joint Session of the Two Houses of Congress, April 2, 1917

GENTLEMEN OF THE CONGRESS: I have called the Congress into extraordinary session because there are serious, very serious, choices of policy to be made, and made immediately, which it was neither right nor constitutionally permissible that I should assume the responsibility of making.

On the 3d of February last I officially laid before you the extraordinary announcement of the Imperial German Government that on and after the 1st day of February it was its purpose to put aside all restraints of law or of humanity and use its submarines to sink every vessel that sought to approach either the ports of Great Britain and Ireland or the western coasts of Europe or any of the ports controlled by the enemies of Germany within the Mediterranean. That had seemed to be the object of the German submarine warfare earlier in the war, but since April of last year the Imperial Government had somewhat restrained the commanders of its undersea craft in conformity with its promise then given to us that passenger boats should not be sunk and that due warning would be given to all other vessels which its submarines might seek to destroy, when no resistance was offered or escape attempted, and care taken that their crews were given at least a fair chance to save their lives in their open boats. The precautions taken were meagre and haphazard enough, as was proved in distressing instance after instance in the progress of the cruel and unmanly business, but a certain degree of restraint was observed. The new policy has swept every restriction aside. Vessels of every kind, whatever their flag, their character, their cargo, their destination, their errand, have been ruthlessly sent to the bottom without warning and without thought of help or mercy for those on board, the vessels of friendly neutrals along with those of belligerents. Even hospital ships and ships carrying relief to the sorely bereaved and stricken people of Belgium, though the latter were provided with safe-conduct through the proscribed areas by the German Government itself and were distinguished by unmistakable marks of identity, have been sunk with the same reckless lack of compassion or of principle.

---

16 *Foreign Relations, 1917, Supplement 1*, pp. 195–203.

I was for a little while unable to believe that such things would in fact be done by any government that had hitherto subscribed to the humane practices of civilized nations. International law had its origin in the attempt to set up some law which would be respected and observed upon the seas, where no nation had right of dominion and where lay the free highways of the world. By painful stage after stage has that law been built up, with meagre enough results, indeed, after all was accomplished that could be accomplished, but always with a clear view, at least, of what the heart and conscience of mankind demanded. This minimum of right the German Government has swept aside under the plea of retaliation and necessity and because it had no weapons which it could use at sea except these which it is impossible to employ as it is employing them without throwing to the winds all scruples of humanity or of respect for the understandings that were supposed to underlie the intercourse of the world. I am not now thinking of the loss of property involved, immense and serious as that is, but only of the wanton and wholesale destruction of the lives of noncombatants, men, women, and children, engaged in pursuits which have always, even in the darkest periods of modern history, been deemed innocent and legitimate. Property can be paid for; the lives of peaceful and innocent people can not be. The present German submarine warfare against commerce is a warfare against mankind.

It is a war against all nations. American ships have been sunk, American lives taken, in ways which it has stirred us very deeply to learn of, but the ships and people of other neutral and friendly nations have been sunk and overwhelmed in the waters in the same way. There has been no discrimination. The challenge is to all mankind. Each nation must decide for itself how it will meet it. The choice we make for ourselves must be made with a moderation of counsel and a temperateness of judgment befitting our character and our motives as a nation. We must put excited feeling away. Our motive will not be revenge or the victorious assertion of the physical might of the nation, but only the vindication of right, of human right, of which we are only a single champion.

When I addressed the Congress on the 26th of February last,[1] I thought that it would suffice to assert our neutral rights with arms, our right to use the seas against unlawful interference, our right to keep our people safe against unlawful violence. But armed neutrality, it now appears, is impracticable. Because submarines are in effect outlaws when used as the German submarines have been used against merchant shipping, it is impossible to defend ships against their attacks as the law of nations has assumed that merchantmen would defend themselves against privateers or cruisers, visible craft giving chase upon the open sea. It is

[1] Wilson had requested authority to arm American ships for defense against U-boats. A senatorial filibuster prevented Congress from acting, but the President discovered existing statutory authority and ordered the arming.

common prudence in such circumstances, grim necessity indeed, to endeavour to destroy them before they have shown their own intention. They must be dealt with upon sight, if dealt with at all. The German Government denies the right of neutrals to use arms at all within the areas of the sea which it has proscribed, even in the defense of rights which no modern publicist has ever before questioned their right to defend. The intimation is conveyed that the armed guards which we have placed on our merchant ships will be treated as beyond the pale of law and subject to be dealt with as pirates would be. Armed neutrality is ineffectual enough at best; in such circumstances and in the face of such pretensions it is worse than ineffectual; it is likely only to produce what it was meant to prevent; it is practically certain to draw us into the war without either the rights or the effectiveness of belligerents. There is one choice we can not make, we are incapable of making: we will not choose the path of submission and suffer the most sacred rights of our nation and our people to be ignored or violated. The wrongs against which we now array ourselves are no common wrongs; they cut to the very roots of human life.

With a profound sense of the solemn and even tragical character of the step I am taking and of the grave responsibilities which it involves, but in unhesitating obedience to what I deem my constitutional duty, I advise that the Congress declare the recent course of the Imperial German Government to be in fact nothing less than war against the Government and people of the United States; that it formally accept the status of belligerent which has thus been thrust upon it; and that it take immediate steps not only to put the country in a more thorough state of defense but also to exert all its power and employ all its resources to bring the Government of the German Empire to terms and end the war.

What this will involve is clear. It will involve the utmost practicable cooperation in counsel and action with the governments now at war with Germany, and, as incident to that, the extension to those governments of the most liberal financial credits, in order that our resources may so far as possible be added to theirs. It will involve the organization and mobilization of all the material resources of the country to supply the materials of war and serve the incidental needs of the nation in the most abundant and yet the most economical and efficient way possible. It will involve the immediate full equipment of the Navy in all respects but particularly in supplying it with the best means of dealing with the enemy's submarines. It will involve the immediate addition to the armed forces of the United States already provided for by law in case of war at least 500,000 men, who should, in my opinion, be chosen upon the principle of universal liability to service, and also the authorization of subsequent additional increments of equal force so soon as they may be needed and can be handled in training. It will involve also, of course, the granting of adequate credits to the Government, sustained, I hope, so far as they can equitably be sustained by the present generation, by well conceived taxation. . . .

While we do these things, these deeply momentous things, let us be very clear, and make very clear to all the world what our motives and our objects are. My own thought has not been driven from its habitual and normal course by the unhappy events of the last two months, and I do not believe that the thought of the nation has been altered or clouded by them. I have exactly the same things in mind now that I had in mind when I addressed the Senate on the 22d of January last; the same that I had in mind when I addressed the Congress on the 3d of February and on the 26th of February. Our object now, as then, is to vindicate the principles of peace and justice in the life of the world as against selfish and autocratic power and to set up amongst the really free and self-governed peoples of the world such a concert of purpose and of action as will henceforth ensure the observance of those principles. Neutrality is no longer feasible or desirable where the peace of the world is involved and the freedom of its peoples, and the menace to that peace and freedom lies in the existence of autocratic governments backed by organized force which is controlled wholly by their will, not by the will of their people. We have seen the last of neutrality in such circumstances. We are at the beginning of an age in which it will be insisted that the same standards of conduct and of responsibility for wrong done shall be observed among nations and their governments that are observed among the individual citizens of civilized states.

We have no quarrel with the German people. We have no feeling towards them but one of sympathy and friendship. It was not upon their impulse that their Government acted in entering this war. It was not with their previous knowledge or approval. It was a war determined upon as wars used to be determined upon in the old, unhappy days when peoples were nowhere consulted by their rulers and wars were provoked and waged in the interest of dynasties or of little groups of ambitious men who were accustomed to use their fellow men as pawns and tools. Self-governed nations do not fill their neighbour states with spies or set the course of intrigue to bring about some critical posture of affairs which will give them an opportunity to strike and make conquest. Such designs can be successfully worked out only under cover and where no one has the right to ask questions. Cunningly contrived plans of deception or aggression, carried, it may be, from generation to generation, can be worked out and kept from the light only within the privacy of courts or behind the carefully guarded confidences of a narrow and privileged class. They are happily impossible where public opinion commands and insists upon full information concerning all the nation's affairs.

A steadfast concert for peace can never be maintained except by a partnership of democratic nations. No autocratic government could be trusted to keep faith within it or observe its covenants. It must be a league of honour, a partnership of opinion. Intrigue would eat its vitals away; the plottings of inner circles who could plan what they would and render account to no one would be a corruption seated at its very heart. Only free peoples can hold their purpose and their honour steady to a common end and prefer the interests of mankind to any narrow interest of their own.

Does not every American feel that assurance has been added to our hope for the future peace of the world by the wonderful and heartening things that have been happening within the last few weeks in Russia? Russia was known by those who knew it best to have been always in fact democratic at heart, in all the vital habits of her thought, in all the intimate relationships of her people that spoke their natural instinct, their habitual attitude towards life. The autocracy that crowned the summit of her political structure, long as it had stood and terrible as was the reality of its power, was not in fact Russian in origin, character, or purpose; and now it has been shaken off and the great, generous Russian people have been added in all their naïve majesty and might to the forces that are fighting for freedom in the world, for justice, and for peace. Here is a fit partner for a league of honour.

One of the things that has served to convince us that the Prussian autocracy was not and could never be our friend is that from the very outset of the present war it has filled our unsuspecting communities and even our offices of government with spies and set criminal intrigues everywhere afoot against our national unity of counsel, our peace within and without, our industries and our commerce. Indeed it is now evident that its spies were here even before the war began; and it is unhappily not a matter of conjecture but a fact proved in our courts of justice that the intrigues which have more than once come perilously near to disturbing the peace and dislocating the industries of the country have been carried on at the instigation, with the support, and even under the personal direction of official agents of the Imperial Government accredited to the Government of the United States. Even in checking these things and trying to extirpate them we have sought to put the most generous interpretation possible upon them because we knew that their source lay, not in any hostile feeling or purpose of the German people towards us (who were, no doubt, as ignorant of them as we ourselves were), but only in the selfish designs of a Government that did what it pleased and told its people nothing. But they have played their part in serving to convince us at last that that Government entertains no real friendship for us and means to act against our peace and security at its convenience. That it means to stir up enemies against us at our very doors the intercepted [Zimmermann] note to the German Minister at Mexico City is eloquent evidence.

We are accepting this challenge of hostile purpose because we know that in such a government, following such methods, we can never have a friend; and that in the presence of its organized power, always lying in wait to accomplish we know not what purpose, there can be no assured security for the democratic governments of the world. We are now about to accept gage of battle with this natural foe to liberty and shall, if necessary, spend the whole force of the nation to check and nullify its pretensions and its power. We are glad, now that we see the facts with no veil of false pretence about them, to fight thus for the ultimate peace of the world and for the liberation of its peoples, the German peoples included: for the rights of nations great and small and the privilege of men everywhere to choose their way of life and of obedience. The world must be made safe for democracy. Its peace must be planted upon the tested foundations of political liberty. We have no selfish ends to serve. We desire no conquest, no dominion. We seek no indemnities for ourselves, no material compensation for the sacrifices we shall freely make. We are but one of the champions of the rights of mankind. We shall be satisfied when those rights have been made as secure as the faith and the freedom of nations can make them.

Just because we fight without rancour and without selfish object, seeking nothing for ourselves but what we shall wish to share with all free peoples, we shall, I feel confident, conduct our operations as belligerents without passion and ourselves observe with proud punctilio the principles of right and of fair play we profess to be fighting for.

I have said nothing of the governments allied with the Imperial Government of Germany because they have not made war upon us or challenged us to defend our right and our honour. The Austro-Hungarian Government has, indeed, avowed its unqualified endorsement and acceptance of the reckless and lawless submarine warfare adopted now without disguise by the Imperial German Government, and it has therefore not been possible for this Government to receive Count Tarnowski, the Ambassador recently accredited to this Government by the Imperial and Royal Government of Austria-Hungary; but that Government has not actually engaged in warfare against citizens of the United States on the seas, and I take the liberty, for the present at least, of postponing a discussion of our relations with the authorities at Vienna. We enter this war only where we are clearly forced into it because there are no other means of defending our rights.

It will be all the easier for us to conduct ourselves as belligerents in a high spirit of right and fairness because we act without animus, not in enmity towards a people or with the desire to bring any injury or disadvantage upon them, but only in armed opposition to an irresponsible government which has thrown aside all considerations of humanity and of right and is running amuck. We are, let me say again, the sincere friends of the German people, and shall desire nothing so much as the early reestablishment of intimate relations of mutual advantage between us — however hard it may be for them, for the time being, to believe that this is spoken from our hearts. We have borne with their present government through all these bitter months because of that friendship — exercising a patience and forbearance which would otherwise have been impossible. We shall, happily, still have an opportunity to prove that friendship in our daily attitude and actions towards the millions of men and women of German birth and native sympathy, who live amongst us and share our life, and we shall be proud to prove it towards all who are in fact loyal to their neighbours and to the Government in the hour of test. They are, most of them, as true and loyal Americans as if they had never known any other fealty or allegiance. They will be prompt to stand with us in rebuking and restraining the few who may be of a different mind and purpose. If there should be disloyalty, it will be dealt with with a firm hand of stern repression; but, if it lifts its head at all, it will lift it only here and there and without countenance except from a lawless and malignant few.

It is a distressing and oppressive duty, gentlemen of the Congress, which I have performed in thus addressing you. There are, it may be, many months of fiery trial and sacrifice ahead of us. It is a fearful thing to lead this great peaceful people into war, into the most terrible and disastrous of all wars, civilization itself seeming to be in the balance. But the right is more precious than peace, and we shall fight for the things which we have always carried nearest our hearts — for democracy, for the right of those who submit to authority to have a voice in their own governments, for the rights and liberties of small nations, for a universal dominion of right by such a concert of free peoples as shall bring peace and safety to all nations and make the world itself at last free. To such a task we can dedicate our lives and our fortunes, everything that we are and everything that we have, with the pride of those who know that the day has come when America is privileged to spend her blood and her might for the principles that gave her birth and happiness and the peace which she has treasured. God helping her, she can do no other.

PART FIVE

Congress Votes for War

The great majority of Americans in all sections of the country reluctantly agreed with the President that Germany actually was waging war upon the United States and that there was no alternative but to recognize that fact. A dissident minority of progressives and pacifists in Congress opposed the war resolution, but it passed the Senate on April 4 by a vote of 82 to 6, and the House of Representatives on April 6 by 373 to 50. The following excerpts from congressional speeches on the war resolution illustrate the range of sentiments and arguments. Gilbert M. Hitchcock of Nebraska, one of the administration's leaders in the Senate, reported the resolution to the Senate and made clear the reluctance with which he and most Americans faced the task ahead. In his view, it was a war of defense against German attacks. Henry Cabot Lodge of Massachusetts, the ranking Republican on the Senate Foreign Relations Committee, spoke for his party in support of the war resolution and for the same general reasons; he also emphasized the ideological concept of the war as a defense of liberty and democracy. Among those Representatives voting against war was William L. LaFollette, a progressive Republican from Washington. LaFollette and his colleagues believed the war to be an unjust one; they feared that war would mean the end of domestic reform and were convinced that the country was being needlessly and unwisely drawn into the conflict by profit-seeking financiers and industrialists.

17 · War for Democracy

The vibrant words of President Wilson were hailed as the voice of the American people when, on April 2, he asked the Congress to "declare the recent course of the Imperial German Government to be in fact nothing less than war against the Government and people of the United States," and to "employ all of its resources to bring the Government of Germany to terms and to end the war," because "the world must be made safe for democracy." "If this, indeed, be not the voice of the nation, we are not fit to be a nation," exclaims the Chicago *Herald;* and Colonel Watterson, in his Louisville *Courier-Journal,* characterizes it as "the most significant and momentous deliverance on the part of the American people since the Declaration of Independence." "The President has heeded the mandate of the people and made their voice his own," says the Boston *Transcript,* and in so doing he "adds another to those golden pages of history which tell the story of the struggle of the sons of men up the slopes that lead to the tableland of liberty." In his words America speaks, declares the Philadelphia *North American,* and "Americans to-day will stand straighter, think clearer, and grasp more firmly the heritage of their citizenship by reason of his ringing interpretation of their decision." "Rarely has the soul of America been interpreted to America, rarely has it been translated into action with greater force, with finer statesmanship, with simpler nobility than in this message of final American revolt against 'that natural foe of liberty,' the German Imperial autocracy," remarks the Chicago *Evening Post,* one of an influential chain of newspapers edited by Mr. John S. Shaffer. He declares this summons to war for democracy "so noble, so generous, that it might righteously lead the German people themselves to join the democrats of the world in the cry of 'On to Berlin!' to destroy the last stronghold of autocracy."

While this far-ranging dream of the Chicago editor may leave probability far behind, there is at least ample evidence that the President's definition of this nation's motives and intention in entering "the most terrible and disastrous of all wars" worked a miracle of crystallization and unification in American sentiment. Even the militant pacifist who assaulted Senator Lodge because he would not promise to vote against a declaration of war profest himself converted by the President's words, as did many German-American papers and other journals whose sympathies had previously seemed more responsive to the sufferings of Germany than to the wrongs of this country. As the Topeka *Capital* remarked the day after the President addrest Congress:

---

17 *The Literary Digest,* 54:1043–1046 (April 14, 1917).

"Until yesterday America was divided into many different groups on the solemn question how best to meet the issues raised by attacks persistently made in defiance of the laws of nations upon American rights and lives at sea. To-day we stand behind the nation's chosen leader in his weighty responsibility and in his reluctant decision to meet war by war."

Thus journals like the Hearst papers, hitherto opposed to taking a firm attitude toward Germany, now advocate a vigorous prosecution of the war and praise the President's stand. "Where the flag leads, all America will follow," declares the Milwaukee *Free Press*, a paper recently thought by some to favor the Washington Administration less than the Government at Berlin. The pacifist San Francisco *Chronicle*, recognizing that now the price of peace is war, admits that "there remains but one course for any loyal American to take, and that is to carve out a peace that will be lasting." The New York *Evening Mail*, which was acquired by its present owners for the avowed purpose of getting a fairer hearing for Germany's side of the case, declares that President Wilson "deserves, and will have, a united America at his back." The leading German newspapers of Chicago, according to a dispatch from that city, "demand that naturalized and unnaturalized Germans in the United States make whatever sacrifice the country asks to conquer the Kaiser," and the *New-Yorker Staats-Zeitung* sees in this hour of bitter gravity "but one duty — America!" Other German-American comment is printed on page 1051. *The Advocate of Peace*, organ of the American Peace Society, admits that there is "one logical excuse for entering this war." It says: "To plunge with a flaming sword into this horror could find no excuse save that peace had become more intolerable and unjust to ourselves and the world than war." Throughout the nation, correspondents report, the response to the President's request for a declaration of a state of war against Germany was "vigorous and unanimous." . . .

18 · *Congress Debates America's Entry into the War*

PRO:

Mr. HITCHCOCK. Mr. President, what I shall say in support of the joint resolution will be short. The time for action has arrived. The time for discussion has passed. The President of the United States has

---

18 *Congressional Record*, Vol. 55, 65th Cong., 1st. sess., pp. 200–201, 207–208, 371–372.

already stated more clearly, more conclusively, and more effectively than I can the reasons which make this great step now to be taken necessary.

The joint resolution provides for war against the Imperial German Government. It is framed on the lines of other war declarations of Congress, in that it directs the President to employ the military and naval forces of the country to carry the war to a successful termination. It also conforms to the precedents of other declarations when Congress has entered upon the solemn business of war by declaring that a state of war already exists. It places the responsibility of this war squarely upon the shoulders of the Imperial German Government, which is charged with having committed repeated acts of war against the United States. Over and above all this, however, the measure is unquestionably also a declaration of war.

Mr. President, in presenting the joint resolution I am impressed with the solemnity of the occasion. Some may be filled with joy at the prospect of war. To me it is depressing and dreadful. The enormous cost which the people must pay, the great increased cost of living which they must meet, the enormous burden of taxes which they must bear, and the still greater heritage of debt which they must incur stagger my mind. The awful sacrifice of life that must follow sickens my heart. I am sure other Senators have the same feeling. I am sure the great body of the American people have it also.

Our country has nothing material to gain by victory. We want no more territory; we demand no indemnity. We have no historic grudges to settle, and no racial antipathies to gratify. . . .

We alone of all the nations, Mr. President, will spend our treasure and sacrifice our lives without possibility of material gain. We are going to war, Mr. President, to vindicate our honor and to maintain our independence as a great nation. We are going to war, as the President has stated, in defense of humanity. Such quarrel as we have with the Imperial Government of Germany was not of our seeking. It was forced upon us. We did much to avoid it.

For nearly three years of this struggle our country has steadily held to its purpose to avoid war if possible. This has been true not only of the President but of Congress; and it has been true of the American people. One desperate act of the Imperial German Government after another has added to the provocation. I do not mean to say, Mr. President, that Germany has desired war with us; I do not believe it; but the German Government has been desperate and has taken desperate chances.

The invasion of Belgium shocked the sense of justice of the whole civilized world and subjected American neutrality to its first great strain. The sinking of the *Lusitania,* with hundreds of innocent passengers, men, women, and children, many of them Americans, sent a thrill of horror through America, and would have produced war had it not been for the moderation of President Wilson and his success finally in securing from the German Government an agreement to modify its methods and conform them to the rules of international law and to the dictates of humanity.

It is customary, Mr. President, to say that this agreement was violated by Germany, but it is more just and more correct to say that Germany had reserved the right to revoke it under certain conditions and exercised that right by revoking it on February first of this year. This also was an act of desperation. It was not intended to provoke war with us, but it was followed by acts of war upon us. They were not made for the deliberate purpose of injuring us, but rather to starve the English people. The effect on us, however, was the same. We were ordered off the high seas. We then dissolved diplomatic relations with Germany. We might then have gone to war. We could not submit; no great nation could remain great and independent if it did so. No great nation could maintain its place in history if it permitted another to order it off the seas; if it permitted another to bottle up its commerce; if it permitted another to dictate to it as to the exercise of its unquestioned right and to impose the penalty of murder of its citizens in case of refusal. . . .

The American people, Mr. President, have clung to the hope through all these months that the dread alternative might be avoided. Like the Savior of man in the garden of Gethsemane, they have prayed that the bitter cup of sacrifice might pass from them. They have prayed that it might not be necessary to make the sacrifice for the protection of humanity and the vindication of national honor. All has been in vain. All patience, all moderation, and all long-suffering have apparently been in vain — not entirely in vain, though, Mr. President, because we have avoided the horrors of war for two years or more; but the time has now come when further delay is impossible. . . .

I can not at this moment cast my vote against war without doing a vain and foolish thing. My act would only serve to weaken my country in the face of the enemy and in the face of inevitable war. Therefore, Mr. President, I have obeyed the instructions of the Committee on Foreign Relations and made this report to the Senate, and I am now ready to take my place with those who will back to the utmost the President of the United States in prosecuting this war for the honor of the country and in the interest of humanity.

Mr. LODGE. Mr. President, no one is more conscious than I that this is a moment for action and not for debate. But, as a member of the Committee on Foreign Relations and having taken part in framing this resolution, I wish briefly to state why I support it with the greatest earnestness of which I am capable.

The most momentous power entrusted to Congress by the Constitution is the authority to declare war, and never has Congress been called to a more solemn exercise of this great function than at this moment. We have submitted to wrongs and outrages from the central powers of

Europe — wrongs which involve not only injury to property but the destruction of American lives — with a long patience. We have borne and foreborne to the very limit of endurance. Now the inevitable end is here and we are about to declare war against Germany.

Speaking for myself and, I hope, for my associates generally on this side of the Chamber, I desire to say that in this crisis, and when the country is at war, party lines will disappear, and this disappearance of the party line will, I am confident, not be confined to the minority. Both Democrats and Republicans must forget party in the presence of the common danger. This is not, and can not be, a party war. It is a war in which all Americans must be united, and no one must ask a loyal citizen, high or low, who seeks to serve his country in the field or in civil life to what party he belongs, any more than it would be possible to ask his religion or his race. . . .

Mr. President, no one feels the horrors of war more than I. It is with no light heart, but with profound sadness, although with hope and courage, that I see my country compelled to enter the great field of conflict. But there are, in my opinion, some things worse for a nation than war. National degeneracy is worse; national cowardice is worse. The division of our people into race groups, striving to direct the course of the United States in the interest of some other country when we should have but one allegiance, one hope, and one tradition is far worse. All these dangers have been gathering about us and darkening the horizon during the last three years. Whatever suffering and misery war may bring it will at least sweep these foul things away. Instead of division into race groups, it will unify us into one Nation, and national degeneracy and national cowardice will slink back into the darkness from which they should never have emerged.

I also believe that on our entrance into this war, under the conditions which it has assumed, our future peace, our independence as a proud and high-spirited Nation, our very security are at stake. There is no other way, as I see it, except by war to save these things without which national existence is a mockery and a sham. But there is a still higher purpose here as I look upon it. The President has said with great justice that Germany is making war on all nations. We do not enter upon this war to secure victory for one nation as against another. We enter this war to unite with those who are fighting the common foe in order to preserve human freedom, democracy, and modern civilization. They are all in grievous peril; they are all threatened. This war is a war, as I see it, against barbarism, not the anarchical barbarism of what are known as the Dark Ages, but organized barbarism panoplied in all the devices for the destruction of human life which science, beneficent science, can bring forth. We are resisting an effort to thrust mankind back to forms of government, to political creeds and methods of conquest which we had hoped had disappeared forever from the world. We are fighting against a nation which, in the fashion of centuries ago, drags the inhabitants of conquered lands into slavery; which carries off women and girls for even worse purposes; which in its mad desire to conquer mankind and trample them under foot has stopped at no wrong, has regarded no treaty. The work which we are called upon to do when we enter this war is to preserve the principles of human liberty, the principles of democracy, and the light of modern civilization; all that we most love, all that we hold dearer than life itself. In such a battle we can not fail to win. I am glad that my country is to share in this preservation of human freedom. I wish to see my country gathered with the other nations who are fighting for the same end when the time for peace comes. We seek no conquests, we desire no territory and no new dominions. We wish simply to preserve our own peace and our own security, to uphold the great doctrine which guards the American hemisphere, and to see the disappearance of all wars or rumors of wars from the East, if any dangers there exist. What we want most of all by this victory which we shall help to win is to secure the world's peace, broad-based on freedom and democracy, a world not controlled by a Prussian military autocracy, by Hohenzollerns and Hapsburgs, but by the will of the free people of the earth. We shall achieve this result, and when we achieve it we shall be able to say that we have helped to confer great blessings upon mankind, and that we have not fought in vain. [Manifestations of applause in the galleries.]

CON:

Mr. LA FOLLETTE. Mr. Chairman, when history records the truth about this awful act we are about to commit here, which means the maiming and dismembering of thousands of our noble boys and the deaths of thousands more, it will record that the Congress of the United States made this declaration of war under a misapprehension of the facts inexcusable in itself and that the people at large acquiesced in it on the theory that the Congress should have the facts, and would not make a declaration of war not justified by every rule of equity and fair dealing between nations, impartially applied by this country to all belligerents, and that after our following that course one of these contesting nations, despite our impartial action, had wantonly destroyed our legitimate commerce and destroyed the lives of some of our people.

I say the people acquiesce in our actions here to-day on exactly that false assumption of the facts. We have not treated, as a Government, these belligerents with any degree of impartiality; but, on the contrary, have demanded of one of them absolute obedience to our ideas and interpretations of international law, and have allowed at least one of the other belligerents to override at will the established rules and practice of all the civilized nations of the world for a hundred years with but feeble protest, and, in many cases, with no protest at all.

We surrendered to Great Britain practically all we contested for in the War of 1812. It is true, as far as we know, that she has not impressed our seamen, but she has seized and appropriated to her own use entire cargoes and the ships that carried them. Not carriers in European trade, but carriers to South America.

One of the underlying causes of the awful holocaust in Europe was because Germany had by her systematized reductions in cost of manufacturing, by subsidization of transportation lines and methods of credits made such serious inroads on Great Britain's trade in South America as to seriously disturb her equanimity and threaten her prestige as well as attendant profits.

Mr. Chairman, this war now devastating Europe so ruthlessly is not a war of humanity, but a war of commercialism, and there is not a student of economic conditions within the sound of my voice but knows that to be the fundamental cause of that war, although there are many primary and intermediate questions entering into it. But I digress, Mr. Chairman. I have said that Great Britain has seized our ships engaged in peaceful commerce on the Western Hemisphere, surrounded by all the hallowed shades of the Monroe doctrine, which we are about to abrogate; has taken them to England and impressed them into her own service, and apparently without protest from our Government now demanding a strict accounting by Germany.

Mr. Chairman, there is no doubt in my mind but that Germany's action in regard to her submarine warfare is reprehensible, is wrong, and would merit punishment; but, Mr. Chairman, can we consistently declare war on Germany and enter into an alliance with "perfidious Albion," who, without regard to international law, laid down a prescribed zone in the Atlantic Ocean and the North Sea sowing those waters with deadly contact mines. Three of our vessels were sunk in this prescribed zone with attendant loss of life; many other vessels were likewise destroyed without protest by our Government, which by indisputable evidence has, to some extent at least, suppressed the facts in regard to the matter.

Mr. Chairman, is a life lost by the destruction of a vessel, coming in contact with a floating mine less dear than one lost on a vessel sunk by a torpedo fired by a submarine? Is the water less cold or wet?

Mr. Chairman, the highwayman who holds you up is less culpable than the coward who sends you a bomb by express or through the mail or sets a spring gun. The floating mine, in my judgment, is more despicable than the submarine, whose operators are at least taking some chances of losing their own lives. We are asked to go into partnership with the belligerent who prescribed a zone and sowed it full of mines to help it destroy the belligerent who prescribed a zone and in that zone uses submarines. Oh, consistency, thou art a jewel! . . .

The President of the United States in his message of the 2d of April said that the European war was brought on by Germany's rulers without the sanction or will of the people. For God's sake, what are we doing now? Does the President of the United States feel that the will of the American people is being consulted in regard to this declaration of war? The people of Germany surely had as much consideration as he has given the people of the United States. He has heard the cry of the Shylocks calling for their pound of flesh; later on he will hear the cry of Rachel weeping for her children and mourning because they are not, sacrificed to make good the pound of flesh in the name of liberty. The exclamation "O Liberty! Liberty! how many crimes are committed in thy name!" was well made.

Ours is the greatest Nation on the face of the globe. We have had a chance, if we had maintained a strict neutrality, to have bound up the wounds of the oppressed and to have upheld the tenets of the highest civilization throughout the world. But, no; we are asked to go into partnership with the country that has never allowed justice and right to have any weight with her when conquest and gold were placed in the balance. In India, which she held by right of conquest, as a punishment to those natives of that country who desired to be free of England's yoke and rebelled, even as did we in our Revolutionary period, she mercifully tied many of the rebels to the mouths of her cannon and humanely blew them to atoms as a sample of English Christianity. She destroyed the Boer Republic by intrigue and force of arms; she forced, for love of gold, the opium trade on China. Christian England, our would-be partner! In the Napoleonic wars she, by force of arms, confiscated the entire shipping of small but neutral nations to her own use, just as she has in a smaller degree appropriated ships of our citizens to her own use within the past two years. During the Civil War she fell over herself to recognize the Confederacy, and gave it every encouragement possible. Now we are asked to become her faithful ally against a country that, whatever her faults, surely has no blacker record than that of Christian England; to contribute our money and our people in the holy name of liberty to destroy one belligerent, which the President designates as Prussian militarism, a menace of the world; but English navalism, which is surely as great a menace, we enter into partnership with. George Washington said, "Avoid European entanglements," but we are recklessly entering a path to the end of which no man can foresee or comprehend, at the behest of, in many cases, a venal press and of a pacifist President.

God pity our country, gentlemen of the House of Representatives, if you desire that this cup be placed to our country's lips to quaff for crimes committed by a country for unneutral actions and that we enter into an alliance with another country which has been much less neutral. You may do so; I can not so vote at this time. . . .

Mr. Chairman, throughout the country patriotic meetings are being held to encourage enlistments of our young men and boys into the Army to engage in this war in advance of our declaration.

Mr. Chairman, I suggest a resolution, which should be passed and adhered to by the young men of our country and by our soldiers who are asked to enter the trenches of Europe:

"I hereby pledge myself to the service of my country and will guarantee to go and uphold its honor and its flag as soon as the sons of all the newspaper editors who have stood out for our entering the war, and who are of age for enlistment, have enlisted for the cause and the proprietors and editors themselves have patriotically enlisted, on the theory that they should feel it their duty to do so as instigators of the act."

Likewise, Mr. Chairman, the sons of manufacturers of ammunition and war supplies, and all stockholders making profits from such trade. They should freely offer their sons on the altar of their country and, in case of their being under military age, go themselves. Likewise, Mr. Chairman, the J. Pierpont Morgans and their associates, who have floated war loans running into millions which they now want the United States to guarantee by entering the European war; after they and all the holders of such securities have offered their sons and themselves, when of military age, on the altar of their country, and, Mr. Chairman, when the above-mentioned persons have no sons and are too old themselves to accept military service, then they shall, to make good their desire for the upholding of American honor and American rights, donate in lieu of such service of selves or sons one-half of all their worldly goods to make good their patriotic desire for our entering the European war in the name of liberty and patriotism.

Mr. Chairman, it will be fitting for those who have really nothing at stake in this war but death to enter into it and give their lives in the name of liberty and patriotism, after the persons covered by the above resolution have done their part as above suggested and many thousands of our citizens will see it that way ere long. . . .

 V

THE WAR IN
RETROSPECT

PART ONE

Propaganda and American Intervention

Although President Wilson stated in his War Address on April 2 that the immediate cause of America's entry into the conflict was German submarine warfare, he emphasized that the struggle was essentially a "war for democracy." Wartime propaganda endlessly reiterated the idealistic objectives of the "Great Crusade": the war to end wars; the universal triumph of democracy over autocracy; the writing of a just peace and the establishment of a League of Nations to ensure its perpetuation. Wilson's hopes were not to be realized, and the postwar reaction in America, and its subsequent effort to return to the prewar pattern of isolation — which culminated in the Senate's rejection of membership with the League — caused many disillusioned citizens to regard the intervention in 1917 as an aberration. Why then had it occurred?

The following selection by historian Horace C. Peterson, published in 1939, reflects a strong conviction widespread in the 1920's and 1930's that emotions aroused by Allied propaganda had played the major role in seducing the nation from its neutral course. Great Britain was keenly aware of the importance of the United States as a supplier of Allied needs and as a potential ally, Peterson points out, and its propagandists left little to chance in their efforts to influence American opinion. A secret ministry of War Propaganda was established in London at Wellington House, under the charge of Charles Masterman. The American section was directed by Sir Gilbert Parker, assisted by, among others, the historian Arnold J. Toynbee. Parker's staff compiled a mailing list of prominent American citizens and organizations, to whom a continuous stream of carefully prepared and selected materials was sent — books, pamphlets, letters, reprinted speeches and pictorial materials, designed to defend the rightness of the Allied cause against the allegedly brutal, militaristic and aggressive Central Powers. In addition, other agencies of the British government censored the mails and cables and deleted all but pro-Ally news to the United States. Since it was the practice — established in pre-war days — of American news services and newspapers to rely upon British and French sources for reports about the continent, the inevitable result was that information reaching the United States about the causes and nature of the Great War had a heavily pro-Ally bias.

Professor Peterson (1902–1952) taught at the University of Oklahoma from 1936 until his death. He was then at work on a study of the opposition to war in America during 1917–1918 that was subsequently revised and published by his colleague, G. C. Fite, in 1957.

1 · Propaganda for War
by H. C. Peterson

The reasons back of the American decision of April, 1917, were not unlike those which had governed the European nations in the crisis of August, 1914. There was the same overcharged atmosphere of hate and distrust; there was the same helplessness resulting from an entanglement of interests; and there was the same stubbornness and political ineptitude on the part of the statesmen. Even the immediate cause for American entrance into the war was brought about by a political impasse similar to that of 1914. Like Grey, Poincaré[1], and the Kaiser, the American and German officials had taken an extreme position from which they could not retreat without a loss of prestige to themselves and their nations. Wilson, like his European contemporaries, chose war rather than accept a diplomatic defeat, and, again like them, justified himself by claiming that the United States was entering the war to uphold peace, liberty, democracy, and the rights of small nations.

The most important of the reasons for the American action in 1917, however, was none of these things — it was instead the attitude of mind in this country — the product of British propaganda. People under the influence of the propaganda came to look upon the struggle of 1914–18 as a simple conflict between the forces of good and evil; they felt that all that was wrong was that certain malevolent individuals had gained control of an autocratic government and were attempting to dictate to the rest of the world. In the minds of American leaders there was developed a blind hatred of everything German. After this hatred had distorted American neutrality, it created a willingness to sacrifice American youth in an attempt to punish the hated nation.

But, even if the propaganda version had been true, no entire nation or race can justly be punished for the actions of single individuals or leaders. Such a course means that the innocent are to be made to pay for the misdeeds of the guilty. In spite of this truth the concept of retaliation was applied in making up the peace treaty and was responsible for making that document vicious. That which made it unworkable also stemmed from the propaganda. Out of an untrue interpretation of what was happening American leaders arrived at an utterly fallacious conclusion as to what could be achieved. In other words the propaganda was not only responsible in a large degree for American entrance into the war, but it was also responsible for the temper and irrationality of the peace treaty and the vindictiveness of the postwar years.

[1] President of France in 1914.

---

1 From *Propaganda for War: The Campaign Against American Neutrality, 1914–1917*, by H. C. Peterson. Copyright 1939 by the University of Oklahoma Press. Pp. 326–330.

The overwrought nature of post-war events is, of course, but a reflection of the extravagance of wartime propaganda, but it is in addition a direct outcome of the warped interpretation of the meaning of the war embodied in that propaganda. The propaganda blinded men completely to the actual forces at work. Economics, nationalism, power politics, and the rise and decline of nations came to mean nothing. American leaders thought that the appalling political crudities of the Germans were the cause for Europe's difficulties instead of realizing that they were merely the outward manifestation of a deep historical force, of a shift in political power. They failed to see that the war was merely one in the long series of wars which the European set-up makes inevitable — that it was a natural concomitant of the political transition caused by Germany's rise to power. . . .

It is useless to criticize Great Britain for the propaganda — for spreading falsehoods and exaggerated interpretations of their own and their enemy's actions. Locked in a life-and-death struggle it was only natural that she should have vilified her enemy and have done everything in her power to gain help. The United States would do the same thing. Criticism can only be directed against America's leaders for failing to see that the propaganda arguments were largely irrelevant and that the causes for Europe's troubles were not given in these arguments.

But the propaganda was accepted largely at face value. With President Wilson it was especially important, influencing him to such an extent that he subordinated the American desire for peace to his own desire for an Anglo-French victory. It caused him to be unneutral, perhaps unconsciously, until it was too late for him to exert pressure to bring about a just peace. It caused him, in the first twenty-one months of the war, to defeat most of the attempts at neutrality which might have been disadvantageous to the Allies.

In order to remove the causes for German submarine warfare, some Americans desired that pressure be exerted on Great Britain forcing her to relax the illegal blockade of the Central Powers. Wilson, however, refused to do anything which would embarrass the Allies. Many Americans wished an embargo on munitions; Wilson objected. Bryan prohibited loans to the warring nations; Wilson lifted the ban. Bryan asked for permission to warn Americans from traveling on foreign ships; Wilson refused. Congress tried to pass a bill preventing Americans from traveling on the armed ships of belligerents; Wilson personally defeated the measure. The President's partisanship was so apparent that even the British stated: "During the period while America was neutral all the issues in dispute between England and America were decided as England wished."

Although no serious attempt was ever made to compel Great Britain to comply with international law, notes were sent to Germany threatening war if she infringed upon what Wilson called American rights. The public was told that the argument with Great Britain was concerned

with property while that with Germany was concerned with lives. This
served to hide the actual claims on the part of Mr. Wilson which today
seem almost fantastic. He was not insisting that Americans were privileged to travel on American ships in peaceful waters. And no Americans
were killed on American ships previous to February, 1917, under circumstances which would have justified war. What he was insisting on, at
the price of war, was the right of Americans to travel in the war zone
(1) on foreign ships of belligerent nationality, (2) on foreign ships
which were armed, and (3) on foreign ships carrying munitions and
other supplies of war. Wilson contended that these were absolutely
inviolable, and that they must be given precedence by the warring
powers even when those nations were struggling for their very existence.
He refused to make any concessions whatsoever — ignoring the fundamental rule of politics, that people and nations live together only by a
patient adjustment of interests.

By 1917 the situation was beyond his control and "he was unprotected
from his own ultimata, which never would have been issued had
peace been his policy. But when finally the dilemmas and confusion led
him into the war, no suggestion appeared that the mishandling of the
American case might have had something to do with our misfortunes.
On the contrary, the American position was pictured as unchallengeable
— a malevolent aggressor had dragged the American people into war.
The débâcle was then rationalized not as a defense of the freedom of the
seas, even against submarine attack, but as a great crusade to end war,
a championship of democracy against autocracy, a kind of religious war
which laid the foundation for that current conflict of ideologies which
threatens new wars. . . .

In the last analysis the American government was forced to join the
Allies in 1917 because it had previously surrendered to them all its
material, diplomatic, and moral support. Norway, Sweden, Denmark,
and Holland refrained from such unneutral conduct and, in spite of the
fact that they suffered a great deal more than did this country, they
escaped becoming involved. Certainly if the United States had emulated
their self-restraint, she also could have remained at peace. The reason
she did not act in the same way was because of the tremendously effective British propaganda campaign. In Europe the agents of Wellington
House[2] had to compete with the propagandists of the Central Powers.
In the United States, however, they had a free field and controlled public
opinion almost as closely as they did within their own boundaries. Consequently there was developed within the United States a climate of
opinion which influenced finance, industry, and government.

To some the history of the "neutrality" period demonstrates that the
United States cannot keep out of war. But the facts do not bear out
any such contention. What it does prove is that it is impossible to be
unneutral and keep out of war.

[2] Headquarters of the British Propaganda Ministry in London.

PART TWO

Unneutrality: Economic
Entanglement

Isolationist sentiment in America reached its peak in the early 1930's, the result of a resurgent spirit of nationalism, a severe economic depression, and ominous signs of new tensions and rivalries in Europe and the Far East. The isolationist cause was further promoted by a series of sensational congressional hearings under the chairmanship of Senator Gerald P. Nye of North Dakota, which began in 1934 and had as their target the allegedly exorbitant profits exacted by the munitions industry during the war. The disclosures of the Nye Committee seemed to many citizens to prove conclusively that the nation had been drawn into World War I by profiteering arms manufacturers and bankers. The growing isolationist sentiment and abhorrence of war was manifested in the neutrality acts of 1935–1937, which sought to preclude another involvement like that of 1917 by prohibiting the sale of arms to belligerents, the advancing of loans to belligerent governments, and American citizens traveling aboard ships of warring nations. In the following excerpt from *America Goes to War*, published in 1938, Charles C. Tansill disclaims being a revisionist or having any particular thesis to advance. Nevertheless his study strongly implies that America became involved in the First World War primarily because her actions had not been those of a genuine neutral. Sentiment, propaganda, pro-Ally views of government leaders, and close economic ties with the Allied Powers all played their part, according to Tansill, in pulling the country into the war.

Professor Tansill (1890–1964) taught at Georgetown University and was the author of a number of works in American diplomatic history. He also published in 1952 what is regarded as the most scholarly study from the revisionist point of view of American involvement in World War II, *Backdoor to War*.

2 · Supplying the Sinews of War by C. C. Tansill

Within a few weeks after the outbreak of the World War it became apparent to competent military observers that victory for either side would largely depend upon the possession of adequate supplies of munitions of war. The nation that labored under the greatest handicap in this regard was Great Britain, whose assistance to France in the early months of the war was sharply limited because of a glaring deficiency in effective artillery and in high explosive shells. Although the production of British factories could be rapidly increased there would remain an alarming shortage of supplies necessary for the conduct of successful warfare. The only means of meeting this situation was through the importation of munitions of war from neutral nations. European neutrals, however, soon placed embargoes upon the shipment of war materials, so the British Government was forced to look to America as the only important neutral that could supply her needs.

In America the rise of "big business" had produced a vast industrial organization that could fill war orders in an amazingly short time, and the very fact that this organization was severely suffering from a widespread business depression meant that these orders would receive special attention. It was not long before immense exports of American munitions were crowding British ports. In 1916 the value of American war supplies to the Allied Governments amounted to more than a billion dollars, and the intimate economic ties thus created served to supplement the sentimental bonds that had long attached America to the side of the Entente Powers. . . .

Further action to clarify popular misapprehensions concerning contraband trade was taken on August 15, [1914] when the Department of State issued a circular which clearly indicated that commerce between the United States and the belligerent governments was not "suspended" because of the existing war. With reference to contraband it was pointed out that the export of such articles was not "prohibited by the neutrality laws or the President's proclamation." Attention was called, however, to the fact that contraband was subject to seizure and confiscation and was not entitled to the protection of the American Government.

Despite this circular there still remained evident uncertainty in the minds of many exporters relative to the status of contraband shipments.

2 Copyright 1938 by Charles C. Tansill. From *America Goes to War* by Charles C. Tansill, by permission of Little, Brown and Co., pp. 32, 36–38, 53–55, 61–66.

Each week the Department of State was deluged with inquiries regarding the legality of contraband trade, and in order to meet this situation the Secretary of State finally issued, on October 15, 1914, a circular which President Wilson referred to as "excellent." Once again it was indicated that "a citizen of the United States can sell to a belligerent government or its agent any article of commerce which he pleases." He is not prohibited from doing this by "any rule of international law, by any treaty provision, or by any statute of the United States." For the Government of the United States in its official capacity to sell to a belligerent nation would be an unneutral act, but

> for a private individual to sell to a belligerent any product of the United States is neither unlawful nor unneutral, nor within the power of the Executive to prevent or control.

These circulars made it unmistakably clear that American citizens had a legal right to sell munitions of war to all the belligerent powers. But the effectiveness of the British blockade soon proved that this was only an abstract right. Unless the American Government took measures to open the lanes of commerce to the Central Powers, it was apparent that the United States would fast be converted into a base of war supplies for the Allied Governments. To many Americans this situation seemed so inconsistent with professed neutrality that pressure was brought to bear upon Congress, and in December, 1914, legislation was proposed which looked toward the prohibition of exports of munitions of war.

In support of his bill prohibiting the shipment of munitions of war Senator Hitchcock remarked as follows: —

> "Our nation stands for peace, and it seems to me outrageous that we should be running our powder-factories and our gunworks night and day to furnish means for carrying on the present war. . . . Two years ago we authorized the President to prohibit the exportation of arms and ammunition to Mexico because we did not feel that this country should help to continue the war there."

Immediately after the introduction of this restrictive legislation in Congress the press throughout the United States began a sharp debate upon every aspect of American neutrality as affected by the export of munitions of war. In January, 1915, the *Literary Digest* submitted to a thousand representative newspapers the following question: "Do you favor stopping by law the exportation of war materials to belligerents?" Of the 440 replies, 244 answered "No"; 167 answered "Yes"; and 20 were noncommittal. The replies, from the cities numbering more than 50,000 inhabitants, were 85 Noes to 24 Ayes. The replies from the cities with a population ranging from 10,000 to 50,000 were 77 Noes to 61 Ayes, while the replies from the cities with a population of 10,000 or less were 86 Noes to 79 Ayes.

It is apparent from this press poll that sentiment with regard to the prohibition of the export of munitions of war varied greatly with reference to the size and location of the cities which answered the question asked by the *Literary Digest*. Large cities in the industrial East were generally opposed to an embargo on exports, while many important cities in the Middle West and on the Pacific Coast were in favor of restrictive legislation. Press opinion in the smaller cities, irrespective of location, tended to be much more evenly divided on the question of an arms embargo. Even in the largest cities the German-American press was almost a unit in its ardent praise of the bill introduced by Senator Hitchcock which the Cleveland *Waechter und Anzeiger* declared would make "American neutrality less one-sided and less serviceable to England."

This vehement support of the Hitchcock bill gave deep concern to the British Government, and Sir Edward Grey protested to Ambassador Page that any legislation of that type would be "unneutral" and would constitute a departure from a "long established" American custom. Secretary Bryan quickly explained that Senator Hitchcock had failed to consult either the President or the Department of State with regard to his bill, and moreover, the Senator himself, in spite of the fact that he came from the State of Nebraska, was not a personal friend of the Secretary of State. . . .

One of the most significant aspects of the rapid growth in the export of American munitions of war to the Allied Powers is the close relationship between this trade and the economic situation in the United States during the years from 1913 to 1915. The first months of the Wilson Administration ushered in a widespread business depression which the far-reaching domestic program of the new Chief Executive seemed to intensify rather than dispel. The outbreak of the World War in August, 1914, made matters considerably worse, and the outlook for economic recovery was distinctly gloomy. Many factories were working at merely sixty per cent capacity. Estimates of the unemployed reached close to a million, with a hundred thousand of these idle men near the starvation level.

An important side-light on business conditions is given in the following letter from Andrew Carnegie to President Wilson, November 23, 1914: —

> The present Financial and Industrial situations are very distressing. I have never known such conditions, such pressing calls upon debtors to pay, and especially to reduce mortgages. Saturday morning last my Secretary reported forty-five appeals to me to meet such calls in one delivery — to-day he tells me that we shall have a hundred or more *at least*. This may change slowly, the Allies purchases from us from Horses down, are certain to be great.

When the Allied Governments began to place in the United States large orders for war materials an improvement in business conditions was soon manifest. But "hard times" persisted well into 1915 with recovery always a little doubtful. In January, 1915, the *Commercial and Financial Chronicle* believed that the "worst is undoubtedly behind us and there is occasion for rejoicing that it is." In March, 1915, some cautious editors still remained a little skeptical about returning prosperity, and *Commerce and Finance* sagely remarked that "the exuberance at first excited by the unprecedented balance in our favor is giving place to an appreciation of the truth that we cannot hope to be permanently prosperous if Europe is to fight on indefinitely." . . .

It was the rapid growth of the munitions trade which rescued America from this serious economic situation. The value of explosives exported from the United States increased from $2,793,530 in March, 1915, to $32,197,274 in November of that year. Manufactures of iron and steel exported during the same period rose from $1,363,693 to $10,776,183, while manufactures of brass mounted from $2,749,835 to $7,528,616.

It was only to be expected that the American Government should be exceedingly anxious to protect this trade that was reviving the drooping American industries. It was also obvious that the German Government would regard with growing concern these vast shipments of war supplies without which the Allied Powers would be in desperate straits. As early as February 14, 1915, Ambassador Gerard warned Secretary Bryan that German public opinion was so aroused over the American exports of munitions of war to the Allies that the situation was "very tense." . . .

As the war continued and American munitions poured into England and France in ever increasing quantities, German sentiment towards America grew more and more bitter. Ambassador Gerard in his volume *My Four Years in Germany* frequently comments upon this feeling of hostility towards the United States which was created by the munitions trade. Even in court circles the sentiment against America was manifest: —

> From the tenth of August 1914 to the twenty-fifth of September 1915, the Emperor continually refused to receive me on the ground that he would not receive the Ambassador of a country which furnished munitions to the enemies of Germany; and we were thoroughly blacklisted by all the German royalties.

In August, 1916, Ambassador Gerard reported a conversation with Gottlieb von Jagow, the German Secretary of State for Foreign Affairs, which clearly reflected the German attitude towards the American shipments of war supplies: —

> He said that the offensive in the Somme could not continue without the great supply of shells from America. He also said that recently a German submarine submerged in the Channel had to allow forty-one ships to pass and that he was sure that each ship was full of ammunition and soldiers but probably had some American (?) also on board and therefore the submarine did not torpedo without warning. He seemed quite bitter.

This attitude of von Jagow is quite understandable when we look at the rising tide of munitions from America during the year 1916. The value of explosives exported from the United States had risen from $14,658,057 in August, 1915, to $74,925,413 in August, 1916. The value of exports of copper had increased during the same period from $7,781,- 487 to $20,319,053, while the exports of brass had mounted from $4,560,- 810 to $45,213,945. According to some authorities the total value of the exports of munitions during the calendar year 1916 reached the astounding figure of $1,290,000,000.

It is no wonder that as Germany became acquainted with the fact that America was supplying the most pressing needs of the Allied Governments at a time when every German need was denied because of the British blockade, the feeling throughout the Central Powers against the United States rose to new heights. A typical expression of this sentiment towards America may be seen in the following excerpt from a volume by Dr. Heinrich Pohl: —

> Germany finds herself in the position of a warrior, hemmed in on all sides, whose enemies are all aiming at his heart. Every time this warrior succeeds in disarming the foe most harmful to him, every time the warrior strikes the sword from the hand of the enemy, a so-called neutral comes running from behind and places a new weapon in the hand of the defeated foe.

America, under the guise of neutrality, was serving the Allied Powers in a manner most suitable to their military plans against Germany. Even British publicists, who usually depreciate the contribution made by America to the Allied cause, have had to admit the decisive importance of the munitions trade, and Sir Edward Grey was frank enough to tell the real story of England's dependence upon American war supplies: —

> Germany and Austria were self-supporting in the huge supply of munitions. The Allies soon became dependent for an adequate supply on the United States. If we quarrelled with the United States we could not get that supply. It was better, therefore, to carry on the war without blockade, if need be, than to incur a break with the United States about contraband and thereby deprive the Allies of the resources necessary to carry on the war at all or with any chance of success.

To the German Government it appeared idle to talk of American neutrality in the face of this significant assistance to the Allied Powers. Moreover, it did seem that America was too prone to forget the attitude of the German Government towards the United States during the Spanish-American War. In 1898, the German Government, upon the request of the American Ambassador, searched a Spanish vessel suspected of carrying contraband from Hamburg to a Spanish port. Apparently, if this ship had been carrying contraband of war it would have been detained until this contraband cargo had been removed.

In 1914 the German Government had hardly hoped that America would follow this German precedent and refuse to permit the shipment of war supplies to the Allied Governments. As the munitions trade continued to grow, however, and it became apparent that America was serving as a base of war supplies that were necessary to Allied success, the German Government believed that this huge and decisive traffic was inconsistent with American neutrality. It was then that the German Government inclined towards the view that, in order to preserve an attitude of strict neutrality in America, the American Congress should be requested by President Wilson to give him the authority to impose an embargo upon the shipment of war supplies. In 1912, Congress had bestowed this authority upon the President with reference to the shipment of munitions to Mexico during the civil war then raging. In 1913 this war was still going on, and President Wilson, in a message to Congress in August of that year, had indicated his views as to the proper manner of preserving American neutrality: —

I deem it my duty to exercise the authority conferred upon me by the law of March 14, 1912, to see to it that neither side to this struggle now going on in Mexico receive any assistance from this side of the border. *I shall follow the best practice of nations in the matter of neutrality by forbidding the exportation of arms or munitions of war of any kind from the United States to any part of the Republic of Mexico.*

If in 1914 the President had followed "the best practice of nations in the matter of neutrality by forbidding the exportation of arms or munitions of war of any kind from the United States" it is very possible that America would not have been drawn into the World War. Before he could have proclaimed such an embargo against shipments of war materials to belligerent nations he would have had to secure the consent of Congress, but there had been no difficulty in persuading Congress to pass the necessary legislation when it came to stopping all exports of arms to Mexico. The industrial East would have fought vigorously against an embargo, but there was a strong pacifist sentiment in many sections of the United States which would have quickly rallied to the support of a restrictive policy. The President, however, never made the "slightest effort to obtain the legal authorization which would be required," and the traffic in munitions soon grew to such proportions that even had he been willing to take steps to curtail this trade it is more than doubtful whether Congress would have adopted his suggestion.

In January, 1916, Professor Charles C. Hyde, one of America's foremost authorities in the field of international law, wrote to Secretary Lansing regarding the dangers involved in the munitions trade. It was apparent to him that the American Government might have to place an embargo upon the export of war materials, and he believed that such action could safely be taken on the ground that Great Britain had refused to heed American protests against unlawful restrictions imposed upon American commerce, or upon the ground that the unrestricted exportation of arms to the Allied Governments would cause Germany to "take steps both hostile and injurious to the United States."

Under existing conditions, the United States was becoming a "base of supplies of such magnitude that unless retarded, the success of armies, possibly the fate of empires, may ultimately rest upon the output of American factories." Such a decisive rôle would inevitably lead America to become "a party to the conflict." This being so, it behooved America to study most carefully the course it should take with reference to the export of arms. There was little doubt that from a strictly legal viewpoint this trade in munitions of war had many precedents in its favor, but it was somewhat questionable whether this mere legal right as a neutral,

> . . . to sell war material to a belligerent state to enable it to cripple an adversary with which the United States is at peace, would . . . appeal to the American people to a degree such that they would consent to make war for the mere purpose of preserving that commercial privilege.

The reply of Secretary Lansing to this letter of friendly warning concerning the obvious implications of the munitions trade is not available to scholars at the present time, but from his acrid notes to Germany and to Austria-Hungary, and from the frank revelations in his *War Memoirs* it is not difficult to imagine the indifferent attitude he assumed towards such a communication. War, and not peace, was his desire. From the moment he became Secretary of State he looked forward to a conflict between the United States and Germany as a necessary incident in the crusade against German militarism. With this idea constantly in mind he was in no mood to listen to suggestions that the exports of American munitions be curtailed. He firmly believed that the Allied Governments should be given all the assistance that was possible under a most liberal interpretation of American neutrality.

America was already well advanced on the road to war, and she was not to be checked by the weak barriers of neutral obligations.

PART THREE

Intervention Defended: The Submarine Thesis

Charles Seymour (1885–1963) was a vigorous oppo-
nent of revisionist thought regarding America's entry into World War I.
A specialist in diplomatic history, he accompanied Wilson to Paris as
one of the American advisers to the commission which was to negotiate
the peace. In the essay below, published in 1935, Seymour denies that
the United States entered the war because of unneutral sentiment, Allied
propaganda, or economic motives. America entered the war, he asserts,
only because German U-boat warfare left it no choice; the submarine
alone was the cause of hostilities.

Seymour served as professor of history and subsequently as president
of Yale University. Among his publications were a biography of Colonel
House, a history of American diplomacy during the World War, and a
book of essays on the neutrality period.

3 · American Neutrality: The Experience of 1914–1917 by Charles Seymour

Threats of war in Europe have raised the question of what steps the United States should take to preserve neutrality and have led to reconsideration of the factors that brought us into the last war in 1917. There is talk of the intrigues of munitions-makers and the greed of capitalists. Less fantastic is the revival of the thesis that if we had treated Germany and the Allies with an even hand in meeting their attacks upon American neutral rights, we might have avoided intervention. A recently published outline of the years 1914–1917, by Mr. Walter Millis,[1] implies that as we had permitted infractions of our rights by the Allies we had no right to protest to the point of war against Germany's use of the submarine. But he suggests no practicable alternatives to the policy followed by President Wilson, no alternatives that would have enabled America to stay at peace. The country slithered into war, he evidently feels, much as Lloyd George once remarked that Europe had slithered into war in 1914. "Among them all," Mr. Millis writes of the Americans of 1917, "none quite knew how it had happened, nor why. . . ."

There was at least one American who was acutely aware of why the United States was brought into the World War. This was the President of the United States, who for nearly three years struggled to maintain neutrality in the face of difficulties that finally proved uncontrollable. Whether as a basis for future policy, or merely to set the historical record straight, it is worth while to review Woodrow Wilson's fight to avoid intervention.

Any inquiry into the causes of American participation in the war must begin with the personality of Wilson. His office conferred upon him a determining influence in foreign policy which was heightened by the troubled state of affairs abroad. His character was such that he never let this influence slip into other hands. He was his own foreign secretary. Conscious of the power and character of public opinion, "under bonds," as he put it, to public sentiment, he nevertheless made the major decisions on his own responsibility. He delivered his "too proud to fight" speech and he sent Bernstorff home without stopping to ask what the

[1] Walter Millis, Road to War: America, 1914–1917 (Boston, 1935).

3 Charles Seymour, "American Neutrality: the Experience of 1914–1917," Foreign Affairs, XIV (October, 1935), 26–36. Reprinted with permission. Copyrighted by the Council on Foreign Relations, Inc., New York.

man in the street would say. Dominant sentiment in the United States
was certainly pro-Ally. American economic prosperity, furthermore,
depended upon the maintenance of our trade with the Allies. But it is
a far cry from these facts to the assumption that because of them we
adopted a policy that pointed toward intervention. It would be necessary to show that they touched the strong pacifistic sentiment of Congress
and people. It would especially be necessary to show that because of
them Wilson first adopted a discriminatory attitude toward Germany and
then surrendered his determination to keep the country out of war.

Ample evidence is now available regarding Wilson's sentiments towards the belligerents. If it reveals an underlying personal sympathy
with the Allies, it also reveals a studied insistence not to permit that
feeling to affect national policy. He was so far successful that he was
attacked in turn by each belligerent group as being favorable to the
other. There can be no question that he regarded the maintenance of
peace as his first duty. Always he held to the double principle he formulated at the moment he was smarting under the news of the *Arabic's*
sinking in August 1915: "1. The people of this country count on me to
keep them out of the war; 2. It would be a calamity to the world at large
if we should be actively drawn into the conflict and so deprived of all
disinterested influence over the settlement." He maintained this attitude
in the face of what he regarded as gross affronts by Germany. "The country is undoubtedly back of me," he wrote privately in September 1915,
"and I feel myself under bonds to it to show patience to the utmost. My
chief puzzle is to determine where patience ceases to be a virtue."

But across the determination to preserve peace ran the equally strong
determination to preserve the neutral rights of the country. There was
a higher principle which the President placed above peace: the honor
of the United States. The outcome of this contradiction would be determined not by Wilson's policy but by that of the belligerents. "I know
that you are depending upon me to keep this Nation out of the war," he
said in February 1916. "So far I have done so and I pledge you my
word that, God helping me, I will — if it is possible. But you have laid
another duty upon me. You have bidden me see to it that nothing stains
or impairs the honor of the United States, and that is a matter not within
my control; that depends upon what others do, not upon what the
Government of the United States does. Therefore there may at any
moment come a time when I cannot preserve both the honor and the
peace of the United States. Do not exact of me an impossible and contradictory thing."

Against both groups of belligerents Wilson steadily maintained American neutral rights. It is by no means a fact that he accepted British and
Allied infractions of what he described as "hitherto fixed international
law." The notes of protest which he sponsored and which so greatly
annoyed those who, like Ambassador Page, frankly favored the Allied

cause, made clear that the United States did not and would not recognize the legality of the Allied pseudo-blockade. In the late summer of 1916 the President secured from Congress wide powers permitting him to prohibit loans and to impose embargoes if retaliatory measures appeared advisable. A few weeks later he asked House to warn Sir Edward Grey "in the strongest terms" that the American people were "growing more and more impatient with the intolerable conditions of neutrality, their feeling as hot against Great Britain as it was first against Germany. . . ."

That he did not actually exercise the pressure of embargoes against the British and French resulted from two factors. The first was that the conflict over Allied interference with neutral trade was pushed into the background at critical moments by the more immediate and intense conflict with Germany over the submarine campaign. "If Germany had not alienated American sympathies," wrote Colonel House, "by her mode of warfare, the United States would not have put up with Allied control of American trade on the high seas." The fact has been emphasized by Winston Churchill: "The first German U-boat campaign," he writes, "gave us our greatest assistance. It altered the whole position of our controversies with America. A great relief became immediately apparent."

The second reason for not pushing the diplomatic conflict with the Allies to the point of retaliatory measures lay in the economic interests of America. Any practicable measures designed to enforce our interpretation of international law would have ruined the interests they meant to safeguard. By our formal protests we protected our ultimate property rights and built up a case for future damages to be proved before an international tribunal. Through private negotiations we secured in large measure the protection of immediate commercial interests. Whatever the inconvenience and delays experienced in our trade with the northern European neutrals, American foreign commerce was deriving rich profits. Allied command of the sea did not touch our pockets so much as our pride. As Ambassador Spring Rice cabled to Grey, it seemed "objectionable not because it is what it is, but because it is so all-pervading." Thus if Wilson had destroyed the basis of our prosperity in order to compel immediate acceptance of the American interpretation of international law, which very few Americans understood and which even now is not entirely clear, he would have provoked something like a revolt against his administration. "If it came to the last analysis," wrote House to Wilson in the summer of 1915, "and we placed an embargo upon munitions of war and foodstuffs to please the cotton men, our whole industrial and agricultural machinery would cry out against it." Wilson's policy was designed not to favor the Allies but to protect the immediate interests of the nation and at the same time to preserve our ultimate legal rights. He yielded no principle and surrendered no claim.

The German attack upon American rights Wilson believed to be of an entirely different nature and one that must be met by different methods. The intensive submarine campaign was the answer to the system of Allied maritime control; logically an excuse might be found for it. But its effects upon neutral rights were far more disastrous. For technical reasons and to operate effectively the submarines must make their attack without warning, destroy blindly, escape as speedily as possible, leaving the sinking merchant ship, which might be neutral or belligerent, which might or might not carry contraband, with no assurance of what would happen to passengers and crew. To Wilson and to dominant American opinion, such wholesale methods of destroying enemy and neutral commerce were shocking. This was no question of "juridical niceties." The submarine campaign, unlike the Allied blockade, involved undiscriminating destruction of American property rights. It permitted no distinction between contraband and free goods. The Allied system gave to the American shipper reasonable assurance of safe passage after he had complied with certain formalities. Under the threat of the submarine the shipper faced the risk of losing his entire cargo. The Allied system did not involve the loss of American ships; if held in a British prize court the owner could find protection for them in legal procedure. The German submarine threatened the loss of the ship and the death of crew and passengers as well.

Thus from the point of view of material interests there could be no comparison between the damage resulting to Americans from the Allied blockade and that from the intensive submarine campaign. If the latter were permitted, under protests comparable to those sent to the Allies, the result would be an almost complete blockade of American commerce, since shippers would not dare send cargoes and crew out to destruction. A clear illustration of the effect of the submarine campaign on American commercial, industrial, and agricultural interests was given by the congestion of our ports that followed the threat of submarine attacks in February and March 1917. Freights were snarled, goods were spoiled, business was menaced with a complete tie-up.

Even so, Wilson might not have taken his firm stand against the submarine if merely property rights had been threatened. He was always careful not to interpret national policy in terms of purely material interests. Despite the difficulties involved, the economic aspects of the diplomatic conflict with Germany might have been adjudicated. But the submarine warfare involved attacks upon American lives, whether sailors on merchant ships or passengers. To Wilson it seemed a war on humanity. Between property interests and human rights there lay a clear distinction. It was brought home to all America when, on May 7, 1915, the *Lusitania* was sunk without warning, over eleven hundred persons drowned, men, women, and children, among them more than one hundred and twenty Americans.

"The sinking of passenger ships," wrote Wilson, "involves principles of humanity which throw into the background any special circumstances of detail that may be thought to affect the cases, principles which lift it, as the Imperial German Government will no doubt be quick to recognize and acknowledge, out of the class of ordinary subjects of diplomatic discussion or of international controversy. . . . The Government of the United States is contending for something much greater than mere rights of property or privileges of commerce. It is contending for nothing less high and sacred than the rights of humanity, which every Government honors itself in respecting and no Government is justified in resigning on behalf of those under its care and authority."

It has been frequently suggested that since the submarine campaign was designed to interrupt the flow of munitions from the United States to the Allies, Wilson might have imposed embargoes upon the export of munitions as a diplomatic bribe to Germany to give up the intensive use of the submarine. There is no indication that the President ever seriously considered this course. He was willing to utilize embargoes, if necessary as measures of retaliation against the Allies in the defense of American rights. But he was not willing to penalize ourselves in order to redress the inherent disadvantage of Germany resulting from Allied command of the seas. He agreed with Lansing that such a policy ran counter to the neutral duties of the United States. It would certainly have ruined not merely the "war babies" of industry, but the cotton and wheat growers, the copper producers, the iron and steel workers, and have thrown the country back into the bleak depression and unemployment from which it had just emerged.

There is no evidence that even the broadest sort of American embargo would have induced the Germans to forego the intensive use of the submarine. They meant to stop British imports of all raw materials, especially foodstuffs, not merely from the United States but from South America, India, and the Dominions. The purpose of the submarine campaign was far wider than the interruption of the Allied "munitions" trade with America; it was, according to the testimony given to the Reichstag investigating committee, designed to throw over the British the deadly fear of complete starvation and thus to compel them to sue for peace on German terms. Hindenburg and Ludendorff made quite plain that, in the winter of 1916–1917, nothing but the prospect of immediate peace on such terms could have prevented the resumption of the submarine campaign.

Wilson, of course, might have avoided a break with Germany by surrendering the right to send American ships and citizens out on the high seas. Thus they would not be sunk by submarines. Such a policy was suggested by Mr. Bryan and was later embodied in . . . resolutions brought before Congress. The President believed that no government was justified in making this surrender. Through his protests to the Allies he had secured, without yielding any principle, a working arrangement that gave reasonable protection to American commercial interests. Now if, under the threat of the German submarine, he withdrew protection on the seas from American goods, sailors, and passengers, he would sacrifice interests that no protests could compensate and yield principles that nothing in the future could make good. "No nation, no group of nations," he wrote to Senator Stone, "has the right, while war is in progress, to alter or disregard the principles which all nations have agreed upon in mitigation of the horrors and sufferings of war; and if the clear rights of American citizens should ever unhappily be abridged or denied by such action, we should, it seems to me, have in honor no choice as to what our own course should be. . . . We covet peace and shall preserve it at any cost but the loss of honor. To forbid our people to exercise their rights for fear we might be called upon to vindicate them would be a deep humiliation indeed."

It was all very well, Wilson pointed out, to argue that the material value of these rights could not be compared with the cost of a war. But if you begin to surrender accepted rights, where do you stop? "If in this instance we allowed expediency to take the place of principle, the door would inevitably be opened to still further concessions. Once accept a single abatement of right, and many other humiliations would certainly follow. . . . What we are contending for in this matter is of the very essence of the things that have made America a sovereign nation. She cannot yield them without conceding her own impotency as a Nation and making virtual surrender of her independent position among the nations of the world."

Such was Wilson's position, written for all the world and especially for Germany to read. He maintained it consistently from the first declaration of submarine warfare in February 1915, two years before the final break, when he warned the German Government that it would be held to "a strict accountability" for acts endangering American lives and property, and that the American Government would take any necessary steps to "secure to American citizens the full enjoyment of their acknowledged rights on the high seas." This warning was translated into specific terms a year later, after the sinking of the *Sussex,* taking the form of an ultimatum which left no further room for negotiation: "Unless the Imperial Government should now immediately declare and effect an abandonment of its present methods of submarine warfare against passenger and freight-carrying vessels, the Government of the United States can have no choice but to sever diplomatic relations with the German Empire altogether."

The Germans yielded, if only for the moment, as a result of this definite warning. During the course of 1915 they had taken von Bernstorff's warnings not too seriously, and heeded them largely because they had not yet themselves realized what a powerful weapon they possessed in the submarine. After Wilson's *Sussex* note they were under no illusions.

"There was no longer any doubt in Berlin," wrote the German Ambassador, "that persistence in the point of view they had hitherto adopted would bring about a break with the United States." But in the early autumn Hindenburg and Ludendorff threw their influence in favor of a resumption of the submarine campaign. The discussions in Berlin were clearly based upon the assumption of war with the United States. Bethmann-Hollweg later testified before the Reichstag committee: "The U-boat war meant a break and, later, war with America. It was on this point that for years the argument between the military and the political branch had turned. The decisive point was that the Supreme High Command of the Army from now on was absolutely determined to assume the responsibility of the risk which an American war meant. . . ."

The one chance of preventing the resumption of the submarine campaign and thus keeping the United States out of war, lay in peace negotiations. Bernstorff judged correctly that neither Wilson nor public opinion would permit America to enter the war on any issue other than the submarine, and that it was vital to secure a postponement of the intensive campaign. "If it once comes to peace negotiations between the combatants," he telegraphed to von Jagow, June 19, 1916, "I regard it as out of the question — even were they to fail — that the United States would enter the war against us. American public feeling in favor of peace is too strong for that. It required the hysterical excitement roused by the *Lusitania* question, and the incidents connected with it, to produce a state of mind among Americans which at times made war seem inevitable. In the absence of similar incidents, such a state of feeling could not be aroused." Hence the eagerness with which he pressed upon Colonel House the importance of peace action by Wilson before it was too late. Hence also the determination with which Wilson, who realized the approaching danger, prepared his peace note of December 18, 1916. He wanted to make it, he wrote House, "the strongest and most convincing thing I ever penned."

In the circumstances the effort was bound to fail. Its effect was confused by the issuance of Bethmann's peace statement on December 12, which made Wilson's note appear to the Allies as part of a plan to rescue the Central Powers from defeat. The Allies were quite unwilling to negotiate with an unbeaten Germany. The Germans were determined to insist upon terms which the Allies would not have accepted until all hope of victory had faded. Neither side wished the mediation of Wilson. The British . . . felt that Wilson merely talked about ideals for which the Allies were dying. "We entertain but little hope," von Jagow had written to Bernstorff, "for the result of the exercise of good offices by one whose instincts are all in favor of the English point of view, and who in addition to this, is so naïve a statesman as President Wilson." The new German Foreign Secretary, Zimmermann, said to the budget committee of the Reichstag: "The good thing about the break with the

United States is that we have finally gotten rid of this person as peace mediator."

Wilson was not discouraged by the failure of the December peace notes. He worked all through January to secure a private statement of German terms, equipped with which he could start negotiations with the Allies. He was determined to save American neutrality. On January 4, 1917, in reply to House's suggestion of the need of military preparation "in the event of war," the President insisted: "There will be no war. This country does not intend to become involved in this war. We are the only one of the great white nations that is free from war today, and it would be a crime against civilization for us to go in." On January 22 he delivered before the Senate the address which he hoped would serve as a general basis for a negotiated peace, a settlement that would leave neither the one side nor the other crushed and revengeful, "a peace without victory." It opened, as British writers later insisted, the "last opportunity of ending the war with a real peace. For America was still pacific and impartial. . . . But unhappily for mankind, the British and Prussian war machines had by then taken charge."

It is possible that if Germany had then held her hand Wilson might have been able to force negotiations. The Allies were beginning to scrape the bottom of the money chest and the time was approaching when they would be dependent upon American credits. He could soon have exercised strong pressure upon them. On the other side the Kaiser, Bethmann, and Bernstorff had no profound confidence in the submarine and were inclined towards compromise. But the decision had already been taken in Germany. On January 9 Hindenburg and Holtzendorf insisted that all chance of peace had disappeared and forced approval of the intensive submarine campaign. On January 31 Bernstorff gave notice that from the following day the engagements of the pledge given after the sinking of the *Sussex* would no longer be observed.

Thus ended Wilson's last effort to achieve a compromise peace, and the rupture between Germany and the United States became inevitable. The President saw no escape from the fulfillment of the warning he had given the previous April. The shock was the worse for Wilson inasmuch as it came just as he hoped to initiate mediation. He said "he felt as if the world had suddenly reversed itself; that after going from east to west, it had begun to go from west to east and he could not get his balance." Resentment against Germany, with whom he had been working for peace, was strong. He felt with House that Germany "desires some justification for her submarine warfare and thought she could get it by declaring her willingness to make peace." Bernstorff himself insists that it was the German declaration of submarine warfare and nothing else that mattered with Wilson. "From that time henceforward — there can be no question of any earlier period, because up to that time he had been in constant negotiation with us — he regarded the Imperial Government as morally condemned. . . . After January 31, 1917, Wilson himself was a different man. Our rejection of his proposal to mediate, by our announcement of the unrestricted U-boat war, which was to him utterly incomprehensible, turned him into an embittered enemy of the Imperial Government."

Even after the diplomatic rupture Wilson waited long weeks, to give every opportunity to the Germans to avoid war. Only actual overt acts would persuade him that they would carry their policy into effect. He was willing to negotiate everything except the sinking of passenger and merchant ships without warning. The Germans showed no sign of weakening. When it was suggested that America might be kept neutral if the submarines "overlooked" American boats, the Kaiser wrote on the margin of the memorandum which disapproved the suggestion on technical grounds: "Agreed, reject. . . . Now, once and for all, an end to negotiations with America. If Wilson wants war, let him make it, and let him then have it." On March 27, following the sinking of four American ships, the President took the decision, and on April 2 he asked Congress to declare the existence of a state of war with Germany.

So far as tests can be applied, Wilson's position was approved by the American people. Like him they were determined to stay at peace so far as the exercise of their acknowledged rights could keep them at peace, but they regarded the submarine attacks as acts of war. They were by no means prepared to sacrifice American rights on the seas and adopt a policy of non-intercourse with European belligerents and neutrals which would have resulted in economic depression or disaster in the United States. . . . On the other hand, whatever the emotional sympathy for the Allied cause in the United States and however close Allied and American commercial interests, the prevailing sentiment of the people was indelibly for peace until the submarines sank American ships. They rewarded the patience with which Wilson carried on long negotiations over the *Lusitania* as well as the firmness with which he issued the *Sussex* ultimatum by reëlecting him President in the autumn of 1916. He owed his victory to the pacifists. So far from being accused of chauvinism because of the stand he had taken against the submarine campaign, he was presented and elected on the basis of having "kept us out of war." But when on April 2, following the destruction of American ships, he declared that peace was no longer consistent with honor, Congress voted for war by tremendous majorities.

It frequently happens that the occasion for an event is mistaken for its cause. Sometimes, however, the occasion and the cause are the same. There is every evidence that the sole factor that could have driven Wilson from neutrality in the spring of 1917 was the resumption of the submarine campaign. On the very eve of his war speech he was seized by his hunger for peace. "For nights, he said, he'd been lying awake over the whole situation. . . . He said he couldn't see any alternative, that he had tried every way he knew to avoid war . . . had considered every loophole of escape, and as fast as they were discovered Germany deliberately blocked them with some new outrage." In the circumstances there was no escape, for the point had been reached which he had long foreseen and dreaded, where he could not preserve both the peace and honor of the United States. "There is one choice we cannot make, we are incapable of making," he told Congress on April 2: "we will not choose the path of submission."

PART FOUR

Wilson and the
National Interests

The outbreak of World War II, with the subsequent
involvement of the United States, caused a number of commentators,
such as journalist Walter Lippmann (*U.S. Foreign Policy: Shield of the
Republic*, 1943), to re-evaluate the nation's entry into the earlier global
struggle and to explain it on the grounds of vital national interests. Since
1945 scholars have examined the thesis that fear of a probable German
victory endangering America's security motivated the decision for intervention in 1917. Edward H. Buehrig, in *Woodrow Wilson and the Balance of Power* (1955), subjects Wilson's neutrality policies to close
analysis and concludes that the President and his advisers were aware
of and shared to a degree the view that a victorious Germany would
jeopardize the nation's security and other national interests. He recognizes, however, that Wilson's idealism and his interest in an international
collective security organization to preserve peace in the postwar world
were of more importance in shaping the President's decision — and,
indeed, that of the nation as a whole. The following article is an adapta-
tion of Buehrig's study.

The author was a member of the American delegation at the San
Francisco Conference on the United Nations and served in the State
Department for a number of years. Since 1955 he has been a Professor
of Government at Indiana University.

4 · Wilson's Neutrality Re-examined by Edward H. Buehrig

Before our entry into the First World War American policy was labeled as one of neutrality, which implied that the proper measure of relations with the belligerents was to be found in international law and, more particularly, in the rules of maritime warfare. The content of that policy failed to correspond with its label, for actually it was sharply inclined to the side of Great Britain. However, the Administration refrained from acknowledging the fact that British naval actions were not being scrupulously subjected to the test of the rules of maritime warfare. Freedom of the seas and support of Great Britain were quite different points from which to proceed. Each might have been used as the basis of separate phases of a changing policy. In fact, however, they were employed simultaneously. Since they not only failed to complement each other but were actually contradictory, the result was to subject American policy to a terrific internal tension.

The confusion over the basic tenets of its policy was not an effect deliberately sought by the Administration. It was the result in part of the historic identification of American policy with freedom of the seas and in part of a badly divided public opinion which threatened constantly to reduce the nation to incoherence. Wilson was painfully undecided over the correct premise to employ. He eventually sought escape by projecting a policy which avoided using neutrality, or German enmity, or British friendship as its point of departure but which sought to find a footing in the general interests of the international community and which aspired to peace without victory. The idea of a league of nations received Wilson's support in his address of May 27, 1916, at a time when freedom of the seas and support of the British cause had become such radically divergent paths that a new formulation of American policy was imperative.

A thread which runs consistently through the tortuous course of American policy is concern for the effect of the war on the future of the nation. Unlike the situation in 1950, security considerations did not come to a sharp focus and failed to impose discipline on public opinion and governmental policies. The people and the government were loath to believe that the nation's future well-being and freedom of action were fortuitously subject to a war whose origins, as Wilson said, did not con-

4 Reprinted by permission from Edward H. Buehrig, "Wilson's Neutrality Re-Examined," *World Politics*, III (1950), 1–19.

cern us. Nevertheless such considerations could not be escaped and exerted a subtle but compelling influence. The present article is concerned with bringing to the attention of the reader various hitherto unused documents, found for the most part in the Wilson Papers, which throw light on the interesting question of the role of political considerations in the formulation of American policy.

It would be a mistake to suppose that the early pro-British turn which American policy took reflected a considered judgment on the implication of the war for the permanent interests of the United States. Our refusal to quarrel seriously with Great Britain over trade was simply in response to a well-established friendship which we were deeply reluctant to disturb. That Germany was also a factor in the equation was given only incidental attention until she forcibly made her presence felt through the submarine. Even then, the absence in the history of American diplomacy of a positive European policy — in the sense, for example, in which it had become customary for the United States to have a Latin American policy — made it difficult for Wilson, and for American opinion generally, to judge American interests in a familiar perspective. In its inception, benevolent neutrality was not a judgment on America's relation to the war as a whole, but to Great Britain in particular.

We have an interesting indication of this British, rather than European, orientation of American policy in an account which Chandler P. Anderson records of a conversation with Wilson in early January 1915. Anderson had just returned from London, where he had been a member of the American Embassy, and at Wilson's request he came to the White House to give his personal impressions. He suggested to the President that there was a "difference between the public interests and private interests involved" in America's reaction to British treatment of neutral commerce. The national interest, he said, "would best be served by reserving all disputed questions for future settlement, instead of trying to force an immediate acceptance of our theory of the law, by threatening our displeasure and unfriendly action at a time when Great Britain was fighting for national existence." Such a position as the latter "might easily involve us in a quarrel with Great Britain, and certainly would have important consequences after the war." As to Wilson's reaction, Anderson records: "The President apparently agreed with all of this, and said that . . . the policy he had laid down was exactly in accordance with the views I had expressed." Anderson also told the President that he "thought the war would be over before the middle of summer, and that the Allies would win." On January 14, Wilson again called Anderson to the White House to repeat these views for Colonel House's benefit.

Events soon demonstrated that the United States was confronted with a much more complicated situation than one which turned exclusively on the question of British friendship with no involvement other than a problematic economic sacrifice. A situation which seemed to have been put to rest by a purely Anglo-American adjustment proved to be subject to German influence by reason of the submarine. Relentlessly, the submarine probed Anglo-American relations and challenged expedient accommodation by the United States to British practices.

Had the submarine been a less exceptionable instrument of naval warfare, the discrepancy between American professions and practice regarding neutrality's injunction of impartiality would have stood out so boldly as to have obliged the United States either to acknowledge her policy as one of benevolent neutrality or seriously to bring pressure to bear on the British. However, the submarine did not serve to clarify the character of Anglo-American relations. On the contrary, the reaction to the indiscriminate and murderous tactics of submarine warfare had the psychological result of reinforcing the reluctance to resist British practices. Less charitably put, the submarine, although it subjected American policy to enormous pressure, made it possible to rationalize the differential in American treatment of the belligerents on the basis of the difference between offenses against property rights (as committed by the British) and offenses against "fundamental rights of humanity" (as committed by the Germans). The former, Wilson said,

> . . . can be vindicated by claims for damages when the war is over, and no modern nation can decline to arbitrate such claims; but the fundamental rights of humanity cannot be. The loss of life is irreparable. Neither can direct violations of a nation's sovereignty await vindication in suit for damages. . . . These are plain principles and we have never lost sight of them . . . The record is clear and consistent throughout . . .

Bearing in mind that the loss of life referred to was that of Americans on *belligerent,* and in some cases *armed,* merchantmen, one is inclined to question whether the force of logic and the horror of the *Lusitania* disaster were the sole motivations giving voice to this often reiterated formula. It served also to disguise the strong political bias present in American policy.

This disguise confounded American and British opinion, while it infuriated German opinion. The whole weight of American interest and policy rested on the distinction between loss of life and loss of property, neither of which resulted from any act directed against the United States as such, but both of which were incidental to the struggle between Germany and Great Britain. This formulation of the issue was emotionally satisfying to Americans at the time, who preferred to accept Germany's submarine policy as a moral rather than as a political challenge. British opinion, for its part, persisted in interpreting American policy as truculent in relation to London and acquiescent in relation to Berlin. German opinion, however, was inclined to see American policy in its true light; and the reiterated insistence of the American Government that it was conducting its relations with both sides on the basis of international law and letting the chips fall where they may could hardly improve the temper of Germany's reaction.

What began as a gesture of friendship toward Great Britain developed into a factor of crucial military importance. The United States refused to put obstacles in the way of the British blockade; facilitated Allied access to American raw materials, foodstuffs, and munitions; and, at the same time, held the German submarine in check — even after the Allied merchantmen were armed for attack. Politico-military considerations were never explicitly taken as a point of departure in the formulation of these policies, but, as the war lengthened, the implications of what the United States was doing were not lost on government officials, nor did the more discerning publicists fail to understand the state of affairs which had come to pass. That this was the case is apparent on the basis of evidence in the Wilson Papers, which we shall now review.

In his conversations with and letters to Colonel House, Count von Bernstorff referred to the differential character of American policy as a matter which was mutually understood and which was not likely to undergo any change. Reporting to Wilson in a letter of April 25, 1916, on a conversation he had had with the German Ambassador, House said that Bernstorff "sees the difficulty in forcing Great Britain to make concessions in her blockade. He sees, too, that war between England and this country would be quite different from war between this country and Germany, and he will impress upon his Government the impossibility of forcing Great Britain to modify her blockade." Bernstorff, having given up hope for a compromise on the submarine mutually satisfactory to his government and the United States, had turned at this time to the possibility of a negotiated peace as the only way in which the United States could be kept out of the ranks of Germany's enemies. Somewhat rashly, he had advised his government, according to House's report to Wilson, "that the position we [the United States] take regarding submarine warfare is a fore-runner to the freedom of the seas which Germany so much desires." The inconclusiveness of this argument, and the small appeal it would have in Berlin, was apparent to House, who commented to the President: "As a matter of fact it is freedom of the seas for England and, as far as I can see, not for Germany, for it would merely restrict depredations by submarines, and the nation that controlled the seas would destroy commerce with their other warships." . . .

The modus vivendi with Germany after the *Sussex* affair, and Wilson's de-emphasis of the rules of neutrality as a point of departure in his address to the League to Enforce Peace (May 27, 1916) and after, shifted the frame of reference of Anglo-American relations. The precise question of the political interests of the United States and how best they might be served became less entangled with the rules of maritime warfare. Wilson's note of December 18, 1916, designed to get peace conversations under way, was viewed with anxiety by Plunkett,[1] who was not among

[1] Sir Horace Plunkett, a prominent Englishman with close connections to the British government.

those Englishmen favoring peace without victory. Plunkett (who was in the United States at the time) warned in a letter of December 27, 1916, against overestimating the influence of "British peace groups." He said also that he had "assured [Balfour] by cipher cable that after full discussion with you [House] I was convinced that, notwithstanding recent utterances of the President, his general attitude toward the war was that which you explained to both of us in London last February." Plunkett said that he understood "the President's difficulties and yet I believe as strongly as I did when I wrote that memorandum to our Cabinet that if the President combined with the humanitarian plea of saving human life a definite stand against the militarist contention the whole American people would follow him as they would follow no other leader." Here he hit upon the formula used by Wilson in his War Address. However, as will be pointed out presently, Plunkett had good ground for his misgivings as to whether Wilson was basing his policy on such a formula in December of 1916.

The incongruity in American policy arising out of its identification with the law of neutrality on the one hand and its politically motivated discrimination on the other is pointed out forcibly by [newsman] David Lawrence in an undated memorandum in the Wilson Papers. Lawrence said that "we must have a definite policy," which should be based on one of two alternatives: "either on consideration of law and absolute fairness to all concerned or on our destiny as it is affected by the cause for which the Allies are fighting." He feared being "dragged into this war" not because of what "Germany is doing to irritate and offend us" but because of the "things which rankle in Germany's mind to make her feel that we are not neutral and that our friendship is not genuine."

Lawrence emphasized that, first of all, this question must be decided: "Is it necessary to the permanent interests and future of the United States that the Allies shall win the war?" He gave his own answer as follows:

If it is not [necessary], our course must be one of relentless neutrality, obviously. If it is necessary that the Allies shall win, we must inquire whether they can win without our help. If they can, we must then too close our eyes to sympathies and traditions and follow the law of self-preservation and by all means remove any possible cause of trouble as between us and Germany and thereby make most remote the chances of our entering the war. I think it is almost axiomatic that if the Allies cannot win without our help, we should be openly a belligerent on their side. We should have a voice in this whole matter if it thus affects us so vitally.

However, Lawrence was "unwilling to believe that the Allies need our help as a belligerent," nor did he believe "that anything we may do as a benevolent neutral" would affect the outcome of the war. He contended that "we must press Great Britain as hard as we have Germany. . . . We must even have crises with Great Britain and talk of a break in diplomatic relations." In this way we could avoid war with Germany:

"as long as Germany can cherish the slightest hope of seeing us in controversy with Great Britain, she will not care to attack us or break with us."

Like Plunkett, Lawrence perceived that American neutrality was leading, paradoxically, to military involvement. But, whereas Plunkett was reticent about the element of discrimination in American policy, choosing to attribute the eventuality of intervention to the defense of humane principles, Lawrence viewed that policy as bent so radically to the British side that it invited reckless German retaliation. Moreover, and herein is the crucial point in his memorandum: Lawrence expressed the view that the "permanent interests and future of the United States" could not best be served by an Anglo-American solidarity which entailed the price of war with Germany. He recalled that "It is the traditional policy of the United States to balance one against another. In our early history we balanced London against Paris." Now, he said, it was "London against Berlin," and it was the resulting "disentanglement from their quarrels that keeps us safe and secure."

This counsel gave expression to an unspoken assumption underlying neutrality: namely, that one's future freedom of action and security need not be a direct object of concern, since they are indirectly taken care of by the divisions among others. One can only speculate on what Wilson's reaction might have been to such a spelling out of the political implications of a neutrality policy. Perhaps he sensed a difference between the situation of the young republic and the one which he faced — that in the earlier instance weakness had made virtue of necessity to which good luck had added the quality of retrospective wisdom. Perhaps, too, he sensed that our unhampered past was due not only to the fortuitous frictions of Europe but also to the positive accommodation achieved with Great Britain.

The posture of German-American relations after the exchange of notes in the *Sussex* affair provided an easy point of departure for American intervention by the route which Plunkett pointed out and anticipated. Wilson, however, became increasingly irreconcilable to such a prospect. Neither was he prepared to use the law of neutrality as a springboard for a balance-of-power policy, after the manner suggested by Lawrence. The freedom-of-the-seas issue had led him into a deep dilemma and he struggled in the summer, fall, and winter of 1916 to construct a European policy which, on the one hand, was not a mere adjunct to the German submarine and, on the other hand, did not require the sacrifice of Anglo-American friendship in order to escape serious trouble with the Germans. In this shift of helm, which began with the address of May 27 and culminated in his address to the Senate in the following January, Wilson did not employ the law of neutrality, nor German militarism, nor Anglo-American friendship as points of departure. He attempted the very difficult feat of judging the war and America's relation to it from the standpoint of Western civilization as a whole. He viewed Germany as a constituent part of the Western community, entitled to a voice in the common future.

This effort to rise above the exigencies of the war crashed to the ground with Germany's declaration of unrestricted submarine warfare, which forced American policy back into the neutrality matrix from which Wilson had tried to escape. Fortunately the issue took a form less awkward than it might have taken. A German declaration confined to belligerent merchantmen would have been sufficient to have invoked the threat of rupture contained in the *Sussex* note of April 18, 1916. However, a vigorous reaction to such a limited declaration would have been hard to justify against our record of benevolent neutrality, which had not stopped short of giving protection to armed Allied merchantmen. The inclusion of neutral shipping in the German declaration made it possible for Wilson to act on the basis of the broadest possible interpretation of the issue defined in the *Sussex* note. Not even Bryan was prepared to argue that the deliberate sinking of American merchantmen could go unanswered.

Nevertheless, the addition of this new facet to Germany's submarine warfare could be of only superficial significance in solving Wilson's dilemma. The uncertainty and confusion over the basic assumptions of American policy remained unalleviated. This perplexing situation, and its implications for what Wilson should do and say, was the subject of a memorandum submitted to Wilson by [journalist] Walter Lippmann on March 11, 1917.

In a covering letter, Lippmann characterizes the "situation it [the memorandum] is intended to meet" as containing three factors:

1. The very deep impression . . . [made on] American opinion by the argument that the United States enforces its rights against Germany but not against Great Britain.
2. . . . this discrimination, while it renders the German people hostile, has failed to win corresponding popular recognition in France, England, and Canada; . . . it . . . confuses popular support [in the United States] by introducing a factitious element of "unfairness."
3. The inability of the pacifist forces to see the correlation between the peace program and warlike measures which may be necessary.

Lippmann continues in his covering letter by suggesting that a statement made by the President along the lines proposed in the memorandum would accomplish the following things:

1. Education of American opinion to the truth that the issue with Germany is not mere legalism or commercialism, but one arising out of America's vital interest in a just and lasting peace.
2. Revivification of the proposal of a league for peace.
3. Capture of liberal opinion in Allied countries.

4. Encouragement of German radicals to force a statement of terms, which might either
   a) start international discussion
   b) or at least tend to divide German opinion.
5. Warn our own jingo elements that American belligerency would still remain subordinate to liberal policy.

Lippmann's memorandum attempted to preserve as a basis for American policy the utterances of Wilson from May 1916 through the following January, which took the international community as the basis of American interest and policy. Accordingly, Lippmann suggested that any statement which Wilson might make should point out that,

> The only victory in this war that could compensate mankind for its horrors is the victory of international order over national aggression. Whatever measures America takes will always be adapted to that end. It has no designs on Germany's life or her legitimate national development. . . .
>   . . . It [America] will reserve freedom of action for itself, and whenever Germany is ready to abandon aggression and enter a league of nations, America will be ready to discuss the matter through open diplomacy.

The greater part of the memorandum is concerned with an attempt to integrate the freedom-of-the-seas issue with this broader conception of American interest and the policy of international organization and co-operation derived therefrom. Lippmann avoids using the distinction between loss of life and loss of property as a justification for America's attitude toward Germany. He points out that "Germany justifies her violent assault on American lives on the ground that America has not succeeded in sustaining certain commercial rights against Great Britain." The American position in reply to this, he suggests, is "that the rights of a neutral are not the possession of a belligerent. It feels entirely free to enforce its rights or suspend them temporarily in accordance with its national purposes." That purpose, Lippmann says,

> . . . is simple and avowed. It consists in the organization of peace on the foundation of consent. To have suspended the right of shipment or travel could be justified only on the ground that Germany's purpose in the war is friendly to America's interest in international order. . . .
>   The controversy with Great Britain is suspended by the more immediate and irreparable injuries inflicted by Germany, by the intrigue and crime committed on American soil, by the refusal of Germany to disavow aggressive ambitions which if achieved would render the future peace of the world unstable.
>   In spite of all this it was the hope of the American Government that a peace could be negotiated without inflaming the whole world. The attempt to secure from Germany a statement of her principles failed to elicit a response, and America was forced to conclude that Germany is fighting for a victory subversive of the world system in which America lives.

Therefore, when Germany broke off the effort to reach some understanding by a proclamation of marine terrorism, America was forced more actively to uphold that portion of its rights which Germany was asking her to forego in behalf of a victory for ends never revealed and justifiably regarded with suspicion.

In his War Address, which was given some three weeks after this communication, Wilson did not acknowledge or rationalize the discriminatory character of American policy. In the last half of the address Wilson speaks most emphatically of accepting Germany's "challenge of hostile purpose" and of the objective of setting up "a concert of purpose and of action" among "the really free and self-governed peoples of the world," whereas in the first half he had taken the German submarine in its relation to the rules of maritime warfare as a point of departure. There was no suggestion of a transition in American policy from freedom of the seas to alliance. These two platforms were erected side by side and used simultaneously as justifications of American intervention, the inference being that they were somehow structurally connected.

Actually the two parts of the address fail to complement each other. To accept either one at face value puts the other in question. If the arguments advanced in the second part have validity, it follows that the only defensible policy was one favoring Great Britain. Yet the arguments advanced in the first part of the address ring true only if it was demonstrable that the American Government had endeavored to apply the rules of maritime warfare without discrimination. This basic anomaly in American policy arose in part from Wilson's own uncertainty over the correct point of departure. More fundamentally, however, it sprang from the inflexibility of historically conditioned policy and from a deeply divided public opinion. Despite his efforts beginning in May 1916, Wilson failed to establish a policy with internal consistency and was confronted in the spring of 1917 with an insoluble dilemma. The stultification of that policy foreseen by Lippmann's memorandum of March 11 could not be satisfactorily overcome. It was too late to straighten out the record; to have tried to do so would have invited fresh debate when circumstances called for action.

PART FIVE

German Mistrust and
American Neutrality

The following excerpt is from a study by a European scholar, K. E. Birnbaum, of the formulation and evolution of German policy toward the United States. His findings, especially those regarding German scepticism about both Wilson's purposes and his neutrality policies, have important implications for the student of American diplomacy in World War I. The author, utilizing extensive archival research in Europe and America, examines the effects of internal politics on German policy and depicts that policy as fluctuating between, on one hand, peace moves, efforts at conciliation and cooperation with the United States to avoid war despite more intensive use of the U-boat, and, on the other, unrestricted submarine warfare even at the price of hostilities with America. Chancellor Bethmann-Hollweg from early 1915 had sought earnestly to avoid a rupture with the United States by making such concessions on U-boat warfare as the domestic political situation and the growing primacy of the military within the German government permitted. The failure of his bid of December 12, 1916, for direct peace negotiations, together with the negative response of Germany's leaders to President Wilson's overtures, finally compelled the Chancellor to acquiesce to a program of unrestricted underseas warfare.

Karl E. Birnbaum is the author of several books. Since 1958 he has been a lecturer in history at the University of Stockholm.

5 · Peace Moves and U-Boat Warfare by K. E. Birnbaum

From the spring of 1916 Germany's policy towards the United States pendulated between peace moves and submarine warfare. These extremes implied two lines of policy that could not be reconciled. German peace moves, of which those via Washington during the autumn of 1916 played a dominant part, could be successful only if peaceful relations were preserved with America. A resumption of U-boat warfare, on the other hand, entailed, after the diplomatic situation created by the *Sussex* crisis, an imminent risk of a rupture with the United States. Before January 1917 Germany's leaders did not definitely decide in favour of either of these alternatives. Bethmann Hollweg did not deem it likely that Germany would win an acceptable peace by means of indiscriminate U-boat action. But neither was he prepared to attempt to enforce a definitive sacrifice of commercial warfare with submarines, since he felt compelled to adapt his position in the U-boat question — this controversial issue in German home politics — to the demands of the internal political situation. In addition the Chancellor seems never really to have been certain that American mediation would not bring a peace unfavourable to Germany; on the other hand, he probably hoped, at least in early December 1916, for a compromise with regard to U-boat warfare in the form of attacks without warning on armed merchantmen. These conflicting tendencies led to a line of action in which peace moves and submarine warfare had a disturbing effect on each other.

Bethmann Hollweg did not oppose the resumption of cruiser warfare with submarines in mid-October 1916, which on account of the difficulty of preventing the submarine commanders, even by the strictest instructions, from mistaking the identity of vessels, constituted a grave danger to the peaceful relations between Germany and the United States. On the other hand the *Marina* and *Arabia* incidents [recently torpedoed] caused the Chancellor to obtain from the Kaiser a new temporary limitation in the freedom of action of the submarines against commercial shipping. Shortly afterwards the Chancellor nevertheless agreed to submarine warfare without warning against armed merchantmen but tried to postpone this considerable intensification of German naval warfare till a time when it would not interfere with the peace move of the Central

5 Reprinted by permission from Karl E. Birnbaum, *Peace Moves and U-Boat Warfare: A Study of Imperial Germany's Policy towards the United States April 18, 1916–January 9, 1917* (Stockholm: University of Stockholm Studies in History No. 2, 1958), pp. 335–339.

Powers. At the beginning of January 1917, when, according to the agreement with the naval and military leaders, the action against armed merchantmen was to commence, it disturbed, however, the continued American peace efforts, which Bethmann at that time seems to have been eager to make use of in order to reach the goal that to Wilhelmstrasse now appeared to be the foremost aim of German diplomacy: to prevent war with America as a consequence of the impending ruthless U-boat campaign.

Ambassador Bernstorff's actions occasionally aggravated the effects of the wavering German policy towards the United States. Bernstorff did not share the scepticism of the German leaders towards Wilson, and strove eagerly to bring about sincere German-American collaboration for peace. The Ambassador tried therefore to emphasize all tendencies in German policy that were likely to promote his efforts. These aspirations, however, led him at times to exceed his instructions and represent his Government's views as being more positive and favourable to American wishes and proposals than they really were. When later Germany reverted to more intensive U-boat warfare and the events on the high seas disclosed this, the discrepancy between German assertions and deeds became even more marked than would have been the case merely on account of the actions and declarations of the authorities in Germany.

While this vacillating German policy towards the United States was in itself one of the reasons for its own breakdown in early January 1917, there are two causes that in the special situation that obtained at the beginning of January 1917 stand out as the decisive factors in the final collapse of Germany's American policy: (1) the scepticism towards Wilson's real intentions that the German leaders could never overcome; and (2) the increasing supremacy of the military and naval authorities and their uncompromising insistence on unrestricted U-boat warfare as from February 1, 1917.

The foundation of the pronounced scepticism of the German leaders towards President Wilson had been laid during the early stages of the war, when the American application of the rules of neutrality turned out to be to the disadvantage of the Central Powers. It was increased by Wilson's differential attitude towards the British blockade on the one hand and German U-boat warfare on the other, which confirmed the impression of the President's partiality among the leaders and public opinion in Germany. The sceptical view of Wilson on the part of those directing German foreign policy was not overcome — not even wholly by Bethmann — during the decisive period at the end of 1916 and the beginning of 1917, when the President in his heart had come very near to the neutrality in thought that he had recommended to his compatriots at the outbreak of hostilities. This was probably due above all to the unsatisfactory communications between the lonely man in the White House and the officials at Wilhelmstrasse, a basic circumstance which in its turn was owing to a number of factors. Wilson's retiring disposition prevented his conferring with the German Ambassador except on very rare occasions. The President's *alter ego*, Colonel House, with whom Bernstorff was in constant contact, usually reported Wilson's views very faithfully. But during the critical period at the end of 1916, House, on account of differences of opinion between himself and his friend in the White House on the peace question, failed in his function as Wilson's most important contact man. To this must be added that Bernstorff, during the whole war could not communicate rapidly and safely with Berlin, and that the main trend of his reports was at times in contrast to certain private communications from America that were now and then received at Auswärtiges Amt, and which at least seem to have had some influence on Zimmermann's estimate of America's policy. These shortcomings were not compensated by American diplomacy. The United States Ambassador in Berlin was a rather incompetent diplomatist, and neither the German Government nor President Wilson had any real confidence in him. His indiscretions during the autumn of 1916 apparently deprived the officials at Wilhelmstrasse of all inclination to employ him as a confidential channel between Berlin and Washington. On the other hand [James W.] Gerard was, owing to the absence of fundamental, general instructions in American diplomatic practice, and on account of Wilson's critical opinion of him, insufficiently informed of the President's intentions and plans during decisive periods.

With regard to the second factor mentioned above, it is sufficient as far as the supremacy of the military and naval authorities is concerned to point once more to the popularity of Hindenburg and Ludendorff in the army and the German public in general and to the position of power that this popularity afforded them. Bethmann Hollweg was therefore unwilling and probably also unable to challenge OHL [Supreme High Command of the Army]. The Kaiser had in the spring of 1916 at least formulated an objective for Germany's policy in the submarine question which took into account the demands of the naval and military leaders as well as those of the political authorities. By the end of the year, however, all traces of independent Imperial initiative in German policy and warfare had definitively disappeared.

The insistence of OHL and the naval leaders on unrestricted submarine warfare was doubtless due in the first place to their determination to take advantage of every chance of winning peace with victory. While further the natural wish of the fleet to activate the rather passive naval forces played some part in this respect, OHL's attitude in the U-boat question should also be seen in the light of the above-mentioned limitations in outlook that were characteristic of Hindenburg and Ludendorff, and which, among other things, seem to have caused them to underestimate the significance of the American danger. The Supreme High Command based its calculations on this point solely on tangible facts such as measurable results and material resources of power: existing American military preparations, U-boat sinkings, available enemy and neutral tonnage and the like. The actual effects of an American entry into the war, even the material, were, however, to a great extent also dependent upon such factors as the psychological reasons for an eventual declaration of war on the part of the United States and the repercussions of American intervention on the morale of the peoples on the Entente side. Hindenburg and Ludendorff seem to have been lacking in understanding of these more subtle but no less important considerations. . . .

PART SIX

Wilson the Statesman

Since the end of World War II scholars have re-
evaluated the causes of American involvement in 1917 from the broader
perspective of developments within the principal belligerent countries as well as from within the United States. Economic factors,
sentiment and propaganda, realistic considerations of the national security, and the forces of idealism have been judiciously examined and
weighed by these writers. The following selection is by Ernest R. May,
Professor of History at Harvard University. A specialist in American
foreign relations, Professor May edited *The Ultimate Decision: the
President as Commander in Chief* in 1960; he is also the author of
Imperial Democracy: the Emergence of America as a Great Power,
published in 1961.

Professor May agrees that without the submarine issue there probably
would have been no involvement in the war for there would have been
no direct conflict of interests and power between Germany and America.
He recognizes that factors other than neutral rights were involved, however, in the formulation of American policy on the submarine issue and
in Wilson's decision to take the nation into war in 1917. The "strict
accountability" policy adopted toward the submarine in 1915, May
contends, reflected the moralistic, legalistic, and economic considerations
of America, in opposition to what seemed to be a flagrant violation of
international law. Moreover, American prestige also was clearly committed after the *Lusitania* crisis.

6 · The Last Crisis
by E. R. May

. . . No one knows or can know what went through Wilson's mind in those decisive days of March [1917]. He talked revealingly to no one. Such letters as he wrote were formal or perfunctory. During much of the time his superb analytical powers undoubtedly sought every possible alternative. He had by this time acquired considerable knowledge and experience in international politics. Few emotional attachments remained to blur the precision of his thought. Over a period of more than two years he had canvassed the subject of German-American relations with a wide range of advisers, especially with his shrewd and perceptive friend, House. It is true that he could not foresee what actually was to happen in 1919 and after. Nor could he foretell Brest-Litovsk, the offensives of 1918, and the expeditionary force of two million men. Otherwise, it can be assumed, he reviewed every consideration that any analyst has been able to imagine in restrospect.

The one clear alternative was that which Wilson had rejected before. He could surrender, asserting that American property losses would be the subjects of postwar claims. . . . There was no longer a compelling economic reason for resisting the German blockade. America had become so prosperous that she could afford to lose part of her trade with the Allies. The unrestricted submarine campaign had seemed thus far to be relatively ineffective. Statistics published at the beginning of March indicated only slight increases in Allied tonnage losses.

Nor was it evident that acquiescence would injure the visible security interests of the United States. Despite the Zimmermann note and other warnings of German activity in Latin America, Wilson had not retracted his earlier assertion to House that no European power offered an immediate menace to the United States. A relatively long period of recovery would be necessary for Germany, he had said, even if she triumphed in Europe. And he had little or no reason to suspect that Germany would win, even if the United States tolerated the U-boat blockade. Page warned him, it is true, that the Allies were on their last legs, but Wilson had long made allowance for Page's excitable temper. Other reports from London, Paris, and even St. Petersburg exhaled confidence. No longer regarding the Allies as upholders of law and civilization, Wilson

6 Reprinted by permission of the publishers from Ernest R. May, *The World War and American Isolation*, Cambridge, Mass.: Harvard University Press, Copyright, 1959, by the President and Fellows of Harvard College. Pp. 426–437.

had said time and again that America's interest lay in a peace without victory. There was no reason for him to believe in March, 1917, that this interest precluded acquiescence in the recent German decree. What did make it impossible was the fact that it would sacrifice America's prestige and moral influence. At the outset of the submarine controversy it had seemed apparent that America would not live up to her potential if she allowed her citizens to be denied the free right of travel. Partly to demonstrate that the United States was a power entitled to respect and deserving of influence, Wilson had taken the cautious gamble of resisting indiscriminate U-boat warfare. Each subsequent diplomatic victory had committed America's prestige more deeply. The submarine issue had also become the symbol of Wilson's willingness to stand up for the rule of law, for international justice, and, as he termed it, for the rights of humanity. If he now retreated he would, in effect, prove America incapable of exercising influence compatible with her population, resources, and ideals. He would demonstrate her Pharisaism, her inability to endure martyrdom for what she believed right. In view of his conviction that her own future turned upon her ability to prevent a recurrence of war, he simply could not accept the pacifist alternative.

Acquiescence was not, of course, the only alternative. Another was armed neutrality. American ships could be provided with guns. They could defend themselves against U-boats. The United States would thus be upholding her principles while waging only a very limited war. Professor Carlton J. H. Hayes of Columbia University had prepared a long and compelling memorandum outlining the virtues of this course. It would make clear that the United States opposed only Germany's illegal and immoral method of warfare. It would allow America to escape military involvement on the continent and leave her unentangled in the intricacies of Allied ambitions and European power rivalries. The President had read this memorandum before asking Congress for power to arm merchantmen. From his address at that time and from other comments, it is evident that this alternative had some attraction for him. While it is comparatively simple to infer his reasons for rejecting pacifism, it is rather harder to sense the rationale that led him away from limited belligerency.

One consideration undoubtedly was the practical difficulty of devising a suitable policy. The Navy Department sketched for him the alternative methods of carrying out an armed neutrality. One was for American ships to acknowledge the legal right of U-boats to conduct visit and search but to resist unlawful attacks. A second was for them to treat German submarines as hostile craft when encountered inside the war zone. A third was to treat U-boats as hostile craft wherever met and to attack them on sight. Each course presented obvious difficulties. One invited torpedoings; the second risked them; the third was not very different from a state of war.

Armed neutrality in any form involved a further danger of blurring the issues. American merchantmen might err in sinking submarines. Especially if the United States were to follow the third of the navy's three forms of armed neutrality, American captains were likely to act in excess of zeal. The result might easily be an American *Baralong* case, which the Germans might employ as a moral pretext for war. Armed neutrality would, in any case, allow Germany to choose her own time and occasion for opening hostilities.

Even so, Wilson could still have elected the alternative. He had always shown a disposition to postpone crises. It would not have been out of character for him to adopt a policy that threw the choice of peace or war back upon Berlin. The keys to his final decision probably lay first of all in his complete mistrust of Germany, secondly in his emphatic desire to preserve domestic unity, and thirdly in his conception of America's probable war effort.

He could no longer expect Germany to be deterred from any action by fear of war with the United States. Responses to the pressures applied during early February had indicated total indifference. Not only had Zimmermann asserted that there was no turning back, but a semiofficial newspaper (the Berlin *Lokal-Anzeiger*), quoted in the United States, had declared, "As to the neutrals — we can no longer be bothered by their opinions." In his message to Congress asking authority to arm ships, Wilson had referred to uncompromising statements by German officials and by the German press. The Zimmermann telegram itself had indicated no more than that Germany anticipated war. Wilson was more shocked apparently by the method of its dispatch. Zimmermann had sent the message to Bernstorff for forwarding, using State Department cable lines which had been opened for the sake of peace discussions. Coupled with Zimmermann's insouciant admission that the telegram was genuine, this revelation seemed to demonstrate that Germany no longer saw any advantage in keeping the peace. The *coup de grâce* for any lingering hope came in Bethmann Hollweg's address to the Reichstag, delivered on the day after Wilson requested power to arm merchantmen. According to the State Department's report of this speech, Bethmann spoke of America's "subjection to English power and control"; he declared that the severance of relations was meant neither to protect freedom of the seas nor to promote peace but only to help "starve Germany and increase bloodshed"; he ended by asserting, "now that our sincere desire to promote peace has met with nothing but ridicule at hands of our enemies there is no longer any retreat for us — nothing but 'Forward.'" It appeared from Wilson's perspective as if there were no longer a moderate party in Berlin. Whether the United States declared war or simply proclaimed an armed neutrality, Germany was likely in either case to treat her as an all-out enemy.

In view of this probability, Wilson undoubtedly foresaw difficulty in maintaining a mere armed neutrality. At the moment it seemed as if most of the country approved such a course. Many neutralists and some pacifists reluctantly accepted armed neutrality as an alternative to war. But chauvinism was visibly on the rise. The Zimmermann telegram and the sinking of the Cunard liner *Laconia* [on February 25], with three Americans among the lost, had created a spreading excitement. The *Literary Digest* reported newspapers all over the country to be joining in a clamor for war. The pacifists who filibustered against armed neutrality were widely denounced as traitors, and Tumulty[1] advised the President that these passions were not likely to cool. The President could also see, of course, the latent strength of pacifism. Bryan had thrown all his enormous energy into an outcry against war. Pacifist and socialist groups across the land joined him. But these forces remained for the moment inchoate and disorganized. The Zimmermann telegram and the *Laconia* sinking had shaken them. It was foreseeable, nevertheless, that a long period of armed neutrality would allow pacifists to regroup. Wilson had reason to believe that German agents were seeking to organize and finance them. Another intercepted German dispatch told of $50,000 to be spent in this cause. Future incidents would meanwhile strengthen and embitter the chauvinists. Other *Laconias* were certain to sink. Even as Wilson sat meditating in the White House, five American ships went down. Other disclosures like the Zimmermann telegram were also probable. There were suspicions, for example, of German activity in troubled Cuba. Armed neutrality was likely therefore to divide the country into irreconcilable groups.

From Wilson's standpoint such a division was dangerous to all his objects. He sought national unity for its own sake. He also sought it in order that the United States might influence the peace settlement. If the extremist factions grew, with erstwhile neutralists and nationalists swinging toward either pacifism or chauvinism, the inner strength of America would weaken. As it was, moreover, the extremist leaders differed with Wilson over the conditions of lasting peace. The winter had seen a queer alliance between pacifists like Bryan and [William E.] Borah and chauvinists like Roosevelt and Lodge. They had joined in attacking the proposed League of Nations. If their respective followings should grow as a result of armed neutrality, the President might find it impossible either to exert significant influence over Europe's peacemakers or even to guide them by his own ideals.

If Wilson had foreseen the AEF of 1918 and the casualties of Chateau-Thierry and the Meuse-Argonne, he might still have chosen armed neutrality as a course that at least postponed full-scale war. His decision to reject this alternative probably grew in part out of a reasonable, if mistaken, estimate of what war would require. No statement by an

---

[1] Joseph P. Tumulty, Wilson's private secretary.

Allied leader had indicated pressing requirements for manpower. . . . The President knew, of course, of the War Department's plan for an expeditionary force, and when the Allies subsequently asked for men he readily complied. But 500,000 was the limit set by army planners, and most of these were to be regular troops or volunteers. The draft, for which Wilson called in his war message, was to replace these men at home stations. He need not have been inwardly shaken by the thought of sending into the trenches men who went there willingly. He evidently conceived of America's war effort as designed primarily to reinforce the Allies with arms, supplies, money, and naval craft.

The relatively small difference that he saw between armed neutrality and war was vividly indicated in a letter written after he had decided on war. It was written, indeed, after he had composed his stirring message to Congress. Answering a Progressive who advocated armed neutrality, Wilson asserted, "To defend our right on the seas, we must fight submarines. . . . Apparently, to make even the measures of defense legitimate we must obtain the status of belligerents." Expecting America to fight mainly with her factories and ships, Wilson chose war in preference to armed neutrality.

This is not to say that the President found the choice easy. No matter how little American blood appeared in his imaginations, war remained horrible to him. He had never ceased to express disgust for its barbarity and for the passions it aroused. He was well aware that divisions into extremist factions would be avoided only at the price of uniting the country in animal hatred of a foreign enemy. He was not at all sure that American institutions and ideals could emerge unscarred. He was simply more sure that they could not survive if the end of the war did not spell the end of all wars. The same dream of peace that had entered into all his diplomacy finally led him paradoxically to a decision for war. . . .

Peace between Britain and the United States had been saved. It had been potentially in jeopardy, if at all, during the early months of the war. At that time there had been no German-American dispute to reinsure it. The American government had been preoccupied with saving the country from economic depression, and the men who made American policy had been unusually ingenuous and doctrinaire. Had the British government then flagrantly disregarded American interests or ideals, it could well have generated tension which not even German recklessness could have relieved.

It is clear that this danger was averted in part by the prudent and skillful diplomacy of Sir Edward Grey. It was he who worked out compromises that avoided offense to America while still safeguarding Britain's future capacity to interrupt German trade. It was he, most importantly, who prevented cotton from going onto the contraband list in the autumn of 1914. But even these concrete acts owed something to conditions beyond his or anyone's control. Grey was able to moderate

British policy because he possessed a momentary hold upon the Cabinet, the House of Commons, and the public, because few people were able to foresee the long years ahead, and because the fleet was temporarily preoccupied.

The preservation of Anglo-American peace resulted in the long run from forces of even more remote origin. It was possible for Grey to effect compromises largely because Britain and the United States shared a community of beliefs. English and American diplomatists spoke the same language, even when using moral abstractions that neither party could define. It is true that Grey maneuvered with great skill to draw the teeth of Wilson's mediation schemes, but he owed his successes chiefly to similarity of English and American ideals. The differences he disguised were, in any case, minor. The peace between America and England stood upon a common heritage. It also rested on foundations of mutual trust which had been built up in the Oregon and *Alabama* negotiations, in the secretaryships of Hay, Root, Balfour, and Lansdowne, in the intermarriages of families, the interchange of books and travelers, and the interplay of English and American reform movements. Grave as were the threats to accord, the forces that made for its preservation were stronger.

After German-American tension developed, the peace between America and Britain was relatively secure. It held despite the triumphs of factions in England that did not prize it. It survived even though considerable elements of the American public were willing, even eager, to risk trouble with Britain. The Anglophobes in America, it is true, were disunited and incapable of pressing a program on the President, and the tradition of Anglo-American friendship exerted some effect upon even the most visceral of the "ginger" group in England. Relations between the two countries could nevertheless have been much sorer if Grey had not continued to exercise a waning influence in the Cabinet and, equally importantly, if Wilson had not been restrained by the hope of bringing general peace through cooperation with England. Tension could have developed if the President, after losing this hope, had not acted with such patience and prudence. But it is a moot question whether Britain and the United States were ever in danger of serious friction after the spring of 1915. The real guarantee of their peace, regrettably, was the trouble between Germany and America.

What Germany and the United States lacked was precisely the underpinning of mutual comprehension and trust that allowed Britain and America to adjust their differences. Not only extremists but even moderates lacked understanding of one another. When Wilson spoke of "lasting peace," he thought of the ages. Most of his countrymen, bred in the Liberal consensus that Louis Hartz has described, understood what he meant. So did most Englishmen. When Bethmann called for "*dauern-den Frieden*," on the other hand, he had in mind a settlement fixing the balance of power for a generation. Despite Kant's famous essay, few Germans shared the Liberal dream of eternal peace. Other words like "rights" and "militarism" posed similar problems. German-American negotiations were always troubled by differences in meaning, intention, and outlook.

In the background of their misunderstandings stood a heritage of unpleasant memories, distorted perhaps but nonetheless vivid. Americans recalled Admiral Diederichs at Manila Bay, Wilhelm's instructions to Waldersee during the Boxer affair ("give no quarter, spare nobody, make no prisoners. . . . Be terrible as Attila's huns."), the frustrated Danish West Indies purchase, the Venezuela crisis, the *Panther*, Agadir, Zabern, and Bethmann's "scrap of paper" interview. Germans, on the other hand, remembered America's discriminatory tariffs, instances of firms that had dumped shoddy goods and infected meat, the seeming hypocrisy of the Monroe Doctrine and the Open Door, Roosevelt's desertion of Wilhelm at Algeçiras, America's cooperation with Germany's enemies at the Hague and London conferences, her missionary zeal in promoting Liberal principles, and Wilson's insistence on the right to sell munitions to the Allies. While mutual misunderstanding and mistrust did not make it impossible for Germany and America to adjust their differences, they did make the task harder.

This heritage of misunderstanding makes it all the more extraordinary that men in Berlin and Washington should have been able for so long to preserve the peace. Bethmann's achievement lay, it is true, in seeing what in retrospect is obvious: if America entered the war Germany was bound to be defeated. But this truth was not apparent to most Germans, even to those who supported the Chancellor. Bethmann was not a great statesman. He was an accomplished courtier and a shrewd politician. At a conference table with Grey, Lloyd George, Wilson, and House, he would not have stood out. He was simply wiser than most of his associates, and he used his arts with remarkable effectiveness. Peace between Germany and America was largely preserved by his prudence and skill. It was lost when his power lapsed.

To credit Bethmann with the chief role in keeping peace between America and Germany is not, of course, to deny Wilson's share. The President's patience in 1915 and 1916 undoubtedly owed something to inertia and timidity and something to divisions in American public opinion. Pacifism and neutralism were powerful forces, even at the end. It is arguable, indeed, that Wilson had little choice except to be both firm and patient. But others would conceivably have done otherwise. House, though an extraordinarily imaginative diplomatist, favored abandoning patience in the *Arabic* and *Sussex* crises. He might have denied Bethmann the time that was always necessary to win a favorable decision from the Kaiser. House might have forced a war when America's aims could still be attained by diplomacy. Bryan, who was in some ways the purest idealist in American politics, would have abandoned firmness. Had his policy been adopted, the U-boats would never have been restrained. America would have suffered a series of injuries and humiliations. While Bryan could have borne them gladly, the public would likely have sent a chauvinist to the White House in 1916. Wilson's mixed firmness and patience offered the only hope in the long run of keeping the peace, and he held to that policy with persistence, foresight, and courage.

It is hard, indeed, to find fault with Wilson's statesmanship. Retrospective analysts have contended that he was unrealistic. He should, it is suggested, have thrown America into the war in order to prevent German victory, preserve Anglo-American control of the seas, and overturn authoritarian and militarist ideologies. But this criticism supposes that Wilson should have acted against a German menace that might never have materialized. Although the President's dreams could look to the eternal future, his diplomacy conformed to Bismarck's rule: it assumed any contingency more than six months away to be out of calculation. Dealing with both Britain and Germany, Wilson concerned himself with the immediate interests of his country. America's security was not threatened in the predictable future. Her economic power and her prestige were in danger. His policy fended off present threats.

His moralism found expression in his quest for world peace. Since peace without victory would have resulted in recreating a balance of power, it has been argued that Wilson was here a *Realpolitiker*. House, who did believe in the balance of power, was so much the manager of Wilson's mediation efforts that his views and the President's mingled. Where Wilson's own ideas emerge with distinctness, the balance-of-power concept is subsidiary. His declaration of war was itself evidence of his belief that eternal peace could be secured even if victory created a power vacuum. He sought lasting peace for its own sake. Since it offered the only sure escape from the dilemmas of his wartime relations with Britain and Germany, it did have its practical side. But the House-Grey understanding and the peace offer of December, 1916, as well as the declaration of war, all indicated his willingness to risk immediate interests for the sake of his dream. If this was realism, it was a sublime realism.

The struggle for peace ended in war. Reviewing its history, one has a sense that it could not have ended otherwise. Bethmann, Grey, and even Wilson were continually pitted against men of less wisdom and compassion. . . . There was no way out. Triumph for the immoderates was only a matter of time. Grey nevertheless saw his hope fulfilled. America and Britain did not become enemies. Bethmann and Wilson kept the peace for more than two years. Despite its tragic ending, the struggle was heroic.

A GUIDE TO FURTHER READING
··

Excellent interpretive guides to the literature concerning American involvement in the First World War is provided by Richard W. Leopold, "The Problem of American Intervention, 1917: An Historical Retrospect," *World Politics*, II (1950), 405–425; Richard L. Watson, Jr., "Woodrow Wilson and His Interpreters, 1947–1957," *Mississippi Valley Historical Review*, XLIV (1957), 207–236; and Ernest R. May, *American Intervention: 1917 and 1941* (Service Center for Teachers of History, Pamphlet 30, 1960), and his "Emergence to World Power" in John Higham, ed., *The Reconstruction of American History* (New York, 1962), 180–196. Also see Leopold's "The Emergence of America as a World Power: Some Second Thoughts," in *Change and Continuity in Twentieth-Century America* (John Braeman *et al.*, eds., Columbus, Ohio, 1964), 3–34. The older multi-volume biography of Wilson by Ray Stannard Baker, *Woodrow Wilson: Life and Letters* (Garden City, N.Y., 1935–39, 8 vols.) is still of value though it is being supplanted by the work of Arthur S. Link: *Woodrow Wilson and the Progressive Era, 1910–1917* (New York, 1954); *Wilson: The Struggle for Neutrality, 1914–1915* (Princeton, 1960); *Wilson: Confusions and Crises, 1915–1916* (Princeton, 1964); and his brief *Wilson the Diplomatist, A Look at His Major Foreign Policies* (Baltimore, 1957). The second volume of Arthur Walworth's *Woodrow Wilson* (New York, 1958) is devoted to foreign policy. A stimulating psychological study, pertinent to an evaluation of American entry into the war, is by A. L. and J. L. George, *Woodrow Wilson and Colonel House* (New York, 1956). Also see the short biographies by John M. Blum, *Woodrow Wilson and the Politics of Morality* (Boston, 1956), and John A. Garraty, *Woodrow Wilson, A Great Life in Brief* (New York, 1956). Some valuable essays on aspects of Wilsonian diplomacy are in Edward H. Buehrig, ed., *Wilson's Foreign Policy in Perspective* (Bloomington, 1957); Arthur P. Dudden, ed., *Woodrow Wilson and the World of Today* (Phila., 1957); and Earl Latham, ed., *The Philosophy and Politics of Woodrow Wilson* (Chicago, 1958). Charles Seymour, *The Intimate Papers of Colonel House* (Boston, 1926–28, 4 vols.), is a biographical and documentary treatment of Wilson's intimate adviser and unofficial foreign minister. J. V. Fuller, "William Jennings Bryan," in S. F. Bemis, ed., *The American Secretaries of State and Their Diplomacy* (New York, 1929, 10 vols.), X, 5–44, should be supplemented by Richard Challener, "William Jennings Bryan, 1913–1915," in N. Graebner, ed., *An Uncertain Tradition: American Secretaries of State in the Twentieth Century* (New York, 1961), 79–100.

For Lansing, see Daniel M. Smith, *Robert Lansing and American Neutrality, 1914–1917* (Berkeley, 1958). Also consult *War Memoirs of Robert Lansing* (New York, 1935).

In the 1920's and 1930's a school of "revisionist" historians began to question the accepted view that America had entered World War I primarily because Germany through ruthless submarine campaigns had forced the United States to fight in self-defense. A pioneer scholarly revisionist work by C. Hartley Grattan, *Why We Fought* (New York, 1929), although without an explicit thesis, implies that involvement in the war should be attributed to the effects of propaganda and the one-sided economic entanglement with the Allies. Walter Millis, *Road to War: America, 1914–1917* (Boston, 1935), tends to concur that the United States was pulled into hostilities by its partiality for the Allied cause and by powerful economic forces. Charles A. Beard, *The Devil Theory of War* (New York, 1936), stresses the economic aspects of involvement in the war. H. C. Peterson, *Propaganda for War, the Campaign Against American Neutrality, 1914–1917* (Norman, Okla., 1939) puts great emphasis on the success of British propaganda in undermining American neutrality. Also see Harold D. Laswell, *Propaganda Techniques in the World War* (New York, 1927); James Duane Squires, *British Propaganda at Home and in the United States from 1914 to 1917* (Cambridge, 1935); and James M. Read, *Atrocity Propaganda, 1914–1919* (New Haven, 1941). For other studies of public opinion, consult C. J. Child, *The German-American in Politics, 1914–1917* (Madison, Wisc., 1939); Edwin Costrell, *How Maine Viewed the War, 1914–1917* (Orono, Me., 1940); J. C. Crighton, *Missouri and the World War, 1914–1917* (Columbia, Mo., 1947); Cedric Cummins, *Indiana Public Opinion and the World War, 1914–1917* (Indianapolis, 1945); and Carl Wittke, *German-Americans and the World War* (Columbus, Ohio, 1936). Alice M. Morrissey, *The American Defense of Neutral Rights, 1914–1917* (Cambridge, 1939); and Edwin Borchard and W. P. Lage, *Neutrality for the United States* (New Haven, 1940 — 2nd ed.), sharply question the extent to which Wilson's neutrality policies complied with the spirit and letter of existing international law and practice. The latest and most exhaustively researched study of the neutrality era from the revisionist viewpoint is Charles C. Tansill's *America Goes to War* (Boston, 1938).

In defense of the administration's course are the works by Charles Seymour, *American Diplomacy During the World War* (Baltimore, 1934), and *American Neutrality, 1914–1917* (New Haven, 1935). Seymour maintained that the submarine alone explains why America went to war in 1917, and that economic and security factors were merely peripheral. Newton D. Baker, *Why We Went to War* (New York, 1936), agrees that Wilson's policies were genuinely neutral and that the country would have remained at peace except for the submarine issue. Harley Notter, *The Origins of the Foreign Policy of Woodrow Wilson* (Baltimore, 1937), presents a careful analysis which generally adheres to the Seymour thesis, as does *Decision for War, 1917* (Rindge, N.H., 1953) by Samuel R. Spencer, Jr.

In addition to Walter Lippmann's *U.S. Foreign Policy: Shield of the Republic* (Boston, 1943), another journalist, Forest Davis, contends in *The Atlantic System: the Story of Anglo-American Control of the Seas* (New York, 1941), that security factors led the United States to enter the war in 1917. Alfred Vagts, "Hopes and Fears of an American-German War, 1870–1915," *Political Science Quarterly*, Vol. 54 (1939), 514–535, and Vol. 55 (1940), 53–76; and Fritz T. Epstein, "Germany and the United States: Basic Patterns of Conflict and Understanding" in G. L. Anderson, ed., *Issues and Conflict* (Lawrence, Kansas, 1959), 284–314, examine the causes of German-American rivalry prior to 1914.

Recent studies have been less concerned with whether intervention in 1917 was wise and unavoidable or not, and more with a balanced economic and political study of the process of involvement. The emphasis also has shifted to an appraisal of the problems of American neutrality within the larger context of political and military exigencies in Great Britain and Germany. Edward H. Buehrig, *Woodrow Wilson and the Balance of Power* (Bloomington, 1955), examined closely the evolution of Wilson's foreign policies and detected elements of a realistic appraisal of the significance of the European balance of power for American security, together with idealistic considerations, in the thinking of President Wilson and his principal advisers. An earlier study by Robert E. Osgood, *Ideals and Self-Interest in America's Foreign Relations* (Chicago, 1953), concurs that there was a small minority of realists within the government in 1914–1917 but maintains that Wilson's approach to foreign affairs was essentially moralistic and idealistic in nature. Also see George F. Kennan, *American Diplomacy, 1900–1950* (Chicago, 1951), chapter IV; and Hans Morgenthau, *In Defense of the National Interest* (New York, 1951). Karl E. Birnbaum, *Peace Moves and U-Boat Warfare* (Stockholm, 1958), focuses on internal politics in Germany and the evolution of the submarine policy. He is critical of Chancellor Bethmann-Hollweg for failing to resist more energetically the pressures from the admirals and for not comprehending adequately the peace hopes and mediation purposes of President Wilson. Ernest R. May's *The World War and American Isolation, 1914–1917* (Cambridge, 1959), utilizes a multi-archival approach to the problem of intervention and concludes that while Wilson was affected by economic and security factors his decision to take the country into the war also involved considerations of prestige and idealistic hopes and plans for a just and stable postwar world. Consult also the latest volumes by Link, previously cited. For an interesting appraisal by a French scholar, see Jean-Baptiste Duroselle, *From Wilson to Roosevelt: Foreign Policy of the United States, 1913–1945*, published in Paris in 1960 and translated for American release in 1963. Duroselle emphasizes Wilson's desire to establish a just postwar world order as an underlying factor in the American involvement.